New Directions in

Urban Public Housing

edited by

DAVID P. VARADY
WOLFGANG F. E. PREISER
FRANCIS P. RUSSELL

CENTER FOR URBAN POLICY RESEARCH
Rutgers — The State University of New Jersey
New Brunswick, New Jersey

Published by the Center for Urban Policy Research
CUPR PRESS
Civic Square • 33 Livingston Avenue • Suite 400
New Brunswick, New Jersey 08901–1982

Printed in the United States of America

Cover design: Helene Berinsky

CUPR Press wishes to thank the Fannie Mae Foundation, Washington, D.C., for permission to reprint chapters 1, 3, 4, 7, 8, and 9 of *New Directions in Urban Public Housing* from the Foundation's journal, *Housing Policy Debate* (Volume 7, Issue 3, 1996). The Fannie Mae Foundation retains copyright to this material.

Library of Congress Cataloging-in-Publication Data

New directions in urban public housing / edited by David P. Varady,
    Wolfgang F.E. Preiser, Francis P. Russell.
        p.   cm.
    Includes bibliographical references and index.

    ISBN 0-88285-160-8 (alk. paper)

    1. Public housing—United States—Congresses. 2. Public housing—
Great Britain—Congresses. 3. Urban policy—United States—
Congresses. 4. Urban policy—Great Britain—Congresses.
I. Varady, David P.   II. Preiser, Wolfgang F. E.   III. Russell,
Francis P.
HD7288.78.U5N48   1998
363.5'85'0941—dc21   97–29600
                                                                   CIP

New Directions in

Urban Public Housing

Acknowledgments

The editors wish to thank the members of the Advisory Board of the International Forum, "Future Visions of Urban Public Housing," held in Cincinnati, November 17–20, 1994, for their dedication and great effort in making the event possible. The International Forum clearly was an important stepping-stone in the evolution of this book. Space does not permit us to list all the contributors, but we would like to gratefully acknowledge the following major supporters in the Cincinnati area: W.O. Brisben Company; Goethe Institut, Cincinnati; University of Cincinnati; Cincinnati Gas and Electric Company; PNC Bank; Procter and Gamble Company; Robert D. Stern Fund; and the Seasongood Foundation.

We thank Donald J. Troendle, Executive Director of the Cincinnati Metropolitan Housing Authority, for his generous support of the International Forum, especially the printing of the *Proceedings* and facilitation of resident participation in both the Forum and the Workshop that preceded the Forum.

Our gratitude to Fannie Mae Foundation for its support of the Forum, which resulted in the publication of a special issue of *Housing Policy Debate* (Vol. 7, Issue 3, 1996). We particularly would like to acknowledge Patrick A. Simmons and Karen A. Danielson for their tireless stewardship and collaboration efforts on that issue. We and CUPR Press thank the Fannie Mae Foundation for permission to reprint the six articles contained in the issue.

Finally, David Varady would like to extend his appreciation to Norman J. Glickman, Director of the Center for Urban Policy Research (CUPR) at Rutgers University; Robert Lake, editor in chief of CUPR Press; Linda Hayes, Anne Henoch, and Arlene Pashman, editors; and other CUPR staff too numerous to mention for providing him with the ideal environment (a Visiting Scholar position at CUPR) to complete the book. Varady would also like to thank his wife, Adrienne (who remained behind in Cincinnati), for her editorial assistance on the book and for her encouragement and endurance during his absence from Cincinnati.

About the Editors

David P. Varady, Professor of Planning at the University of Cincinnati, has written extensively on public housing, community conservation, and residential mobility. He is author of *Selling Cities: Attracting Homebuyers Through Schools and Housing Programs*; *Neighborhood Upgrading: A Realistic Assessment*; and *Ethnic Minorities in Urban Areas: A Case Study of Racially Changing Communities*. Dr. Varady has been a Visiting Scholar at the University of Glasgow, Scotland; the U.S. Department of Housing and Urban Development; the Montgomery County (Maryland) Housing Opportunities Commission; the National Association of Realtors™; and the Center for Urban Policy Research at Rutgers University. He holds a doctorate in City Planning from the University of Pennsylvania.

Wolfgang F. E. Preiser is Professor of Architecture at the University of Cincinnati. He holds a doctorate in Man–Environment Relations from Pennsylvania State University and master's degrees in Architecture from Virginia Polytechnic Institute and State University and the Technical University Karlstuhe, Germany. He has authored or edited numerous articles and books, including *Facility Programming*; *Post-Occupancy Evaluation*; *Design Intervention: Toward a More Humane Architecture*; *Professional Practice in Facility Programming*; and *Directions in Person–Environment Research and Practice* (forthcoming).

Francis P. Russell (Frank) is director of the Community Design Center at the University of Cincinnati, where he organizes collaborative interdisciplinary community/university partnerships for the research and design of physical improvements that serve the university's urban mission. He holds a master's degree in Architecture from Harvard University.

Contents

DAVID P. VARADY

Introduction

Background

The chapters of this book comprise papers presented at an international forum, "Future Visions of Urban Public Housing," held in Cincinnati, November 17–20, 1994. The germ of an idea for the forum can be traced back to 1991, when a post-occupancy evaluation of Cincinnati's Laurel Homes (the country's second-oldest public housing development) was undertaken by Wolfgang Preiser. Like many other public housing projects, Laurel Homes had experienced sharp demographic changes over the years—from white to black, and from a working-class population to a welfare-dependent population; it also had suffered the attendant declines in neighborhood and housing quality. Although the post-occupancy evaluation was intended to lead to a remodeling of the entire development, including a reduction in density and a mix of different size dwelling units, it identified issues that went beyond the scope of the original evaluation. These included the need for comprehensive neighborhood planning, better urban design, infrastructure improvements, more active resident participation, and enhanced family self-sufficiency. The forum became a mechanism for addressing these broader issues.

Initially the forum was intended to be primarily a local event with considerable input and involvement from residents of Cincinnati Metropolitan Housing Authority housing. When I joined the planning group in 1993, I involved international academics and policy officials. The positive reaction to this global event probably reflected the fact that it was independent of any government agency, professional organization, or academic group.

Even though a number of innovative, and in some cases controversial, worldwide housing programs had been implemented in the 1980s, little had been written about them. Among the innovations were: (1) design and safety programs that promote "defensible space"; (2) vouchers and rent certificates to deconcentrate the poor; (3)

family self-sufficiency programs; (4) integration of the elderly with mentally handi-capped younger people; (5) comprehensive strategies to revitalize severely distressed developments; and (6) tenant management and resident empowerment. As members of the organizing committee, we saw the forum as a way to stimulate discussion regarding these programs. We also recognized that in contrast to the United States (where public housing is typically viewed as a failure), public housing programs have been successful overseas (e.g., the high-rise housing in Hong Kong and Singapore). An international event could facilitate learning from these successful approaches.

The International Forum

More specifically, the purposes of the international forum were to identify, debate, compare, and analyze practices and urgent issues in urban public housing in industrialized nations. The event was to be preceded by a four-day workshop with Cincinnati public housing residents. Other components of the forum included an international traveling exhibit from Germany, "Modernist Visions of Urban Housing," and an art competition by local artists who had installed art work at two local public housing developments in Cincinnati.

Consultants, policymakers, public housing officials, and academicians from the United States and overseas, as well as local public housing residents, attended the forum. Fifty-five papers were presented, and a number of keynote addresses were given by such policy leaders as Dwight Robinson from the U.S. Department of Housing and Urban Development; Richard Best of the Rowntree Foundation in York, United Kingdom; Dr. Yasuyoshi Hayashi of the Research Center for Planning Technology in Tokyo, Japan; Hans-Jörg Duvigneau of the Gemeinnutzige Siedlungs- und Wohnungsbaugesellschaft (GSW) in Berlin; and Bertha Gilkey, an urban public housing activist known for her work on tenant management at Cochran Gardens in St. Louis, Missouri.

The first published product resulting from the forum was the proceedings, *Future Visions of Urban Public Housing.* Next, six papers from the *Proceedings* were published in 1996 in a special issue of Fannie Mae's *Housing Policy Debate,* entitled "Managing Devolution in Public Housing: The New Landscape" (vol. 7, no. 3). *New Directions in Urban Public Housing* includes the six papers from *Housing Policy Debate,* together with five other papers presented at the Cincinnati conference and an epilogue by James Stockard prepared specially for this volume.

These twelve chapters touch on a broad range of public housing issues from the origins of American public housing design and policy to the current policy climate, and they anticipate future directions of public housing. Some of the issues that the United States is just beginning to wrestle with, such as the impact of public housing homeownership, the United Kingdom has been grappling with for more than a decade. This book includes a chapter that highlights recent U.K. experience in public housing policy and the lessons that can be drawn for American policy. Special attention is given in the epilogue to the problems of "radical devolution" (assigning to the states and localities the funding and implementation of the program) and the merits of "moderate devolution" (providing greater flexibility to local public housing authorities but maintaining a strong monitoring role for HUD).

New Directions in Urban Public Housing and the Changing Public Housing Environment

By scheduling workshops in conjunction with the more traditional academic forum, and by inviting policy and design experts, both foreign and domestic, the organizers of the forum anticipated maximizing the possibility of developing recommendations at both the local and national levels. As it turned out, policy changes occurred more rapidly than had been expected—and for reasons that could hardly have been anticipated.

Republican victories in the 1994 elections—held just before the forum convened—resulted in a massive shift in political power in the United States Congress. Henry Cisneros anticipated correctly that Republican leaders would seek to do away with HUD as part of a broader effort to cut back federal social programs. Consequently, in December 1994, HUD produced its *Reinvention Blueprint,* which spelled out how the agency should be overhauled. The HUD recommendations for transforming public housing went way beyond what Dwight Robinson recommended in his speech at the November 1994 forum. The HUD proposal, in brief, sought to discontinue subsidies to public housing projects and buildings and, instead, to provide subsidies to residents in the form of rent certificates and vouchers. This proposal went nowhere, however—largely because of cost considerations. As this introduction was written, the Clinton administration was proceeding to modify the character of public housing by implementing proposals for eliminating or substantially rehabilitating some of the most troubled developments, reducing regulations, and encouraging more mixed-income developments. The twelve papers in this volume present state-of-the-art wisdom on how these programs should be designed and implemented.

New Directions in Urban Public Housing: A Quick Overview

HISTORICAL PERSPECTIVES

The review of American public housing design, written by von Hoffman, studies the relationship between political/social development and physical development. Von

Hoffman looks at the early, environmentally deterministic assumptions that under-lay the architectural visions of public housing during the 1930s (when the Zeilenbau style was imported from Europe). He then turns his attention to the 1950s and 1960s, when the modernist vision produced the high-rise "slabs" and "superblocks" that have become the icon of public housing. He ends with an evaluation of current thinking on heterogeneous community building that prescribes a lower-density, mixed-income approach to public housing. Von Hoffman convincingly argues that environmental determinism from these earlier periods has been replaced by today's social determin-ism—the belief that income mixing can transform the poor into middle-class citi-zens.

Based on a review of American public housing's fifty-five–year history, Peter Marcuse argues that public housing has never been part of the mainstream of hous-ing policy. Instead, it has been a by-product of policies with goals other than the improvement of housing. In the mid-1930s, with the Depression and the New Deal, public housing came closest to being part of the mainstream. Those who were ill-housed and those who identified with them constituted a large proportion of the population. During only two other periods has public housing been relatively pro-gressive: in the years after World War II, when veterans demanded decent housing; and in the years around 1968, as part of the effort to address the causes of ghetto violence. During three other periods, public housing policy has been relatively ret-rogressive: just before World War II, when economic conditions were improving; in the 1950s and 1960s, when urban renewal (which used public housing to meet re-location requirements) led to widespread social disruption; and lastly, in the shift to conservatism at the beginning of the Nixon administration, with calls for the elimi-nation of the program altogether. The unmistakable lesson from this history is that for public housing to thrive it will have to serve a broader spectrum of residents and forge broad coalitions of low- and middle-income people around a variety of hous-ing issues ranging from housing affordability to homeownership for young couples. (This issue—bringing public housing into the mainstream—is further discussed in the epilogue.)

SOCIAL ISSUES

Resident management corporations (RMCs) have often been touted as the best way to simultaneously improve the management of public housing developments and "em-power" low-income residents. William Peterman shows that it is no simple matter to empower low-income residents. Resident management corporations first must achieve a creative tension between managing, which stresses working within the sys-tem—and organizing, which involves fighting the system. Few RMCs have succeeded in balancing these objectives. Furthermore, as Peterman observes, it is hard to say whether RMCs empower anyone because there is so little agreement on what the term "empowerment" means. The term implies homeownership for conservatives; shared responsibility with housing authorities for liberals; and community organization and community control for progressives.

Through a Decatur, Illinois, case study, Leonard F. Heumann highlights the folly of mixing the elderly with younger people, some of whom have mental illnesses and some of whom have drug and alcohol problems. While this type of mixing was undoubtedly well-intentioned, and might have seemed like a good idea in theory, it turned out to have disastrous negative effects: high levels of dissatisfaction among the elderly; high levels of staff "burnout"; and difficulties in achieving cost efficiencies due to the reduced level of interest in the housing by the elderly.

DESIGN ISSUES

Karen Franck identifies and discusses the changes in values occurring during the three stages of public housing in the United States: (1) low-rise housing separated from the surrounding neighborhoods (1930s); (2) high-rise housing separated from surrounding areas (1950s and 1960s); and (3) low-rise housing integrated into the surrounding areas (late 1970s until the present). She points out, for example, that in stage two, the design of individual buildings emphasized "openness," but the projects as a whole were still separate and distinct from the surrounding neighborhoods. A key implication of this chapter is that having a single-minded vision for public housing is not necessarily optimal; community revitalization requires an emphasis on variety and sensitivity to different local situations.

David Schnee's post-occupancy evaluation of a 203-unit public housing development in San Francisco is decidedly positive and uplifting in comparison to most of what has been written about public housing recently. The development, Robert Pitts Plaza, is one of the few examples of new public housing in the United States and is unique because of the high degree of involvement of residents in the design process. Using a combination of techniques (a behavior-trace survey to assess uses of space, resident surveys, key informant interviews), Schnee describes and then evaluates the eight different design guidelines for the development. Some of the results are counterintuitive and indicate the value of post-occupancy–evaluation methodology. For example, whereas the parking lots were expected to be perceived as dangerous, they actually turned out to be conducive to informal gatherings and social interaction. Furthermore, not only was it cheaper to rebuild than to modernize, but new construction was more in line with residents' aspirations and preferences. Thus, in some cases it might make more sense to use a "demolish and rebuild" strategy rather than to modernize. PHAs should be given the flexibility to make the choice between modernization and new construction. The case study also suggests that if planners and architects listen to residents, they might avoid the disasters of the 1950s, 1960s, and 1970s, when individual project designs were based on the idealized visions of modernist architects. A final implication is that public housing developments for families can succeed when adequately funded, properly designed, and competently managed. (Several other showcase family developments are also mentioned in this book. See chapters by Epp, Vale and Stockard.)

RESTRUCTURING SEVERELY DISTRESSED PUBLIC HOUSING

Gayle Epp provides a good introduction to the subject of restructuring severely distressed public housing. After reviewing the national efforts to address this issue, including the work of the National Commission on Severely Distressed Public Housing and the more recent Urban Revitalization Demonstration program (also known as HOPE VI), she describes two case studies—Holly Park in Seattle and the Near Westside in Indianapolis. Epp argues that improved design and layout can contribute to improved quality of life.

Lawrence Vale compares the redevelopment efforts undertaken in three Boston public housing projects during the 1980s as part of HUD's Urban Revitalization Demonstration Program. One of the three, the Commonwealth development, was particularly successful with respect to management, tenant organizing, implementation strategy, and in dealing with security measures. Commonwealth's success implies that projects in relatively good condition may be more appropriate targets for redevelopment than distressed ones. Unfortunately, for political and bureaucratic reasons, most housing authorities probably will not follow this wise advice.

FUTURE DIRECTIONS

Mary Nenno's chapter, "New Directions for Federally Assisted Housing," seems to be out of synch with recent political changes in the United States. Nenno critiques HUD's shift away from supply-side initiatives (e.g., building more public housing and improving communities) toward demand-side programs like rent certificates and housing vouchers. She sketches out various roles that HUD could play in a broad supply-side/community-oriented strategy (e.g., advancing the field of housing market analysis, supporting mixed-income housing initiatives, encouraging better design in low-income housing). Though her ideas do not coincide with current political realities, her proposals hopefully will contribute to the coming debate on long-term housing policy.

Benjamin Disraeli quipped that "there are three kinds of lies—lies, damned lies, and statistics." Irving Welfeld's provocative criticism of the Gautreaux housing voucher demonstration underlies the wisdom of this statement. Under the HUD-funded demonstration program in Chicago, Section 8 slots were made available to those in pub-

lic housing or on waiting lists who are willing to relocate to areas of the city or suburbs that were less than 30 percent black. Welfeld argues convincingly that the enthusiasm of James Rosenbaum (Northwestern) and his colleagues who have written
extensively on the program "outran their findings"—particularly those dealing with
economic impact. Rosenbaum emphasizes that among those who were unemployed
before the move, those who relocated to the suburbs were significantly more likely
to become employed than those remaining in the city. Welfeld points out, however,
that, given suburban job growth, the suburban movers did not do all that well. Within
the suburban mover group, fewer had jobs after the move than before. Further,
Welfeld correctly asks: If the city-to-suburbs move had such a positive effect, why
would the hourly wages of those who moved to the suburbs and the number of hours
worked per week be the same as for those who remained in the city? Although Welfeld
questions the long-term economic impact of Gautreaux-type programs, the political
feasibility of the approach is also uncertain. HUD's 1994 decision to relocate 285
inner-city Baltimore residents to suburban Baltimore County through Baltimore's
Moving to Opportunity (MTO) program provoked such controversy that a Senate
Committee, prodded by Barbara Mikulski of Maryland, eliminated 1995 funding
for the program. The findings presented in this chapter imply that there is a continued need for public housing, but the housing needs to be better designed and managed.[1]

Many similarities exist between the British and American public housing programs.
Because of the frequency of cross-Atlantic sharing of ideas, a chapter by Richard Best
that describes the shrinkage of Britain's public housing sector since 1979 is included
in this book. Public housing in Britain accounts for one-third fewer homes now than
it did a decade ago. The main reason for this shrinkage is that many residents have
exercised their right to purchase their units. As Best points out, the policy has produced mixed results. Many of the new owners take special pride in their homes and
have made substantial investments in upgrading. The policy's downside is that it has
reduced the pool of apartments for rent and that the new owners have a high incidence of default on mortgage payments. Local housing authorities now see their role
as extending beyond providing rented homes to include providing the nucleus of
urban regeneration efforts, such as City Challenge. The latter program is distinctive
because it has introduced competition for funding by cities. The program has also
succeeded in fostering partnerships among the public, private, and nonprofit sectors—a prerequisite for any successful endeavor. Recent evaluations indicate that the
program has not revitalized the worst-off public housing estates because it has not
alleviated poverty and other social problems in these areas. The implication—similar to the one offered by Vale in his chapter on Boston—is that public housing purchase programs may be best suited for developments (or "estates" as they are called
in the United Kingdom) where social problems are still relatively manageable and
where facilities are still in good condition.

Epilogue

James Stockard provides an upbeat assessment of the future of public housing in the United States; much of what he says is also applicable to the United Kingdom and other advanced societies. Since the public housing program has been a partial success (it has provided decent and affordable housing to millions; only a small minority of authorities are mismanaged), the program should be revised, not replaced. Stockard's vision of public housing (one the editors share) involves bringing public housing into the mainstream of housing and social policy. This means: (1) allowing PHAs to undertake a wider range of activities (e.g., administering homeownership programs as well as owning and managing rental housing); (2) providing a full range of options (e.g., cooperatives, transitional housing) so that families can shift along the continuum until they are independent; (3) moving toward more mixed-income properties; and (4) allowing money earmarked for public housing to be used more flexibly. Whether PHAs will be given this flexibility and, if so, whether they will use the flexibility effectively, remains to be seen.

Notes

1. The interested reader should see Welfeld's paper on the future of the public housing program contained in the 1994 *Proceedings* (Welfeld 1994).

References

Preiser, Wolfgang F.E., David P. Varady, and Francis P. Russell (eds.). 1994. *Future Visions of Urban Public Housing*. Proceedings of "Future Visions of Urban Public Housing: An International Forum," held at the University of Cincinnati, Cincinnati, Ohio, November 17–20.
U.S. Department of Housing and Urban Development. 1994. *Reinvention Blueprint*. Washington, DC: HUD.
Welfeld, Irving. 1994. Public housing: The need for a new framework. *Future Visions of Urban Public Housing*. Proceedings of "Future Visions of Urban Public Housing: An International Forum," held at the University of Cincinnati, Cincinnati, Ohio, November 17–20.

PART I

Historical Perspectives

ALEXANDER VON HOFFMAN

1   *High Ambitions: The Past and Future of American Low-Income Housing Policy*

Introduction

This chapter explores the often unexamined assumptions that shape and delimit discussions about housing policy. Usually policy debate focuses on the efficacy of specific programs, but such debate, which often takes place in the midst of political struggles, leaves little time to examine the logic and philosophy that drive policy. To understand the underlying thinking behind American housing policy, the chapter examines the public housing program during the 1930s, the midlife of public housing in the 1950s, and the present situation.

The argument presented here is that the failures of public housing have been less in the area of housing (despite the well-publicized disasters of a minority of projects) than in the area of expectations. The disillusion, which has dogged the program, arose in large part from the high and idealistic ambitions of its proponents. The idealism of public housing advocates has often taken the form of environmental determinism, a belief that an ideal or improved residential environment will better the behavior as well as the condition of its inhabitants.

In the 1930s, advocates of the new federal public housing program hoped to cure the social ills of the city and aspired to rehouse up to two-thirds of the American people in European-style public housing projects that would eliminate slums forever. Although they established a public housing program, they were unable to escape political controversies over location of the projects, and their design innovations

Reprinted from *Housing Policy Debate* 7, 3 (Washington, D.C.: Fannie Mae Foundation, 1996). This copyrighted material is used with the permission of the Fannie Mae Foundation.

3

would later come back to haunt the program. After the passage of the Housing Act of 1949 created a much larger public housing program, visionaries attempted to help by placing the poor in high-rise buildings, an experiment that was soon deemed a disaster.

In the face of frustration and failure, housers reluctantly accepted that a single public housing program for the majority of Americans was unfeasible and abandoned the notion of introducing new architectural styles through low-income housing projects. Yet visionary idealism, in particular environmental determinism, persists in the housing movement. Today heterogeneous communities are latter-day versions of the public housing and high-rise environments that housers once believed would eradicate the evils of the slum. Thus, some contend that programs of mixed-income housing development, scattered-site public housing, and geographical dispersal of low-income families will achieve social betterment for the urban poor.

But the shattered dreams of the past are a warning that today's popular housing policies are not panaceas. The future of public housing and related programs depends on setting goals that the movement can reasonably and readily address.

Early Public Housing Programs

The idea that living environments influence people's lives has been a part of the housing movement from its earliest days. Beginning in the mid–nineteenth century, idealistic philanthropists and moral reformers attempted to solve problems related to the housing of the urban poor. They firmly believed that the slums of the city were a malevolent environment that threatened the safety, health, and morals of the poor who inhabited them. By clearing slums and convincing or coercing property owners to improve the housing in the slum, reformers hoped to create a better environment that would uplift the poor. By the time of the New Deal, housing reformers had accomplished the passage of stringent building regulations, the construction of dozens of model tenements and industrial villages, and, most important, the dissemination of the belief that housing reform was necessary to solve the social problems related to urban poverty (Birch and Gardner 1981; Cousineau 1989; Lubove 1962; Wright 1981).

The economic crisis of the Great Depression created a favorable climate for federal government intervention in the housing industry. The housing industry had been in recession since the late 1920s, unemployment rates reached painfully high levels, and many American homeowners could not make their mortgage payments. Overwhelmed by soaring demand for relief and by plummeting tax revenues, local governments could only look on helplessly. During the 1930s, the administration of Franklin D. Roosevelt responded by propping up the financial system of credit that supported homeownership.[1]

At the same time, Roosevelt's New Deal programs intervened directly in the production and maintenance of housing for middle- and lower-class Americans. Besides the planning experiments of the Resettlement Administration and the Tennessee Valley Authority, the government's initial housing production program came as part of an employment program. When New Dealers and their congressional supporters drafted a jobs bill during the spring of 1933 to cope with the unemployment crisis, veteran housing reformers such as Mary Kingsbury Simkhovitch and Edith Elmer Wood persuaded them to include provisions for slum clearance and low-income housing. The result was the Housing Division of the Public Works Administration (PWA). During a tenure that lasted until 1937, the PWA Housing Division built 51 public housing projects containing 21,800 dwelling units (Cole 1975; Keith 1973; McDonnell 1957; Straus and Wegg 1938).

Housing reformers were not satisfied with the PWA because they felt that it was a temporary agency committed to creating employment, not low-income housing. With the support of such groups as the American Federation of Labor and the National Conference of Catholic Charities, reformers lobbied successfully for the Wagner-Steagall Housing Act of 1937, which established the United States Housing Authority (USHA) and put public housing on a permanent footing in this country. The USHA had built 100,000 units in more than 140 cities by 1942 (when it was folded into the National Housing Authority) (Biles 1990; Keith 1973; McDonnell 1957).

Visionary goals inspired the advocates of New Deal public housing. As heirs to the environmentalism of the 19th century, the housers of the 1930s condemned the slum districts for breeding disease, delinquency, and crime and believed that the elimination of the slums would cure urban social ills. They argued that the government should fight the problems of the slums by providing good homes furnished with abundant light and air, sufficient space for privacy for family members, adequate plumbing, and adequate heating, at a cost that unskilled workers could afford (Bauer 1933, 1934b; Ford 1936; Walker 1938; Wood 1931).

Housing experiments in Europe and Britain inspired breathtaking ambitions in the leaders of the movement for public housing. Elizabeth Wood and the brilliant young writer Catherine Bauer, among others, envisioned a massive housing program that would house not just the working poor, but two-thirds of the American population. They believed that private enterprise constructed good homes only for families whose income placed them in the top third of the population. This view relegated those in the lowest income group to the dangerous slums and those in the middle income third to shoddy subdivisions that were frequently potential or incipient blighted slums. The audacious goal to house all but those in the luxury market exceeded both the popular understanding of the need for a housing program and the liberal agenda of political leaders such as PWA director Harold Ickes and President Roosevelt (Bauer 1934a; von Hoffman 1995; Wood 1931).

To create an environment antithetical to the urban slum, housers mixed American architectural traditions with European modernist styles that, for better or worse, gave public housing its distinctive image.[2] For decades, reformer architects had experimented with single-family houses planned in Garden City–style groupings (after the innovations of Unwin and Parker), perimeter apartment blocks, and garden apartment buildings. In the 1930s, Bauer and designers such as Henry Wright heralded recent European innovations in housing, applauding the streamlined functional-looking image championed by the modernist or international school. The modernist-oriented designers particularly celebrated the German Zeilenbau style, in which parallel rows of two- to four-story apartment buildings were aligned along an east-west orientation and situated in superblocks (large blocks that exceed standard city block sizes) (Bauer 1934a; Plunz 1990).

During the 1930s, public housing architects and officials fashioned the Zeilenbau style to American cities and created a mold for much subsequent public housing. Oscar Stonorov created an early prototype of the American Zeilenbau style at the Carl Mackley Houses, built from 1933 to 1934 in Philadelphia for the Hosiery Workers Union.[3] His design softened the severe Zeilenbau lines of the apartment buildings with indentations and added American amenities such as courtyards, laundries, and parking garages (see figures 1.1 and 1.2) (Bauer 1934a; Bauman 1987; Plunz 1990; Pommer 1978; Sandeen 1985).

The aesthetic designs and amenities in some early public housing projected an image of superior housing, especially when compared with the old, dilapidated housing of the slum districts. Particularly good designs characterized, for example, Techwood Homes in Atlanta, a handsomely landscaped project that included parking garages and modern kitchens; Harlem River Houses, an attractive restatement of the garden apartment typology; and Lakeview Terrace in Cleveland, Ohio, where the Zeilenbau style was adapted to a sloping site above Lake Erie. These projects compared favorably with commercially produced apartment building complexes of the day (*Architectural Forum* 1938; Pommer 1978).

Many, perhaps most, of the first generation of public housing projects, however, fell short of these high architectural standards. The apartment blocks in developments such as Old Harbor Village in Boston, the Jane Addams Houses in Chicago (see figure 1.3), and Willert Park in Buffalo lacked the graceful doorways and roof lines and the varied landscaping found in the better-looking projects. Their interpretations of functional-looking modern design appeared austere rather than elegant. If mediocre in architectural terms, these projects were quite serviceable nonetheless and well appreciated by their communities and residents. A few projects such as Parklawn in Milwaukee, La Salle Place in Louisville, and Cheatham Place in Nashville resembled traditional domestic architecture. Adorned with familiar pitched roofs, doorways, and backyards, these intimately scaled one- and two-story row houses were more homey than many of the modernist projects (*Architectural Forum* 1938).

Whatever the quality and type of design, the idealistic planning principles used in all early public housing developments also helped endow them with the "project" identity that public housing would wear for decades afterward. To distinguish pub-

FIGURE 1.1
View of children's wading pool, Carl Mackley Houses, Philadelphia, PA,
W. Pope Barney, Architect

Source: Architectural Record 78(5), November 1935. Photograph by F. S. Lincoln. Copyright 1998 by The McGraw-Hill Companies. All rights reserved. Reproduced by permission of the publisher.

lic housing complexes from the tawdry environment of the slums and to incorporate the community planning principles espoused by Henry Wright, Clarence Stein, and others, the government developments invariably were designed as discrete residential entities. By placing the housing complexes in superblocks, the designs separated them from surrounding streets and neighborhoods (Plunz 1990; Pommer 1978). The fact that the new housing developments were composed of apartments also contributed to the distinctive image of public housing. At the time, over three-quarters of all American families lived in single-family houses; public housing projects presented a contrast with the types of residences occupied by most Americans.

Despite the deviations of public housing in type and appearance from other American homes, early academic research into the effects of public housing seemingly confirmed the principles of environmental determinism. Chapin (1940), for example, claimed that public housing actually improved the social behavior of the poor. How-

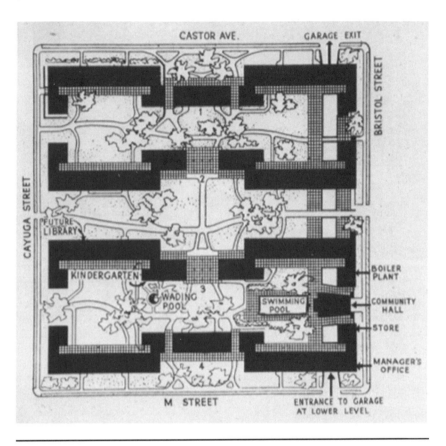

FIGURE 1.2
Plan, Carl Mackley Houses, Philadelphia, PA, W. Pope Barney, Architect

ever, his use of sophisticated mathematical analysis of survey data disguised methodological assumptions that were heavily biased toward the optimistic findings.

The establishment of a public housing program in the United States was a remarkable achievement, but the vaulting ambitions of public housing's supporters created pitfalls for the program. Location of the projects, for example, proved vexing. Many of the supporters of public housing planned to build most new public housing on inexpensive land on the outskirts of cities and let the inner-city slums gradually wither away on their own. This approach, however, flew in the face of their own rhetoric about the need to solve the immediate crisis of the slums and contradicted

FIGURE 1.3
View of Jane Addams Houses, Chicago, IL

Source: *Architectural Forum* 68(5), May 1938. Photograph by Wesley Bauman.

the wishes of conservatives who believed government should house the very poor only in inner-city low-income neighborhoods. As a result, the program soon became embroiled in disputes over the location of housing projects (Bauman 1987; Fairbanks 1988; Straus and Wegg 1938). In addition, the principles of modern design, originally intended to distinguish the projects in a positive way, would in time become a stigma for public housing.[4]

Troubled Midlife of American Public Housing

After a hiatus in the low-income housing program caused by World War II and rising conservative political sentiment after the war, the passage of the Housing Act of 1949 restarted public housing in the United States (Davies 1966). Reflecting mainstream reformist thought and the demands of the real estate industry, the 1949 law renewed the war against the slum through provisions for slum clearance and new construction, under the rubric of urban redevelopment. Although Congress never met the Act's ambitious goal of appropriations for 810,000 new public housing units or 135,000 per year, tens of thousands of new units were built annually during the Truman and Eisenhower administrations.

Continuing the design traditions of earlier projects, public housing (except in a few large cities) usually consisted of buildings of no more than three stories. Such complexes may have appeared dull from an aesthetic viewpoint and often contained small apartments, but at least they offered some convenience to their inhabitants. The low-rise designs provided a human scale and allowed tenants to view the playgrounds, courts, and gardens under their windows. Thus, the designs allowed residents to supervise their children and maintain surveillance over common areas (Newman 1972).

Contrary to Pommer's (1978) assertion that the public housing program produced no interesting architecture from the late 1930s to the 1960s, the government sponsored some noteworthy projects in the 1950s. The city of San Antonio, for example, produced an interesting variety of one- and two-story row houses and flats that offered ventilation and hillside views, and in Greenwich, Connecticut, city and state housing authorities sponsored a complex of three-story apartment blocks that reiterated Zeilenbau principles on a hill above the New York, New Haven, and Hartford railroad tracks (*Progressive Architecture* 1952a, 1952b).

During the late 1950s and 1960s, nonetheless, high-rise projects came to dominate the image of American public housing. Again European modernism provided the inspiration, but rather than its low-rise Zeilenbau manifestation, it now took the form of Le Corbusier's airy visions of towers rising out of vast expanses of grass and greenery. Le Corbusier, a Swiss-born modernist-style architect, exerted a powerful influence on a generation of designers who were mesmerized by his bold drawings of what he called the contemporary city. The movement for tall modernism also gained support from city officials and developers who saw sleek skyscrapers as a way of modernizing the aging urban landscapes of postwar America (Hall 1988).

The arguments that housing should take the form of tall modernism had little to do with reality. Before the war, Le Corbusier, Walter Gropius, and other modernists had argued for a new urban environment made up of "towers in the park" by appropriating traditional housing reformers' rhetoric about the need for low population densities and open space in the city (Le Corbusier 1947, 1967; Sert 1947). In a bizarre twist on the community planning tradition that had informed Garden City–style housing projects in the United States and Europe, tower-in-the-park theorists subscribed to the notion that elevator buildings would reproduce earthbound neighborhoods in the air. Accordingly, wide, often external, building corridors would somehow duplicate the complex functions and vitality of sidewalks and streets in the city below (*Architectural Forum* 1951; Yamasaki 1952). From the early 1950s, some designers and housers expressed qualms about what Bauer condemned as supertenements, but in New York, Philadelphia, St. Louis, and Chicago, officials embraced high-rise design with an almost insane tenaciousness (Bauer 1952, 1957; Bauer et al. 1957; Jacobs 1961; *Journal of Housing* 1952; Plunz 1990).

The ambitions of the housers of the 1930s pale when placed next to the idealism of the housing officials, designers, and planners who believed that city dwellers had to live in skyscrapers. In cities such as St. Louis and Chicago, the high-rise apartment building was a key component in sweeping urban redevelopment plans meant to turn back deteriorating physical and social conditions. Without discussion and perhaps without much thought, the supporters of high-rise redevelopment simply assumed that modern structures would transform the low-income people who were streaming into America's large cities (Chicago Housing Authority 1956–1963; *St. Louis Post-Dispatch* 1950, 1961; Teaford 1990). Explaining long-standing policy in 1965, the chairman of the Chicago Housing Authority declared, "Families who must or want to live in the inner city will have to learn to live with the high-rise building" (Brodt 1986, 18). Economy was often alleged as the reason for such large-scale structures, although the costs of sinking caissons, building elevators, and maintaining open spaces made tower-in-the-park public housing more expensive than low-rise developments.

The new public housing schemes defied both common sense and the overwhelming evidence of Americans' housing preferences. As it turned out, only the wealthy in luxury apartment buildings and the poor in public housing projects actually adopted this supposedly inevitable new form of urbanism. The well-to-do occupied their luxury apartments for only part of the year and used their wealth to dine out, hire nannies, and otherwise make their lives easier. In contrast, low-income residents had to live in their high-rise apartments year-round without such conveniences. For them, the task of supervising children was complicated by living in high-rise buildings where neither the galleries with their loud acoustics nor the great expanses of open spaces were particularly apt recreation areas (Jacobs 1961; Newman 1972).

The point here is not that effective child rearing is impossible in high-rise buildings—families live contentedly in the high-rises of Hong Kong and even New York City—but rather that the commitment to tall buildings was unrealistic and out of keeping with American tastes and values. While officials insisted on high-rises, the working and middle classes were rejecting apartments and flocking en masse to inexpensive single-family homes in the suburbs of every American city.

To be sure, designers produced some interesting interpretations of tall modernism. At Philadelphia's Mill Creek housing project, for example, Louis Kahn designed three 17-story apartment buildings so that only four units shared a common corridor on each floor. In addition, Kahn's plan included adjacent clusters of low-rise apartment buildings with their own courtyards and related tall and low buildings to one another within the larger site plan (Bae 1995; Bauman 1987).

More typical, however, were the severe slabs with rows of apartments lining either side of a central corridor. In St. Louis, the housing authority hired the well-connected local firm Hellmuth, Leinweber, and Yamasaki. After Minoru Yamasaki's design for the John J. Cochran Garden Apartments (an arrangement of 6-, 7-, and 12-story buildings with balconies to serve as porches) won honors in architectural circles, the authority built his design for the mammoth Pruitt-Igoe project of thirty-three 11-story buildings (see figure 1.4). Along one outer wall, the firm included deep hallways or "galleries" that were to function as playground, porch, and entry-

FIGURE 1.4
View of Pruitt-Igoe Housing Project, St. Louis, MO, Hellmuth, Leinweber, and Yamasaki, Architects

Source: Courtesy of the Frances Loeb Library, Graduate School of Design, Harvard University. Reproduced with permission.

way to laundry and storage rooms, attracting residents and creating "vertical neighborhoods." In Chicago, housing officials over a period of years constructed a four-mile strip of public housing high-rises along South State Street, climaxing in 1963 with the completion of the world's largest public housing project, the Robert Taylor Homes, a two-mile stretch of twenty-eight 16-story buildings containing more than 4,300 units (see figure 1.5) (*Architectural Record* 1954; Bailey 1965; Bowly 1978).

Within a few years, such behemoths were beset by a myriad of serious problems. When federal authorities held down unit costs, local housing authorities compensated by increasing the number of apartments in high-rise complexes. In St. Louis, as Eugene Meehan has shown, authorities called for small apartments when the low-income demand was for large ones. To make matters worse, landholders, contractors, and unions progressively inflated their charges in every large project. Caught between stingy federal unit cost ceilings and skyrocketing project costs, the authorities skimped, eliminating such basic construction and safety elements as insulation for heating pipes (Meehan 1975, 1979).

FIGURE 1.5
Bird's-eye view of Robert Taylor Homes, Chicago, IL, Shaw, Metz, and
Associates, Architects

Source: Courtesy of the Chicago Historical Society. Photograph by Bill Engdahl, Hedrich-Blessing.

The open spaces evolved into dangerous no-man's-lands. At Pruitt-Igoe, vandalism and crime made a mockery of Yamasaki's galleries and other aesthetic pretensions. In 1965 the project, which by then had a significant number of vacant apartments, was deemed a failure, and the federal government initiated a $7 million rescue effort. Yet as late as 1966 the Chicago Housing Authority insisted, over the objections of federal housing officials, on building 22- and 16-story towers at the Raymond Hilliard Center (*Architectural Forum* 1966; Bailey 1965; Bowly 1978).

Social problems also plagued the public housing program. In the 1930s, the clientele for public housing was working-class families who had adjusted to city life and were seldom recent immigrants. After the war, the constituency for public housing became lower-class rural migrants from the South and Puerto Rico, many of whom were uneducated and had little experience with the city and its institutions. Much to the dismay of local public housing authorities, in the late 1940s conservatives in

Congress and the federal housing authority pushed through a federal policy of evicting families whose income exceeded poverty-level ceilings. The enforcement of income limits excluded many stable and upwardly mobile tenants. To make matters worse, housing acts of the 1950s forced the admission into public housing of people who had been uprooted by urban renewal and highway projects. Some of those families were plagued with problems of instability, violence, and alcoholism (Friedman 1968; Gelfand 1975; Wood 1982).

At the same time, officials attempting to integrate existing public housing or locate new projects in outlying neighborhoods encountered stiff, sometimes violent, resistance. In response, housing authorities chose to situate most family projects in the slums. Public housing became associated with the inner city, impoverished dependency, African Americans, and crime. The design of projects as separate environments—a legacy of the idealism of the 1930s—and the monumental institution-like quality of the high-rise developments underscored the role of public housing developments as stigmatized warehouses for the poor (Hirsch 1983).

In the 1960s, public housing had begun to project an image of disaster. Caught between rising costs and falling rents, city officials began to cut maintenance and security budgets for the deteriorating projects. Then the Brooke Amendment to the 1968 Housing Act placed a ceiling on rents of 25 percent of the tenants' income, further reducing the amount of funds available for operating expenses. In the late 1960s and early 1970s, public housing became the subject of fierce attacks. In his book, sociologist Lee Rainwater (1970) condemned Pruitt-Igoe and other giant projects as human disaster areas. Portraying a bleak world of crime and violence where the strong persecute the weak, the architect Oscar Newman (1972) disparaged the design of the high-rises for their lack of security. The demolition of the Pruitt-Igoe project in the early 1970s, after repeated efforts to rehabilitate it had failed, symbolized the despair that surrounded the program. When Richard Nixon placed a moratorium on federal funding for all housing programs in 1973, many felt that it seemed appropriate to end a bad program.

Yet despite the well-publicized failures, the disrepute of public housing was not all justified. From the 1960s, many local housing agencies produced elderly housing that was accepted without controversy and that, along with the Social Security and Medicare programs, helped enhance quality of life among older Americans. Moreover, many thousands were and are content to live in the inexpensive apartments that public housing projects offered, as long as some semblance of personal security was included in the bargain. The failure of public housing, although few seemed to realize it, was simply that the program by itself could not solve social problems, integrate society, or usher in a new high-rise urbanism.

From the 1960s, housing advocates and officials began to retreat from the concept of public housing as an appropriate response to the problems of the urban poor. Policymakers devised new programs that provided indirect and direct subsidies to private, not public, developers and landlords of new and rehabilitated low-income housing. For example, the Section 221(d)(3) program (as it was first passed in 1961) and the Section 236 program (enacted in 1968) allowed mortgage lenders to dispense low-income housing mortgages at rates below the current market. Later Section 221(d)(3) was amended to provide direct subsidies to cover the difference between a calculated potential rent and 20 percent of the tenants' income. Section 8 of the Housing and Community Development Act of 1974 created a complicated set of subsidies and tax incentives for constructing, rehabilitating, and maintaining buildings with low-income rental units. (The privatized construction programs were also bedeviled by problems, especially financial scandals.) In the 1980s, the Reagan administration began to promote Section 8 rental vouchers for tenants as a housing program that would avoid spending public monies on construction of low-income housing (Hays 1985; Listokin 1991).

Meanwhile, the designers of low-income housing began to reject the distinctive modernist-style architecture that had characterized, and now stigmatized, public housing. The new thinking about the form of low-income housing, foreshadowed in the criticisms of Bauer and others in the 1950s, received official standing in 1968 when a presidential commission condemned the idea of large-scale high-rise projects (National Commission on Urban Problems 1968). Although some monumental housing projects continued to be built during the 1960s and 1970s, designers groped for more responsive subsidized housing forms. In Boston's Villa Victoria, John Sharratt mixed building sizes by combining towers with row houses. Other projects—such as the Martin Luther King Community designed by Hartford Design Corporation in Hartford and Woodlawn Gardens designed by Stanley Tigerman in Chicago—consisted of courts of low-rise buildings that retained some of the austere image of public housing (Bowly 1978; *Progressive Architecture* 1971, 1980).

But architect Hugh Stubbins demonstrated the wave of the future in the late 1960s when he designed Warren Gardens in Boston's Roxbury neighborhood as a town house development. Abandoning the extreme modernist style altogether, Stubbins demonstrated that low-income housing could be made to look indistinguishable from housing for the middle-class market (see figure 1.6) (*House and Home* 1972). In the 1970s, architect Oscar Newman published a set of design principles formulated to ensure the maximum amount of safety through private entrances and enclosed semi-private open spaces (Newman 1972). Applying Newman's principles, designers began to build new housing and rebuild old public housing in ways they hoped would give their low-income residents a sense of connection to, not isolation from, the community at large.

Persistence of High Ambitions

During the 1980s, the advocates of good low-income housing responded to the budget retrenchment of the Reagan administration by finding new ways to produce hous-

FIGURE 1.6
View of Warren Gardens, Roxbury, MA, Hugh Stubbins and Associates,
Architects

Source: Photograph by Jonathan Green. Courtesy of the Frances Loeb Library, Graduate
School of Design, Harvard University. Reproduced with permission.

ing. Community development corporations and other nonprofit groups emerged as
leading developers of subsidized low-income housing. Funded at first primarily by
foundations and corporations and later, under Presidents Bush and Clinton, by government, these groups now produce about 30,000–40,000 units of housing annually, equal to the levels of production of public housing during the 1950s.

Although housing advocates of today have learned much from the experiences of
the past, the visionary idealism that has characterized the housing movement in the
past persists in new forms. The idea that the manipulation of the environment can
improve the social circumstances and behavior of the poor still persists, but not in
the form of a vast public housing program or avant-garde architecture and urban
design. Instead many housers believe that they can address the problems of the poor
by placing them in economically and ethnically heterogeneous residential areas.

Mixed-income tenancy, for example, is now seen as a road to uplifting the poor.
In its more moderate form, this argument makes a great deal of sense. The departure of stable working- and middle-class households from areas where low-income

people live has deprived the poor not only of role models but also of churches and other organizations that promote the order and values necessary to a healthy community (Wilson 1987). To combine the residences of the poor with those of somewhat better-off households, housing advocates and officials have called for removing the maximum limits to income in housing projects and setting aside units for varying income levels in low-income housing projects (for example, see Spence 1993). These are practical policies that have helped to counteract the effects of population shifts in recent years.

But the more extreme versions of mixed-income housing call for combining elements of the population that differ radically in class and ethnicity. Like the earlier enthusiasms for policies related to the public housing program, the arguments for this policy are vague about precisely how the poor will benefit from living next to wealthy neighbors with whom they have little in common (Mulroy 1991). The virtue of recent urban housing developments that combine luxury market units with low-income units (Tent City, a project completed in 1988 in Boston's South End, is one example) is that they provide poor families with good homes they would not otherwise have. By itself, however, the mixing of extremely diverse income groups does not solve any social problem other than that of housing.

Similarly, the policy of scattering the sites of low-income housing across the city aims at uplifting the poor through contact with the financially better-off. Although a great improvement on the policies that concentrated masses of single-parent families on relief, this program often attracts adventurous and upwardly mobile families who probably would persevere in any case. In addition, scattered sites of low-income public housing can be developed only in small numbers and, according to Fuerst (1985), are more expensive than centralized projects to maintain and provide with social services.

The most impractical and therefore perilous version of contemporary environmental determinism is the policy of aggressively dispersing low-income families into middle- and upper-income suburbs. That policy is based on the idea that thriving suburban locales will impart superior schooling and employment to the poor who are moved there. Pioneered as the Gautreaux program in the city of Chicago, the dispersal policy originated as a civil rights, not a housing, initiative. A court order devised the Gautreaux program as a remedy to the patterns of racially segregated tenant placement of the Chicago Housing Authority. The program found available units in the suburbs and placed low-income households with Section 8 certificates in them. The Gautreaux program was implemented with great care; officials found cooperative landlords and screened tenants for reliable rent payment, good housekeeping, and large families. Despite its origins, housing advocates soon celebrated Gautreaux as a way that poor urban dwellers could improve school performance and obtain better jobs (Rosenbaum 1991).

Demonstrating the historic tendency of housers to overreach, the Bush and Clinton administrations instituted the Moving to Opportunity demonstration program to expand the Gautreaux-style dispersal policy to Baltimore, Boston, Chicago, Los Angeles, and New York. The task of duplicating the carefully constructed Gautreaux program all over the country will not be an easy one. The implementation of large and complex government programs in housing and other fields has rarely run smoothly. Indeed the program stumbled at the outset when officials failed to educate the residents of blue-collar suburbs outside Baltimore about the limited scope of the plan. Because of the ensuing storms of protest, the Clinton administration delayed the implementation of the program in Baltimore (De Witt 1995; U.S. Department of Housing and Urban Development 1996).

As its early problems indicate, the Moving to Opportunity program risks the kind of political disasters that beset the public housing program. In blue-collar neighborhoods, the words "Section 8"—like the words "public housing"—have become a pejorative term associated with loud, unruly, and possibly dangerous tenants. (Only a minority of subsidized families fit this description, but as with public housing, a few bad actors ruin the reputation of the whole group.) In Boston, for example, neighborhood residents became aggravated over the influx of holders of Section 8 rental certificates into buildings owned by absentee landlords and complained so bitterly that the mayor convened a special task force to calm the situation (Committee on Subsidized Housing/Absentee Landlord Issues 1993). Just the threat of an influx of inner-city poor triggered large-scale protests in Baltimore. If resumed, an aggressive dispersal program will only provoke more controversies and resistance. At a time when many are fighting to keep basic social programs alive, right-wing commentators have begun to use the threat of a campaign to enforce socioeconomic heterogeneity throughout metropolitan America as ammunition to suppress all government housing programs (Bovard 1994).

Yet even if the Moving to Opportunity program had been able to copy Gautreaux perfectly, it would have failed to solve the problems of the poor. A second look at survey data shows that Gautreaux achieved far less impressive results than earlier conclusions suggested. Although more likely to obtain jobs, low-income arrivals in the suburbs neither earned nor worked more than their counterparts located in the city. As might be expected, the new suburbanites complained that they were isolated from child care, adequate public transportation, and the kinds of support provided by a shared community. But most important of all, individuals who had been on welfare for a long time or felt they had little control over their lives—the crucial group that such a program is supposed to help—had a harder time finding jobs in the suburbs and made less money when they did find work (Popkin, Rosenbaum, and Meaden 1994).

The preceding analysis of the flaws in recent policies should not be interpreted as an objection to either socioeconomic integration or vigorous prosecution of fair housing laws. Rather it demonstrates the continuing tendency of housers to view housing policies as panaceas and, in particular, to overstate the importance of environment in determining social behavior. Perhaps the intensity of political debate encourages this inflation of claims for policies. Nonetheless, advocates of good low-income housing might be better off admitting that the physical environment is only one of a complex of problems—including cultural values and individual behavior patterns— that block the upward mobility of the poor. To do otherwise is to court bitter disillusionment and perhaps even jeopardize the housing movement.

Lessons of the Past

History does not provide precise prescriptions for the future, but it does indicate that, to be successful, housing advocates should not promote large-scale politically controversial programs (such as Moving to Opportunity) as panaceas for deep-rooted social problems. Instead history suggests that flexibility and political pragmatism are the best guides to shaping housing policy. Thus, since current housing programs enjoy considerable, although not overwhelming, political support, housing advocates should try to protect government funding to preserve and renovate viable public and subsidized housing developments and to maintain the number of rental vouchers and certificates. In addition, advocates should work to preserve tax credits to assist nonprofit community-based low-income housing efforts.

In an era of drastic reductions in government expenditures for social programs, the success of housing developments as safe havens and places of social betterment will depend not on new, expensive social programs but on screening tenants and coordinating with local social service agencies, schools and educational services, and the police. And if, as President Clinton has stated, the era of big federal government is over, then advocates for effective housing policy now should refocus their energies on state and local governments and the private sector.

For many housing advocates, such pragmatic approaches to policy may seem too modest. The simple goal of providing decent and safe housing to low-income people where they now live is not as lofty as creating modern housing, a high-rise civilization, or a socially heterogeneous society. Yet it is just as worthy and, in these perilous times for social policy, has the advantage of being remotely possible.

Notes

1. The Federal Home Loan Bank Board supported savings and loan associations. Its offspring, the Home Owners Loan Corporation, offered long-term loans to homeowners, and the Federal Housing Administration insured long-term mortgages offered by housing lenders.

2. The literature concerning the modern movement in architecture is vast. In a recent work, Peter G. Rowe defines the important characteristics as follows:

> The by now familiar modern functionalist doctrine consisted of four central considerations: material integration and suitability; the expression of contemporary building construction and fabrication techniques; efficient use and layout of buildings; and the propagation of a new spatial order devoid of all references to the past. (Rowe 1993, 43)

3. The Carl Mackley Houses project was begun before the start of the public housing program and was financed in part by a loan from the PWA (Straus and Wegg 1938).

4. Another grievous fault was the tendency to segregate public housing tenants by race. Although the supporters of public housing were liberals and certainly did not consider racial segregation as part of a housing program, Ickes inaugurated a policy, later followed by many federal and local officials, that allotted projects to a single racial group according to the previous composition of the neighborhood.

References

Architectural Forum. 1938. Public Housing. 68(5):356–424.

Architectural Forum. 1951. Slum Surgery in St. Louis. 94(4):128–36.

Architectural Forum. 1966. Goldberg Variations. 125(4):25–33.

Architectural Record. 1954. Multi-family Housing: Building Types Study Number 211. 115(6):170–87.

Bae, David Y. 1995. Mill Creek Housing—Louis I. Kahn and Housing Reform. Seminar paper. Cambridge, MA: Harvard University Graduate School of Design.

Bailey, James. 1965. The Case History of a Failure. *Architectural Forum* 123(5):22–25.

Bauer, Catherine. 1933. "Slum Clearance" or "Housing." *The Nation* 137(3575):730–31.

Bauer, Catherine. 1934a. *Modern Housing.* Boston: Houghton Mifflin.

Bauer, Catherine. 1934b. Slums Aren't Necessary. *American Mercury* 31(123):296–305.

Bauer, Catherine. 1952. Clients for Housing: The Low-Income Tenant—Does He Want Supertenements? *Progressive Architecture* 33(5):61–64.

Bauer, Catherine. 1957. The Dreary Deadlock of Public Housing. *Architectural Forum* 106(5):140–42.

Bauer, Catherine, James W. Rouse, Ellen Lurie, William L. C. Wheaton, Charles Abrams, Henry Churchill, Stanley Tankel, Elizabeth Wood, Vernon Demars, Lee F. Johnson, and Carl Feiss. 1957. The Dreary Deadlock of Public Housing II. *Architectural Forum* 116(6):139–41, 218, 222–32.

Bauman, John F. 1987. *Public Housing, Race, and Renewal: Urban Planning in Philadelphia, 1970–1974.* Philadelphia: Temple University Press.

Biles, Roger. 1990. Nathan Straus and the Failure of U.S. Public Housing, 1937–1942. *The Historian* 52(1):33–46.

Birch, Eugenie, and Deborah Gardner. 1981. The Seven-Percent Solution: A Review of Philanthropic Housing, 1870–1910. *Journal of Urban History* 7(4):404–38.

Bovard, James. 1994. Suburban Guerrilla. *The American Spectator* 27(9): 26–32.

Bowly, Devereaux. 1978. *The Poorhouse: Subsidized Housing in Chicago, 1895–1976.* Carbondale and Edwardsville: Southern Illinois University Press.

Brodt, Bonita. 1986. Dream of Progress Died Quickly at Taylor Homes. *Chicago Tribune*, December 3.

Chapin, F. Stuart. 1940. An Experiment on the Social Effects of Good Housing. *American Sociological Review* 6(5):868–79.

Chicago Housing Authority. 1956–1963. *Annual Report.* Chicago.

Cole, Mary Susan. 1975. Catherine Bauer and the Public Housing Movement, 1926–1937. Ph.D. Diss., George Washington University.

Committee on Subsidized Housing/Absentee Landlord Issues. 1993. *Setting the Course: A Plan for Housing Policy Reform.* Boston: City of Boston.

Cousineau, Christine. 1989. *Tenement Reform in Boston, 1870–1920: Philanthropy, Regulation, and Government Assisted Housing.* Hilliard, OH: Society for American City and Regional Planning History.

Davies, Richard. 1966. *Housing Reform during the Truman Administration.* Columbia: University of Missouri Press.

De Witt, Karen. 1995. Housing Voucher Test in Maryland Is Scuttled by a Political Firestorm. *New York Times*, March 28.

Fairbanks, Robert. 1988. *Making Better Citizens: Housing Reform and the Community Development Strategy in Cincinnati, 1890–1960.* Urbana and Chicago: University of Illinois Press.

Ford, James. 1936. *Slums and Housing.* Vol. 1. Cambridge, MA: Harvard University Press.

Friedman, Lawrence M. 1968. *Government and Slum Housing: A Century of Frustration.* Chicago: Rand McNally.

Fuerst, J. S. 1985. Scattered-Site Housing: No Panacea. *Planning* 51(2):21–23.

Gelfand, Mark I. 1975. *A Nation of Cities: The Federal Government and Urban America, 1933–1965.* New York: Oxford University Press.

Hall, Peter. 1988. *Cities of Tomorrow: An Intellectual History of Urban Planning and Design in the Twentieth Century.* Oxford, England: Basil Blackwell.

Hays, R. Allen. 1985. *The Federal Government and Urban Housing.* Albany: State University of New York.

Hirsch, Arnold R. 1983. *The Making of the Second Ghetto: Race and Housing in Chicago, 1840–1960.* Cambridge, England: Cambridge University Press.

House and Home. 1972. Project Portfolio: Warren Gardens, Roxbury, Massachusetts. 442(1):80–83.

Jacobs, Jane. 1961. *The Death and Life of Great American Cities.* New York: Random House.

Journal of Housing. 1952. High-Rise Housing—Does It Have a Place in the Public Housing Program? 9(2):46–47, 60.

Keith, Nathaniel S. 1973. *Politics and the Housing Crisis since 1930.* New York: Universe Books.

Le Corbusier. 1947. *The City of Tomorrow and Its Planning.* Translated by Frederich Etchells. London: John Roher. 1929. Reprint, London: Architectural Press.

Le Corbusier. 1967. *The Radiant City.* 1933. Reprint, London: Faber and Faber.

Listokin, David. 1991. Federal Housing Policy and Preservation: Historical Evolution, Patterns, and Implications. *Housing Policy Debate* 2(2):157–85.

Lubove, Roy. 1962. *The Progressives and the Slums: Tenement House Reform in New York City, 1890–1917.* Pittsburgh: University of Pittsburgh Press.

McDonnell, Timothy L. 1957. *The Wagner Housing Act—A Case Study of the Legislative Process.* Chicago: Loyola University Press.

Meehan, Eugene J. 1975. *Public Housing Policy—Convention Versus Reality.* New Brunswick: Center for Urban Policy Research.

Meehan, Eugene J. 1979. *The Quality of Federal Policymaking: Programmed Failure in Public Housing.* Columbia: University of Missouri Press.

Mulroy, Elizabeth A. 1991. Mixed-Income Housing in Action. *Urban Land* 50:2–7.

National Commission on Urban Problems. 1968. *Building the American City: Report of the National Commission on Urban Problems to the Congress and to the President of the United States.* Washington, DC: U.S. Government Printing Office.

Newman, Oscar. 1972. *Defensible Space.* New York: Macmillan.

Plunz, Richard. 1990. *A History of Housing in New York City: Dwelling Type and Social Change in the American Metropolis*. New York: Columbia University Press.

Pommer, Richard. 1978. The Architecture of Urban Housing in the United States during the Early 1930s. *Journal of the Society of Architectural Historians* 37(4):235–64.

Popkin, Susan J., James E. Rosenbaum, and Patricia M. Meaden. 1994. Labor Market Experiences of Low-Income Black Women in Middle-Class Suburbs: Evidence from a Survey of Gautreaux Program Participants. *Journal of Policy Analysis and Management* 12(3):556–73.

Progressive Architecture. 1952a. Clients for Housing: The Public Authority. 33:65–70.

Progressive Architecture. 1952b. San Antonio Public Housing. 33:15–18, 20–22.

Progressive Architecture. 1971. The Low-Income Family as Client: Who's Going to Live Here Anyhow? 52:106–11.

Progressive Architecture. 1980. Villa Victoria. 14:13–19.

Rainwater, Lee. 1970. *Behind Ghetto Walls*. Chicago: Aldine-Atherton.

Rosenbaum, James E. 1991. Black Pioneers: Do Their Moves to Suburbs Increase Economic Opportunity for Mothers and Children? *Housing Policy Debate* 2(4):1179–213.

Rowe, Peter G. 1993. *Modernity and Housing*. Cambridge, MA: Massachusetts Institute of Technology Press.

St. Louis Post-Dispatch. 1950. Progress or Decay—Supplement. March–May.

St. Louis Post-Dispatch. 1961. Special Progress Section: The Fight Against Decay. May 7.

Sandeen, Eric. 1985. The Design of Public Housing in the New Deal: Oscar Stonorov and the Carl Mackley Houses. *American Quarterly* 37(5):645–67.

Sert, José Luis. 1947. *Can Our Cities Survive?* Cambridge, MA: Harvard University Press.

Spence, Lewis H. 1993. Rethinking the Social Role of Public Housing. *Housing Policy Debate* 4(3):355–68.

Straus, Michael W., and Talbot Wegg. 1938. *Housing Comes of Age*. New York: Oxford University Press.

Teaford, Jon. 1990. *The Rough Road to Renaissance—Urban Revitalization in America, 1940–1985*. Baltimore: Johns Hopkins University Press.

U.S. Department of Housing and Urban Development, Office of Policy Development and Research. 1996. *Expanding Housing Choices for HUD-Assisted Families*. Washington, DC.

von Hoffman, Alexander. 1995. Slums and Housing in the 1930s: The Fateful Marriage. Paper read at the annual meeting of the Organization of American Historians, March 30–April 2, Washington, DC.

Walker, Mabel. 1938. *Urban Blight and Slums—Economic and Legal Factors in Their Origin, Reclamation, and Prevention*. Cambridge, MA: Harvard University Press.

Wilson, William Julius. 1987. *The Truly Disadvantaged: The Inner City, the Underclass, and Public Policy*. Chicago: University of Chicago Press.

Wood, Edith Elmer. 1931. *Recent Trends in American Housing*. New York: Macmillan.

Wood, Elizabeth. 1982. *The Beautiful Beginnings, the Failure to Learn: Fifty Years of Public Housing in America*. Washington, DC: National Center for Housing Management.

Wright, Gwendolyn. 1981. *Building the Dream: A Social History of Housing in America*. New York: Pantheon.

Yamasaki, Minoru. 1952. High Buildings for Public Housing? A Necessity. *Journal of Housing* 9(7):226, 229–32.

PETER MARCUSE

2   *Mainstreaming Public Housing*

A Proposal for a Comprehensive Approach to Housing Policy

Introduction: The Nature of the Problem

Housing for the ill-housed (primarily the poor, although not only the poor[1]) has never been the central feature of United States housing policy, not even of public housing policy. Historically, public housing[2] has always been the tail of some other dog:

- First, of the effort to create jobs, in the original United States Housing Act of 1937;
- Second, of the needs of war production, during World War II;
- Third, of the demands of returning veterans for decent housing after that war ended;
- Fourth, of the relocation and slum clearance requirements of urban redevelopment and urban renewal programs;
- Fifth, of the anti-poverty program and attempts to still the racial unrest in the ghettos;
- Sixth, of the ideologically driven effort to extricate the government from housing for the poor, in production, management, and ownership;
- Seventh, of the pressure to reduce social expenditures by decentralization and the passing of responsibilities so far as feasible to nonprofits and residents; and
- Eighth, of the general drive for privatization of governmental functions and the reduction of "big government."

These are obviously oversimplified descriptions. The conflict between private market and big government has been a recurrent theme in housing debates; public housing has had to deal with racial issues from its inception; slum clearance played a role as far back as the 1930s; the anti-poverty program strongly stressed decentralization in many areas; and so on. But concern for housing for poor people has always been simply one among many forces that have driven national housing policy, never the sole and rarely the most important force shaping it.[3]

This is so for two reasons; one is narrowly economic, the other broadly political/ideological. The economic self-interest of the private real estate industry has long been recognized as a major force in limiting the role of public housing.[4] From the very outset, the requirement that the incomes targeted for admission must be 10 percent less than those necessary to find housing in the private market was openly designed to prevent public housing from competing with private housing, regardless of whether such competition might have benefited poor people. The power of private real estate interests in shaping national housing policy is visible in many aspects of public housing: the limitations on construction costs that have plagued it throughout its history; the refusal to allow amenities (even toilet seat lids or closet doors, in the early days, and air-conditioning later on) and any but minimal forms of decoration; the objections to the use of eminent domain;[5] and, above all, the constant budgetary restrictions on expenditures for public housing, culminating in Nixon's freeze on all new construction funds. The reasons for the limited role of public housing go beyond the simple and rational economic self-interest of the real estate industry, for anyone in real estate will recognize that there are some whose incomes are so low that there is no profit to be made from supplying housing to them. The most hardened and self-interested opponents of rent control in New York, for instance, have come out unequivocally in favor of public housing for those unable to afford private rentals (in lieu of holding private rentals down). Other private market economies with strong real estate industries—Germany, for example, and Great Britain[6]—have been able to adapt quite well to substantial government provision of housing, at levels ten to twenty times the scope of that in the United States. Even within the public housing program, private provider interests have been able to find sources of profit for themselves; the turnkey construction programs are a prominent example. And, beyond this, for a significant part of the real estate industry, public housing is no competition in any event; it is simply concerned with a different portion of the housing market. Poor people will never be able to afford new construction on their own; construction firms, therefore, have nothing to fear from public housing, and in fact may gain contracts from it that would not have been available otherwise.

The restrictions on the provision of housing publicly thus go deeper than real estate opposition. They lie in a political position that has powerful ideological roots. The ideological position is phrased in deceptively simple terms: The market is in the long run the most efficient provider of housing for the large majority of people, and the government should intervene in the market only where there is a market "failure," and then as little as possible. Market provision is the mainstream; public provision needs to be rigorously justified as a deviation from that mainstream. In other countries in which housing, once publicly provided, has been subject to privatization, that policy has likewise been grounded in a broad "free market" philosophy, not limited to housing or derived from analyses of the housing market. Margaret Thatcher, the Christian Democrats in Germany, the liberals in Eastern Europe, have all been avowed and ideologically committed advocates of the widest possible extension of market approaches.

The free market position as to housing is ideological, not because its premise as to the efficiency of a theoretically "free" housing market is wrong (although it has certainly been debated),[7] but because it draws from this premise a conclusion, as to the desirability of government action, that involves judgments that the premise cannot support or even illuminate. How important is what happens to poor people between the short and the long run? If government action is inefficient, is the additional cost for improving the housing of the minority the market does not serve worth that cost? Are the distributional effects of a smoothly functioning private market socially more or less desirable than those produced by governmental allocation? To what extent should monopolistic practices, whether of private real estate interests, landowners, or public authorities, be regulated or eliminated? These are not questions that have "right" or "wrong" answers. There have been a multiplicity of often excellent evaluations of public housing, either in its own terms or in comparison to other programs,[8] but it would be a foolhardy political scientist that would argue that they have ever determined public policy. Indeed, the more cynical would argue just the reverse. President Nixon suspended public housing construction funds before, not after, his administration produced reports justifying the suspension; no one ever doubted the direction President Johnson's Commission, or President Reagan's, would go on public housing.[9] And, of course, basic decisions on public housing were made by political leaders under pressure from private groups on both sides of the issue, whose positions have remained the same through thick reports and thin.

If an ideological commitment to the private market has combined with the narrower self-interest of portions of the real estate industry to limit the role of public housing, that limitation has had several effects. One is the small number of units built—small, certainly, in comparison to need, to the numbers of those eligible for occupancy, and to the numbers on the waiting list in many cities.[10] The limited role of public housing has also divided its potential beneficiaries and caused constant concern with precisely who should obtain the limited supply. Rigid income limits and complex formulae for priorities in admission have divided the very, very poor from the only very poor, the homeless from the publicly housed, the elderly from both groups, and large families from small families and singles. Where public housing might have housed a broad band of beneficiaries, those of relatively higher income have been dealt with through other programs: the old Sections 235 and 236 moderate-income programs, rehabilitation programs, financing assistance for homeownership, and, most egregiously, tax benefits afforded owner-occupants. The limited scale of public housing construction and the restricted incomes of its residents have combined to restrict the political strength of any "public housing beneficiaries' lobby," opening the door to a stronger influence by provider interests. Developers, for instance, were able to build turnkey housing to make a profit on otherwise unsalable land or on housing construction contracts, overriding the locational or quality concerns of the future residents and thereby contributing to public housing's ill repute.

Let us look at the history of public housing to see what dogs have wagged the public housing tail in the past. Understanding the past may help suggest better approaches to designing a public housing program that will be both viable and socially effective in the future.

The History: Dividing Public Housing from the Mainstream

Going back to the eight-part division of the sources of public housing at the beginning of this chapter (see also Marcuse 1994 and Marcuse [forthcoming]), there were three periods when housing policies were dramatically more progressive than during other times: the mid-1930s, the few years immediately after World War II, and the years around 1968. During three other periods, they were dramatically more retrogressive: as the Great Depression was drawing to a close, in the post–World War II period of redevelopment and urban renewal, and in the swing to conservatism under President Nixon and thereafter, following the decline of the civil rights movement. But in none of these cases was the progressive or retrogressive nature of the policy part of an overall and comprehensive concern with the housing conditions of the ill-housed, even when, as in the three progressive periods, discussion of those housing conditions was high on the political agenda.

During the Great Depression, many of the working class *were* very poor. The sharp line of distinction that was often drawn earlier between the "deserving" and the "undeserving" poor, or that is often drawn today between the "underclass" and working people, was not a topic of debate. Too many people were poor; even many who saw themselves as comfortably established working people were concerned about the possibility of eviction, the possibility that they themselves might be looking for work, might be panhandling, might be "down-and-outers." The homeless seemed no different from the housed except that the latter for the moment had roofs over their heads. The division between very poor and poor did not cut deeply; no one could blame the unemployed for their unemployment; those with jobs could not look disparagingly at those without them. At protests and rallies and demonstrations—and at voting booths—everyone came together, and their united strength achieved the New Deal reforms that laid the foundations of so much social policy today, including public housing. In President Roosevelt's famous phrase, "one-third of the nation

[was] ill-housed." The ill-housed and those who identified with their problems were a large enough part of the population so that programs addressed at their needs might be considered truly mainstream programs.

Yet the Housing Act of 1937, which established the public housing program (note: 1937, not in those first 100 days that set the New Deal agenda), stated in its preamble that its purpose was to relieve unemployment. Its New York City predecessor was justified on the twin grounds of slum clearance and giving jobs to the unemployed. The requirement in the federal legislation of equivalent demolition, both to establish the link to slum clearance and to remove any possible threat to demand in the private real estate market, reinforces the implication that expansion of the housing supply for the poor was not the dominant concern of the Act. Certainly not housing for the very poorest; public housing, at its inception, was a broad-based program for the working poor.[11] Rents were based not on income but on the costs of the housing: amortization of subsidized capital costs plus maintenance and operating expenses. Those earning too little to afford those rents could not get in.

By the end of the Depression, the situation had changed. As the economy picked up, the crisis atmosphere that large-scale unemployment had produced abated. Programs justified as job creation stimuli were no longer seen as necessary, and the conservative attack on public housing largely carried the day. Budgets for public housing were slashed and would perhaps have been eliminated entirely by 1941 had the new war effort and then World War II not revived demand. The attack on the standards of public housing and the cost-cutting that required faceless projects rather than homes were in any event successful. And the enforcement of more and more rigid income limits—the confinement of public housing's eligibles to only the very poorest—had the same result. Conservatives in Congress were ideologically committed to the primacy of the market; as employment picked up, the need for nonmarket solutions should abate, and presumably disappear entirely in the foreseeable future. Public housing was attacked as inherently socialistic, acceptable only in an emergency.[12] Its brief moment of mainstream acceptability had already passed by the time the United States entered World War II.

The war effort, of course, created a housing emergency, even in the view of conservatives. Authorization for expenditures to provide housing for war workers in the Navy yards and elsewhere was noncontroversial. Public housing built during the war was not directed toward the poor; income limits were irrelevant, place of employment and connection with the war effort were crucial. Emergency housing built directly by government under such legislation as the Lanham Act was to be only temporary, and by congressional mandate was to be sold off—privatized, we would say today—as soon as possible after the end of World War II, just as housing built by federal agencies during United States involvement in World War I was required to be, and was, sold off immediately after the end of that war.

But immediately after World War II, neither the political nor the housing situation allowed for such a conservative approach. Everyone was confronted by a hous-

ing shortage—the very poor, working people, the middle class, and above all the returning veterans. They had fought for their country in the war; they had no doubt
about their own right to be decently housed on their return. Nor would they brook
conservative opposition on the grounds of "defense of the private market." For many
veterans, exposure to a whole range of different political approaches in Europe had
opened their eyes to possibilities the mainstream of American politics did not reveal; veterans' organizations became eloquent proponents of governmental action for
housing (Keith 1973; Lawson and Naison 1986). The combination was formidable
and produced, in New York City, more local and state government-built housing
between 1948 and 1951, without any federal assistance, than was built by government in any other similar period in that city's history with all funding sources—
federal, state, and city, combined (Hopper 1994). Nationally, pressure from veterans
was responsible both for direct emergency federal action and for the Veterans Administration mortgage insurance program (and expansion of FHA programs) that
supported homeownership expansion on a large scale.

The 1950s saw the end of the upsurge of progressive action that had followed
the war. Prosperity and fuller employment reduced discontent; rapid home building
eliminated critical housing shortages; pressures for redevelopment and urban renewal
put public housing at the disposal of relocation requirements; continued cost restrictions and architectural preconceptions that seemed consistent with them produced
concentrated high-rise "projects." Race became, again, a friction point, but now not
because blacks were not obtaining a fair share of public housing, but because public
housing was turning predominantly black, under pressure both of urban renewal relocation needs and the continuing shortage of affordable housing available to blacks.
The mix made public housing widely unpopular.[13] And the McCarthyite attack on
"reds" and the whole Cold War mind-set that swept the country in the early 1950s
undermined the legitimacy of the defenders of public housing.[14]

The civil rights movement, the ghetto riots/rebellions, and the resurgence of street-
level political protest around the time of the Vietnam war resulted in the third period of more progressive housing policy. Housing issues were seen as part of larger
issues: employment, education, race relations, grassroots democracy. As such, they
entered the mainstream of political debate and social policy considerations. Interests
of the very poor and the poor were widely seen as linked; so were interests of blacks,
whites, and Hispanics, men and women (with increasing feminist consciousness).
The fight against displacement by urban renewal, subsidized housing construction,
or other government acts united poor, middle-income, and often high-income groups
in a common cause. The broader view had successes, both through militant action
and through fears of militant action. The neighborhood or community housing movement—the many organized, locally based housing groups, tenants' organizations,
nonprofit corporations, church-affiliated groups, and community organizations—got
access to and funding from government. Better designed, better managed, better integrated, more accessible housing, with lower rents, resulted, not just for the very

poor, or just for the regularly employed, but for both. Public housing was seen as having a key role in a comprehensive approach. The picture should not be painted in too glowing terms; many efforts went astray, and some were bitterly criticized as misguided from the outset.[15] But, comparatively, public housing had a higher status and was more nearly integral to housing policy than at any time in the decade before or the two decades after.[16]

The 1970s witnessed a swing of housing policy in the opposite direction, but not the swing of a natural pendulum caused by some inevitable law of gravity. Rather, it was a shift in political power, with sides quite clearly drawn and conscious of the conflicts. The use of the police, the National Guard, and armed force to put down ghetto disturbances represented a quite different approach, by a quite different leadership, than did the anti-poverty civil rights–oriented approach of the 1960s liberals. On the other side, ghetto protesters lost support among their earlier allies, and the earlier tenuous alliances of the 1960s broke apart: Blacks became separate from whites; welfare recipients separate from the poorly paid; inner-city residents separate from those further out; public employees separate from taxpayers; and liberals separate from radicals (Schwartz 1992). The coup de grace was the "fiscal crisis"; working people were told that if those less well-off got the benefit of significant public expenditures, working people would have to pay for them through higher taxes and fewer jobs. A division between "taxpayers" and "the poor" was reinforced, at the expense of the poor.

Today the pendulum is vibrating but has not changed its essential position. Although the leadership of HUD has frequently expressed its desire to embed a comprehensive housing policy within a comprehensive urban policy, the political situation has not permitted it to implement such an approach. The Clinton administration's primary concerns with housing policy appear to be framed by budgetary rather than housing issues; indeed, urban policy as a whole has not figured significantly in the administration's public positions. The "urban" vote, a term often used as a euphemism for the black and liberal vote, is not an attractive target for an administration competing for the center with an aggressive opposition to its right. Thus the limitations imposed on what can be considered viable proposals for housing policy today derive from considerations outside the housing sphere. That result is not remarkable in itself; obviously, considerations other than those of housing have to be weighed in determining national housing policy. But such considerations have today not only limited but also distorted the ultimate goals and perspectives of housing policy. HUD's 1995 blueprint for housing, *Renewing America's Communities from the Ground Up* (commonly known as Reinvention I), at first abandoned the vision of public housing as an integral part of housing policy and proposed phasing out subsidies for public housing in favor of certificates (vouchers) for its residents (HUD 1995, 42). With the phasing in of certificates, "public housing would be indistinguishable from conventional housing from the renter's point of view" (HUD 1995, 7). Under the later revision of the proposal (Reinvention II), some existing public housing would in fact survive in substantially its present form but as an unwanted stepchild, not a member of the family (HUD 1996).

No detailed critique of the presently pending proposals for changes in HUD policies and programs, whether emanating from HUD or expressed in pending legislation, is possible here. There are significant differences between the two HUD "reinvention blueprints," and between them and various bills introduced in Congress. But two elements run through them all. The most important is budgetary; and HUD's proposals are defensive.[17] They envisage a severe cutback in funding, accept the elimination of new public construction as a given, and look for alternate ways of meeting housing needs. The other key element that runs through the legislation—about which HUD is also defensive—is the retreat from public ownership and management of housing, in favor of a variety of nongovernmental alternatives. Part of those proposals have the full support of public housing tenants and most backers of public housing: the increase in tenant involvement, for example, and the decrease in bureaucratic, particularly federal bureaucratic, controls. But another part of the proposal is consistent with an overall hostility to public support for housing in any form, and includes the anticipation of a reduction of subsidies, increases in rents (repeal of the 30%-of-income cap on rents) for tenants, demolition of publicly owned units, and a gradual reduction of the publicly owned stock altogether.

The lesson that seems to me to emerge from this history is simple: To the extent that public housing is concerned with the housing needs of a broad segment of the nation, a politically and economically important constituency, its programs will be accepted and supported. To the extent that the constituency of public housing is perceived as limited, politically and economically unimportant, or, worse yet, to the extent that public housing is perceived simply as a drain on the federal treasury and the taxpayer, its programs will be neglected and sidelined. The debate as to the advantages and disadvantages of public housing becomes, in this context, almost irrelevant; for the goal is not to find the most successful program to house the ill-housed, but rather to minimize government's involvement in helping that constituency altogether. If housing policy is piecemeal, there will be a Nehemiah program for this group, public housing for that group, tax abatement for the elderly, reduced interest rates for first-time homeowners, mortgage guarantees for others, tax-exempt bond financing for one group, tax credit financing for another. A whole set of separate and separated interests are developed, and no support behind a comprehensive program ensues. In the process, the presumptive beneficiaries of public housing will be on the losing end of the competition for limited resources.

The Remedy: Mainstreaming Public Housing

The logic, then, is that if the housing needs of the most ill-housed are to be addressed, they must be addressed as part of a comprehensive housing policy that deals both with the large range of groups facing housing problems and situates public hous-ing within the mainstream[18] of housing policy. As a general principle, the point is hardly new, although out of favor today. Mary Nenno's recent summary points out how long ago the problem was recognized:

> As early as the 1960s a widely agreed-upon diagnosis of the ills of the public housing program was its isolation from both the operations of the total housing market and from the economic and social forces that direct community life. (Nenno 1996, 121)[19]

The policy implications drawn below interpret mainstreaming in three senses: policy, practice, and politics. In policy, public housing needs to be seen as an inte-gral if not central part of overall governmental housing policy, rather than an unfor-tunate minor program for a special group, a minority of the very poor. In practice, public housing needs to be situated, built, and equipped as part of the community in which it is located; it needs to serve a broad spectrum of residents, rather than be isolated in stigmatized "projects" for the poor. In politics, public housing policy must be taken up as part of a coalition effort to deal with the broad range of housing issues, from affordability for lower-paid working households to homeownership for young couples, to neighborhood security, to environmental quality, to tax fairness, to red-lining, to interest rate and mortgage insurance policies.

We are returned to an issue taken up earlier in this chapter: the impact of the concept that the market is the mainstream, that government action should be lim-ited to remedying market "failures." The most ill-housed, the poorest, are then rel-egated to treatment "outside" the market; all others are dealt with "inside the market." The poor are thus out of the mainstream, everyone else in it. The division between the very poor and all others in need of some assistance through housing policy is thus reflected in a division between what is done through and within the housing market and what is done outside it. One solution might be to deal with the prob-lems of the very poor also through the market; vouchering out represents such an approach. But, as even HUD recognizes in Reinvention II, vouchering out completely will not improve the position of most of the poor. The supply of affordable housing is too limited to provide choice; much of public housing is poorly located or other-wise unattractive to middle-income families and will not be rented by them. Besides, in other cases public housing is functioning very well as is (HUD estimates more than 3,000 local authorities are "well-performing"; only some one hundred are "se-verely distressed"); the investment in public housing is great and would be jeopar-dized by a switch to "market" forces; social services are needed by many; racial discrimination limits alternatives; and private and public management incentives are divergent.[20]

If public housing is to be retained in any form, then, the remedy for its present isolation and neglect involves overcoming the treatment of anything outside of the market as being outside of the mainstream, as an unwelcome intruder in a frugal society. Housing policy could develop an approach to public provision of housing

that would distribute benefits in a rational manner based on need, integrate market
and nonmarket housing in a comprehensive manner (bringing it into the policy mainstream), fit public housing into the context and fabric of the communities in which
it exists in ways satisfactory both to its residents and their neighbors (bringing it
into the practice mainstream), and address in coordinated fashion all those who would
benefit from a greater public role (bringing it into the political mainstream). It is
indeed an approach consistent with the views of many in HUD and the Clinton
administration.[21]

The view of the private market as the "natural" and "right" way of providing housing, and the consequent denigration of public housing and those benefiting from it,
need to be reexamined. It is an illusion that the housing market is a free, private
market today. Government is integrally involved in housing from beginning to end:
from street and infrastructure provision to the services that make residential life possible (police, fire, sanitation, and the like), to taxation, to judicial enforcement of
property rights, to zoning and building code restrictions. What the private housing
market has accomplished for many Americans—and it is quite a bit—it has accomplished with the support of very extensive governmental action. The conception that
the default setting for housing provision is simply "private market" is ideological and
harmful, both for the formulation and for the implementation of housing policy.

It is not a criticism of the private market to say that it functions as it does; there
is simply a need to recognize that the market can, and can only be expected to, care
for a limited segment of the population, although its consequences affect all. It should
operate within a publicly determined framework, not independent of it. Public housing could function as a yardstick for the private market, in much the same way as
the TVA does for private utilities. By direct competition, the influence of decent housing can be spread outside public housing itself.[22] Even standards for rent controls
in the private market could be established on the basis of controlled costs in public
housing. Increasing the affordability of private housing can help substantially improve the housing situation of many households.

On the other side, the ideological conviction that either government officials, housing experts, or tenants and community residents, separately, know all the answers to
housing problems also needs to be reexamined. Very few today advocate "big government" for its own sake. But there is an inherent tension between the desire to set
federal standards and the desire to provide resident or community control, between
the need to allocate centrally available resources centrally and the desire to decentralize expenditures and decision making. HUD's new concept of performance-based
bonuses may be a sensible approach to that tension: It permits decisions to be made
locally, but it also leaves in federal hands the judgment of the effectiveness of their
results. "Locally," however, may mean mayors, or city councils, or community groups,
or public housing residents. The anti-poverty program, in the opinion of many, floun-
dered on just that tension: what "maximum feasible participation of the poor" really
meant (Moynihan 1970; Piven and Cloward 1974), and how mayors and bureau-

crats reacted (Marris and Rein 1967). The arguments about federal preferences in admission to public housing today show that the tension involved is alive and well.

What would such an approach look like? We may contrast it with the present treatment of public housing, in which public housing is seen as a separate program catering with public funds to those at the bottom end of a housing market, excluded from the market by lack of effective demand, while the balance of housing provision is privately undertaken. Diagrammatically, it may be imagined thus:

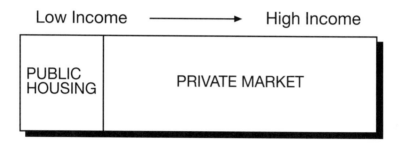

If one were to visualize a policy that saw housing provision as a whole, both public and private efforts within a single mainstream, it might look as follows:

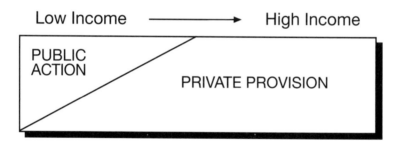

These are, of course, simply schematic diagrams, intended to suggest approaches rather than present data. But a comprehensive approach to housing might well consider beginning in this way: detailing the relationships between governmental expenditures, from whatever source, and housing needs, of all parts of the population. The data to move from a conceptual and schematic approach to an empirically based comprehensive analysis is available.[23] There are some difficult issues in performing the analysis—the handling of general income support payments not tied to but usable for housing, for example; the calculation of infrastructure transfer payments; the relationship between income and wealth; the adjustment of need to household size; measuring the benefit of non-taxation of imputed rental income, and so on. Grappling with such issues is the meat of housing policy analysis; even if it cannot be done perfectly, we can get much closer than we are.

In approximate terms, the findings would likely show a present distribution with substantial benefits to a fraction of the very poor, declining benefits for moderate income, and then increasing benefits for the well-to-do. Diagrammatically, it would look somewhat as follows, arraying benefit by income:

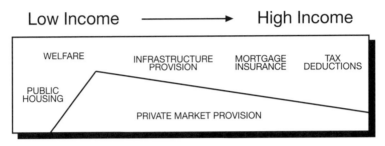

What a desirable distribution should be can then be intelligently debated. Definitions of equity vary widely.[24] Two principles seem both intuitively fair and politically palatable: (1) that no one should live below some threshold of safe and sanitary housing (and thus that the very poorest should receive enough to be brought up to such a minimum standard); and (2) that thereafter, distribution should be proportional to need, the rich getting less than the not-so-rich. It might also be well to establish that some relationship between earned income and housing quality (and extent of subsidy) continues to exist above the minimum threshold, so that the perennial complaint of some in the middle class—that they are worse off than their poorer cousins—can be avoided. Instead of arguing only negatively against tax benefits for the wealthy, a broad call for examination of the equity of all subsidies to housing would create less political antagonism from residents. Rather than having one set of untouchable mainstream programs, like income tax benefits for homeownership, and another set of marginal programs, like public housing, each would be seen in the context of the other.

In particular, tax policy needs to be integrated with housing policy. Tax subsidies to homeowners through mortgage interest and local real property tax deductions from the federal income tax, as well as non-taxation of imputed income, are far and away the largest government subsidy going to housing today.[25] At the local level, neither the Comprehensive Housing Affordability Strategy (CHAS) nor the Consolidated Plan guidelines ask about the levels of real property taxation applicable to different categories of property, let alone their distributive effect. Yet appraisal policies and tax benefits (abatements, exemptions) at the local level, and tax expenditures at the federal level, significantly influence the cost of housing. Today, at both federal and local levels, they favor homeowners. Whether that is the desirable result could be much more intelligently (and effectively) debated if the figures were, comprehensively and in context, on the table.

Obviously all this requires extensive debate, and no general resolution is likely in the foreseeable future. But a debate looking at these issues all together, each in the context of the other, would be a major step in the right direction.

In general, comprehensive planning has long been espoused in theory in federal legislation dealing with housing—but, strikingly, only for local governments. Planning has been required in a long series of federal legislation, running from Urban Renewal Plans, General Neighborhood Renewal Plans, 95-a Plans, Housing Affordability Plans, and most recently Comprehensive Housing Affordability Strategies. Under current legislation a variety of separate plans required for different programs are folded into a single planning document, the Consolidated Plan. But, regardless of their utility at the local level (they are often done perfunctorily to meet requirements imposed from the outside, are not binding, and are not pursued[26]), they have had no counterpart at the national level. Legislation enacted in 1968 called for establishment of "national housing goals"; however, the requirement was steadily downplayed after adoption and was finally merged into the requirement for a "National Urban Policy Report." It now consists of little more than an annual report by the agencies involved of their activities during the year covered. Comprehensive planning and analysis need to be taken seriously, and as much at the federal level as at the local.

A mainstream role for public housing would also require some changes in the public housing program as it now exists. The most obvious changes are quantitative:[27] the total amount of public housing—housing publicly owned and maintained—should be substantially expanded, although in forms significantly different from that of the stereotype today.

Four arguments are generally leveled against such a proposal: cost, inequity, market interference, and supply/demand relations. As to costs, the United States now spends proportionately much less on publicly aided housing than other countries, many of them less prosperous than ours; the cost issue is really one of the level and distribution of tax burdens, and that is a political problem. Our society is certainly rich enough to pay the costs; the question is whether there is the desire (and whose desire it is) to do so. As to inequity, there is indeed a serious problem if middle-income people see poorer people obtaining, as of right, better housing than they themselves have. The answer here, however, lies precisely in the comprehensiveness of approach; proportional benefits should be available to middle-class people also, presented in such a way that the overall equity of the distribution is evident. The ideological aspect of the market interference issue is discussed above.

The demand- versus supply-side debate is a more difficult one, and relates to the form in which housing assistance is provided. In most European countries, housing production and housing allowances are integrated in a single system (Harloe 1994). Social housing is built, with limited subsidies and with either no income limits or limits set to cover "the broad sectors of the population," in the language of the German program. The same rentals are then set for all. (This was also the system used at the inception of public housing in the United States.) Households that cannot pay are given assistance in meeting the rent. A housing allowance system, in other words, is integrated with a public housing production system. Thus, a much greater income mix is possible than where there are income limits for continued occupancy; yet, subsidies are broadly proportional to need. The principle is widely acknowledged in the United States also, but here, in practice, demand subsidies are treated as substitutes for supply subsidies, not as supplemental to them;[28] the twisting needed to make the Section 8 program useful to expand the housing supply is an example of the problem.

The "vouchering out" system that has had its ups and downs in HUD's recent deliberations is an attempt to find a similar approach. The basic approach of permitting a range of occupants within publicly owned housing, and permitting a range of housing for those eligible for public housing, is sound. The Gautreaux experiments have shown the advantages for some families of a move from the normally restricted areas of low-income, minority residence.[29] But if the net effect is simply to reduce the amount of public housing available to those with low incomes, and instead to provide those otherwise eligible for public housing with limited subsidies to search for housing in a constricted market, the approach will end by narrowing, rather than expanding, opportunities. It must be tied into a program to expand the supply of housing—public housing as such but also affordable housing in general— to provide a fully functioning housing market in which even lower-income people have a real chance of finding decent housing. Further, given the limited attractiveness of much of the present public housing, a situation produced in large part by limitations on expenditures designed to make clear the lower status of that housing to all the world, the likelihood of producing a real income mix is slim. Today those with incomes adequate to find housing in the private market are not likely to consider seriously moving into public housing; not income limits, but limited quality, narrows the band of occupancy today. Problems of housing quality, architecture, location, and services must be addressed if the largely commendable goals of expanding choice for the ill-housed are to be implemented.

Other changes in the public housing system are also needed. Few doubt today that giving residents greater control over their living environment can have significant positive effects.[30] Much is known and many things have been done at a building level—even though the line between public relations "tenant involvement" and real control is still an often visible one. What is needed is an integration of building and neighborhood involvement, a participation by residents in the control of their communities, not just their housing. The pattern today is often tenant associations in public housing on the one side, and block associations or homeowners associations on the other, with the two sides often going in different directions. Yet, it is precisely their joining together that will make a difference in the environment of public and of not-so-directly-public housing. Then, the issue of integration into citywide and national priorities must be dealt with. Not all cities, indeed not all communities, look favorably on public housing residents in their midst, let alone residents who are managing their own projects. But if federal guidelines are oriented toward improving local democratic processes for decision making in housing, for instance by improving the selection procedures for housing authority commissioners, there should be no conflict between federal standards and decentralized control.

Other changes are also needed. Public housing projects today often stand in splendid isolation from their surroundings, whether the surroundings are better or worse off. Architectural design can produce either isolation or integration; New York City's authority has been innovative in exploring the latter (Marcuse, Burney, and Tsitiridis 1994). Management practices can either close off or open up on-site facilities to the neighbors. Tenant associations can work together with block or community associations in dealing with problems of location and management. Commercial space can be planned to bring people together. Neighborhood preference in admission is tricky, but nondiscriminatory forms are conceivable and would have advantages. Certainly contextual design is desirable. The possibilities are many.

Infrastructure and services must also be integrated with housing provision. That seems obvious, but it is rarely done except when the basic necessities are provided for new development. Social services, education, and recreation are particularly important. The policy of triage, in which the neighborhoods with the most desperate needs are written off as hopeless and investment is concentrated in neighborhoods that can be "rescued,"[31] is self-defeating when viewed from the perspective of the city as a whole. The accusation that public housing has contributed to the formation or expansion of ghettos has some truth to it (Hirsch 1983; Massey and Denton 1993), but it need not be so.

Location is another critical issue that needs to be considered in any attempt to bring public housing into the mainstream of housing in practice. The integration of public housing into neighborhoods has three aspects: site selection, comprehensive planning, and neighborhood planning.

The Department of Housing and Urban Development has struggled with the dilemmas of site selection for years, with varying degrees of good faith.[32] On the one hand, there is a desire to avoid increasing segregation. On the other, there is a desire to avoid community opposition and build in supportive neighborhoods. An "oasis" strategy has been both applied and repudiated. Clear standards should be established and applied in a comprehensive planning process rather than case by case. A community might be required to propose some minimum number of available sites for entry into the program; NIMBY-type opposition (which should be less with an integrated and comprehensive program) should be legally overridden; and fears of displacement and/or gentrification should be made subject to community decision.[33]

Using site selection criteria to determine where public housing should go is a second-best answer. The best answer is a program for the location of housing generally: an integrated zoning, infrastructure, and services plan that will locate not only public housing but also middle-class and upper-class housing, single-family as well as multifamily housing, schools, libraries, and fire and police stations, in efficient and

democratic relationship to each other. This has always been the goal of city planning, but generally it considers land uses independently of the class and social character of the users. Experience is still surprisingly limited in what kinds of mixes, what
kinds of densities, what distributional spreads, work well in residential neighborhoods.
That is because the market, left to itself, produces income as well as racial segregation. A public policy pushing in the opposite direction could accomplish much.

Administrative integration of the variety of housing activities conducted at each
level of government would seem a minimal measure for a coordinated, let alone comprehensive, housing program. Yet, it is remarkable how few governments have undertaken such measures. Housing authorities, in particular, are rarely integrated
administratively with other local housing activities, such as the handling of munici-
pally owned property, code enforcement, support of voluntary and nonprofit efforts,
housing finance, urban renewal, comprehensive neighborhood revitalization, and the
like. Bad experiences with the centralization of housing-related powers that were at
the height of national concern thirty years ago (in Newark, for example, where the
"federal bulldozer" got its bad name) may be part of the explanation. But more recent efforts, for instance in Montgomery County, Maryland, where the Housing Authority was given broadly expanded jurisdiction and renamed the Housing
Opportunities Commission (Tetreault et al. 1994), show what could be done.

Mainstreaming public housing is quite a different thing than implementing the
varied "solutions" now being discussed for "distressed" public housing projects (redesign, demolition, privatization, tenant control or control of tenants, and police
sweeps; see Gayle Epp's contribution to this volume), but it is not inconsistent with
most of them. While useful as immediate Band-Aids in crisis situations, if these "solutions" are seen as a substitute for a housing policy, they go in the wrong direction.
They divide problems into discrete categories and look for separate solutions to separate problems.[34] They are not solutions (most who advocate them do not claim they
are, although some do), but ameliorations. As solutions, they misperceive the causes
of the problems they address. They focus on problems *within* public housing; they
accept its division from the mainstream of housing provision; they accept the division of those eligible for public housing from the rest of the population; they seek
solutions within the program, rather than trying to integrate that program into a
comprehensive attack on the problems of the ill-housed.

Conclusions

To put these recommendations in their broader context: The division of our cities
into discrete groups and the resulting segregation into mutually exclusive ghettos and
enclaves are among the most visible manifestations of the troubles of our society today (Marcuse 1989). Policies that cross boundaries, that integrate, that affect the
majority of our communities with a fair distribution of benefits and burdens, are

thus centrally important. Ideological obeisance to the private market as the mainstream of housing provision accentuates divisions; public housing, as a legitimate, permanent part of the mainstream of housing provision, can help overcome these divisions. In practice, the way in which housing policies are implemented—in design, construction, management, location, financing, tenant selection—have tended to aggravate problems of social division and inequality; they can be used explicitly to confront those problems and help alleviate them. And politically, if the division of the ill-housed into discrete beneficiary categories has been a key factor in weakening support for public housing, then a focus on program initiatives that join interested groups together, that benefit them comprehensively rather than separately, is wise. As long as the housing problem is viewed (and sold) as one affecting the bottom 15 percent, 20 percent, or even, as in Germany, the bottom 33 percent of society, the remaining majority is not likely to act decisively to solve it. But if the housing problem is shown to affect a true majority of society (in different ways), a comprehensive policy that benefits that majority (in different ways) should have a better chance of success.

The answer to the problems of public housing, it seems to me, is to bring public housing into the mainstream of housing provision—to view it, and to press for it, as part of an integrated effort to address the housing problems of the majority of the American people.

Notes

1. Harvard University's Joint Center for Housing Studies 1995 Report lists, among "unmet needs," varying by area: declining homeownership rates for young households; high housing costs relative to income; lack of a suitable housing stock; lack of access to mortgage capital for minority and immigrant households; affordability of rents; structural inadequacy; and the concentration of low-cost and assisted housing, limiting locational choice and social stability.

2. I use "public housing" here to refer to housing built under the Housing Act of 1937, as amended from time to time, and owned by and managed by/for a local housing authority under the Act. It is an interesting but not particularly productive debate whether indeed public housing, as thus defined, is a single program or a series of different programs; it is here treated as a single program.

3. I have examined various episodes in the history of housing policy in the United States in a number of earlier studies: first in Marcuse (1978), which makes the same point as to governmental regulatory programs going back to the turn of the century, then in Marcuse (1986), which examines the first five years of public housing in New York City, and in Marcuse (1988), which examines New York City's housing policies. Marcuse (forthcoming) is a detailed history of the New York City Housing Authority.

4. See McDonnell (1957), for instance, for the early period, or Freedman (1969) for the post-war controversies.

5. It was, of course, the challenge to the federal government's right to use eminent domain for housing construction (*United States v. Certain Lands*) that led to the shift from a

direct, federally run program to one established under state laws and only funded (and regulated) by the federal government.

6. While Great Britain is not yet at the end of a policy of privatization that has severely reduced the proportion of Council housing in its housing stock, during its heyday social housing was one-third of that stock, under Conservative as well as Labor governments, coexisting with a robust private market in the balance of the stock; even today the proportion of publicly owned housing is some five times that in the United States.

7. For an argument couched in classical economic terms, see Smith (1970).

8. One of the most comprehensive is that of Arthur Solomon (1974), but virtually every national administration has appointed a commission that has provided commentary in one fashion or another on this question. A comprehensive review of such evaluations, and their context, would be very illuminating, but space does not allow for it here. Most such studies are vulnerable to fatal criticism as "objective" guides for public policy (and the best make no such claims), for they ultimately involve value judgments: e.g., the valuation of long-term public ownership as against benefits limited in time, with its necessarily arbitrary choice of discount rates to apply not only to financial investments but also to the human benefits of good housing; the measurement of intangibles such as racial integration or segregation; decisions as to employment or contracting practices having non-housing impacts; and others. Again, a housing purposes should be included, and if so whether as cost or benefit; and so on.

9. See Johnson and Reagan Commission reports.

10. The New York City Housing Authority, for instance, has more names on its waiting list than it has units of housing in its inventory. That is not typical: Waiting lists are not updated similarly by all authorities; many authorities have waiting lists for some projects and massive vacancies in others. Changes in the broader housing market influence demand in each sector of that market. But the overall magnitude of the numbers can fairly be taken as an indicator of the fact that public housing is for many the best possible opportunity for obtaining decent housing, even if it does not provide a good measure of the exact extent of the need.

11. In New York City, for example, the Housing Authority did employment checks to make sure applicants had the financial ability to pay the necessary rents (Marcuse 1986).

12. It is an unhappy irony that, as this is being written, Bob Dole has called public housing "one of the last bastions of socialism in the world" (*New York Times*. April 30, 1996, B8).

13. Bauer (1957) both encapsulated the description of the situation and began the process of change, which only the political changes of the 1960s allowed to bear fruit.

14. In some cities, including Los Angeles and New York City, attacks on "reds" decimated the ranks both of public housing advocates and of housing authority employees. See Parson (1984); the New York story is told in absorbing detail in Caro (1974).

15. Moynihan (1970) is probably the best known of the informed criticisms by those directly involved; Murray (1984) is a classic conservative criticism.

16. A comparison of major federal commission reports is illuminating; the reports of the Eisenhower, Nixon, and Reagan Commissions all sought ways to diminish or eliminate the role of public housing; the Kaiser and Douglas Commission reports both saw it as a necessary part of a national housing policy.

17. Many of the top officials at HUD have, in previous times, been eloquent advocates of increased new construction of public housing. See, for instance, Stegman (1988).

18. Mary Nenno's book (1996), using the same approach and terminology about "the

mainstream," appeared after this chapter was written, and is entirely consistent with the approach used here. Its recommendations, however, are more modest (or perhaps more immediately realistic): a National Commission on Cities and Urban Regions; programs expanding information and research; improved design and livability of housing; a greater international orientation (chapters 12 and 13).

19. Nenno cites the policy statement of the National Association of Housing and Redevelopment Officials (1963), issued as early as 1963, as one comprehensive formulation.

20. Criticisms of the vouchering-out proposal are many, ranging from questions raised by the General Accounting Office (US GAO 1995) to analyses by the National Low Income Housing Coalition (1996). Many are taken up in Nenno (1996), parts I-IV; see especially p. 270.

21. See, for instance, the August 3, 1995, statement of Judy A. England-Joseph, Director—Housing and Community Development Issues, Resources, Community and Economic Development Division of the United States General Accounting Office, Washington, D.C., describing with approval a number of comprehensive initiatives.

22. Kemeny has worked out the implications of one scenario for such competition in what he calls a "unitary" market in Kemeny (1995).

23. Many attempts have been made to analyze systematically numbers of housing policies viewed either as a whole or in comparison with each other, and certainly many efforts have been made to formulate more comprehensive approaches than the current legislation embodies. To name only a few: Aaron 1972; Solomon 1974; Stegman 1988; Appelbaum and Gilderbloom 1988; Schwartz et al. 1988; Bratt 1989. Analyses of the distributive impact of various federal actions affecting housing are undertaken periodically by the Congressional Budget Office and the Office of Management and Budget, and by Cushing Dolbeare for the National Low Income Housing Information Service.

24. See Gans (1973) for a broad discussion.

25. The issues were first highlighted years ago in Aaron (1972).

26. See Columbia University Housing Policy Seminar (1992), and the analyses of the Center for Community Change, Washington, D.C.

27. That was, in fact, the recommendation of many past Commissions and studies of national housing problems; it is, for instance, the first of the recommendations in NAHRO 1963, and figures prominently in the recommendations of both the Kaiser Committee (President's Committee 1968) and the Douglas Commission (National Commission 1968).

28. See, for instance, the conclusions of President Reagan's Commission on Housing (President's Commission 1982).

29. They have also shown some of the limitations, of course: the importance of counseling, the relevance of location, the general availability of housing, the level of support. The most recent overview by HUD gives a balanced assessment. See Goering (1995), especially p. 80.

30. See William Peterman's discussion in this volume for some of the limitations on what should be expected.

31. Roger Starr was the most outspoken advocate of such a policy in New York City; see Starr (1978). For discussion, see Marcuse, Medoff, and Pereira (1982).

32. Goering (1986) is by far the best discussion.

33. For one proposal of how this might be done through the use of special district zoning controls, see Marcuse (1984–85).

34. For a trenchant analysis of the very concept of "distressed" public housing projects, see Vale (1993).

References

Aaron, Henry. 1972. *Shelter and Subsidies: Who Benefits from Federal Housing Policies?* Washington, DC: Brookings Institution.

Appelbaum, Richard, and John I. Gilderbloom. 1988. *Rethinking Rental Housing.* Philadelphia: Temple University Press.

Bauer, Catherine. 1957. The Dreary Deadlock of Public Housing. *Architectural Forum* CVI(5):138–148. May.

Bauman, John F. 1987. *Public Housing, Race, and Renewal: Urban Planning in Philadelphia, 1920–1974.* Philadelphia: Temple University Press.

Bickford, A., and D. S. Massey. 1991. Segregation in the Second Ghetto—Racial and Ethnic Segregation in American Public Housing. *Social Forces* 69(4):987, 1011–1036. June.

Bratt, Rachel G. 1989. *Rebuilding a Low-Income Housing Policy.* Philadelphia: Temple University Press.

Caro, Robert A. 1974. *The Power Broker: Robert Moses and the Fall of New York.* New York: Knopf.

Columbia University Housing Policy Seminar. 1992. Analysis of the New York City CHAS. Mimeo.

Fairbanks, Robert B. 1988. *Making Better Citizens: Housing Reform and the Community Development Strategy in Cincinnati, 1890–1960.* Champaign, IL: University of Illinois Press.

Fisher, Robert Moore. 1975. *Twenty Years of Public Housing: Economic Aspects of the Federal Program.* New York: Harper and Brothers.

Freedman, Leonard. 1969. *Public Housing: The Politics of Poverty.* New York: Holt, Rinehart and Winston.

Gans, Herbert. J. 1973. *More Equality.* New York: Pantheon Books.

Goering, John M. 1986. *Housing Desegregation and Federal Policy.* Chapel Hill: University of North Carolina Press.

Goering, John, A. Haghughi, H. Stebbins, and M. Siewart. 1995. *Promoting Housing Choice in HUD's Rental Assistance Programs.* Washington, DC: U.S. Department of Housing and Urban Development. April.

Harloe, Michael. 1994. *The People's Home: Social Rented Housing in Europe and America.* London: Blackwell.

Hartman, Chester. 1975. *Housing and Social Policy.* Englewood Cliffs, NJ: Prentice Hall.

Harvard University Joint Center for Housing Studies. 1995. *The State of the Nation's Housing, 1995.* Cambridge, MA: The Center.

Hirsch, Arnold. 1983. *Making the Second Ghetto: Race and Housing in Chicago, 1940–1960.* New York: Cambridge University Press.

Hopper, Leonard. 1994. *Brief History of the New York City Housing Authority.* New York City Housing Authority. Manuscript.

Institute for Policy Studies. 1988. *The Right to Housing.* Washington, DC: The Institute.

Jencks, Christopher, and P. E. Petersen. 1991. *The Urban Underclass.* Washington, DC: Brookings Institution.

Keith, Nathaniel. 1973. *Politics and the Housing Crisis Since 1930*. New York: Universe Books.

Kemeny, Jim. 1995. *From Public Housing to the Social Market: Rental Policy in Comparative Perspective*. London: Routledge.

Lawson, Ron, and Mark Naison. 1986. *The Tenant Movement in New York City, 1904–1985*. New Brunswick: Rutgers University Press.

Marcuse, Peter. 1978. Housing Policy and the Myth of the Benevolent State. *Social Policy* (Jan./ Feb.). Reprinted in Roger Montgomery and Daniel Mandelker. 1979. *Housing in America: Problems and Perspectives,* 2nd edition. Indianapolis: Bobbs-Merrill. Also reprinted in *Critical Perspectives on Housing*. 1986. Rachel Bratt, Chester Hartman, and Ann Meyerson, eds. Philadelphia: Temple University Press.

Marcuse, Peter. 1984–85. To Control Gentrification: Anti-Displacement Zoning and Planning for Stable Residential Districts. *New York University Review of Law and Social Change* XIII(4):931–952. Reprinted in *Yearbook of Construction Articles*. Washington, DC: Federal Publications.

Marcuse, Peter. 1986. The Beginnings of Public Housing in New York. In *Journal of Urban History*. 12(4):353–390. August.

Marcuse, Peter. 1988. Divide and Siphon: New York City Builds on Division. *City Limits*. XIII(3):8–11. March.

Marcuse, Peter. 1989. "Dual City": A Muddy Metaphor for a Quartered City. *International Journal of Urban and Regional Research* 13(4):697–708. December.

Marcuse, Peter. 1995. Interpreting "Public Housing" History. *Journal of Architectural and Planning Research* 12(3):240–258. Autumn.

Marcuse, Peter. forthcoming. *A History of the New York City Housing Authority*. Manuscript.

Marcuse, Peter, David Burney, and Eftihia Tsitiridis. 1994. New York City: Historical Perspectives, Current Policy, and Future Planning. In Wolfgang F. E. Preiser, David P. Varady, and Francis P. Russell, eds., *Future Visions of Urban Public Housing*. Proceedings of "Future Visions of Urban Public Housing: An International Forum," held at the University of Cincinnati, Cincinnati, Ohio, November 17–20.

Marcuse, Peter, with Peter Medoff and Andrea Pereira. 1982. Triage as Urban Policy. *Social Policy* 12(3):33ff. Winter.

Marris, Peter, and Martin Rein. 1967. *Dilemmas of Social Reform: Poverty and Community Action in the United States*. New York: Atherton Press.

Massey, Douglas S., and Nancy A. Denton. 1993. *American Apartheid: Segregation and the Making of the Underclass*. Cambridge: Harvard University Press.

McDonnell, Timothy L. 1957. *The Wagner Housing Act*. Chicago: Loyola University Press.

Moynihan, Daniel Patrick. 1970. *Maximum Feasible Misunderstanding: Community Action in the War on Poverty*. New York: The Free Press.

Murray, Charles. 1984. *Losing Ground*. New York: Basic Books.

National Association of Housing and Redevelopment Officials. 1963. New Concepts for the 1960's: NAHRO's Proposed Low Income Housing Program. *Journal of Housing*. 20(5,6,7):253–65, 307–16, 371–85.

National Commission on Urban Problems (The Douglas Commission). 1968. *Building the American City*. Washington: U.S. Government Printing Office.

National Low Income Housing Coalition. 1996. *Roundup* 179. Washington, DC. March/April.

Nenno, Mary. 1996. *Ending the Stalemate: Moving Public Housing into the Mainstream of America's Future*. Lanham, MD: University Press of America.

Parson, Don. 1984. *Urban Politics During the Cold War: Public Housing, Urban Renewal and Suburbanization in Los Angeles.* Ph.D. Dissertation, University of California at Los Angeles.

Piven, Frances Fox, and Richard A. Cloward. 1974. The Case Against Urban Desegregation. In *The Politics of Turmoil.* New York: Vintage Books. 200ff.

President's Commission on Housing. 1982. *Report.* Washington: U.S. Government Printing Office.

President's Committee on Urban Housing (The Kaiser Committee). 1968. *A Decent Home: Report of the President's Committee on Urban Housing.* Washington: U.S. Government Printing Office.

Rohe, William M., and Michael A. Stegman. 1992. Public Housing Homeownership: Will It Work and for Whom? *Journal of the American Planning Association.* 144ff. Spring.

Schwartz, David C., Richard C. Ferlauto, and Daniel N. Hoffman. 1988. *A New Housing Policy for America.* Philadelphia: Temple University Press.

Schwartz, Joel. 1992. *The New York Approach: Robert Moses, Urban Liberals, and the Development of the Inner City.* Columbus, OH: Ohio State University Press.

Smith, Wallace. 1970. *Housing: The Social and Economic Elements.* Berkeley: University of California Press.

Solomon, Arthur P. 1974. *Housing the Urban Poor: A Critical Evaluation of Federal Housing Policy.* Cambridge: The MIT Press.

Starr, Roger. 1978. Making New York Smaller. In George Sternlieb and James W. Hughes, eds., *Revitalizing the Northeast: Prelude to an Agenda.* New Brunswick, NJ: Center for Urban Policy Research, Rutgers University. 379.

Stegman, Michael A. 1988. The Role of Public Housing in a Revitalized National Housing Policy. M.I.T. Center for Real Estate Development, Housing Policy Project. April.

Tetreault, Bernard L., Patrick Maier, and Joyce Siegel. 1994. Lessons for the Future: What We've Learned in Montgomery County, Maryland. In Wolfgang F. E. Preiser, David P. Varady, and Francis P. Russell, eds., *Future Visions of Urban Public Housing.* Proceedings of "Future Visions of Urban Public Housing: An International Forum," held at the University of Cincinnati, Cincinnati, Ohio, November 17–20.

United States Department of Housing and Urban Development [HUD]. 1995. *HUD Reinvention: From Blueprint to Action.* Washington, DC: The Department. March.

United States Department of Housing and Urban Development [HUD]. 1996. *Renewing America's Communities from the Ground Up.* Washington, DC: The Department. February.

United States General Accounting Office. 1995. *HUD's Reinvention Blueprint Raises Budget Issues and Opportunities.* Testimony submitted to Subcommittee on the Veterans Administration, Department of Housing and Urban Development, and Independent Agencies. U.S. Senate, Committee on Appropriations. July 13.

United States v. Certain Lands in the City of Louisville, 78 F. 2nd 684 (1935)

Vale, Lawrence J. 1993. Beyond the Problem Projects Paradigm: Defining and Revitalizing "Severely Distressed" Public Housing. *Housing Policy Debate* 4(2).

PART II

Social Issues

WILLIAM PETERMAN

3   *The Meanings of Resident Empowerment*

Why Just About Everybody Thinks It's a Good Idea and What It Has to Do with Resident Management

Introduction

The notion of resident management as a tool for empowering public housing residents seems to appeal to almost everyone. Images are invoked of "empowered" tenants, overcoming tremendous social and economic obstacles, taking control of and redirecting their developments from crime- and drug-ridden slums to safe and productive communities. It is a new version of the Horatio Alger story, with adult black women as Horatio.

This chapter arises from my reflections on several years of working with residents, public officials, and activists on the issue of resident management. It focuses on the word "empowerment" and the different meanings given to it by different groups of people—conservatives, liberals, and progressives. Different meanings result in different goals and objectives for resident management programs, and these differences lead to confusion over what can be expected of resident management and how such programs should be fashioned. No matter which meaning of empowerment is invoked, resident management is neither the best nor necessarily even an appropriate means for achieving it. Because resident management by itself is not an empowering act, it should not be the sole or even the major focus of efforts to revitalize both the residents and the structures of public housing.

Reprinted from *Housing Policy Debate* 7, 3 (Washington, D.C.: Fannie Mae Foundation, 1996). This copyrighted material is used with the permission of the Fannie Mae Foundation.

A Brief History of Resident Management in U.S. Public Housing

Resident management, originally called tenant management, appeared in the early 1970s, first in Boston and then in St. Louis when residents were forced to assume control to keep from losing their homes. In Boston, residents at Bromley-Heath, an 1,100–unit development of town houses and high-rise buildings, organized in the mid-1960s to improve health services. In time, they took over operation of social services in the community, formed a crime patrol, and developed a drug center (Hailey 1984). In 1969, the resident organization proposed taking over management of the development, which was accomplished on January 1, 1971. Bromley-Heath is the first of 11 pioneering resident management corporations (ICF 1992) that have been managing their developments since before 1988.[1]

In St. Louis, tenant management grew out of the settlement of a 1969 rent strike. In all, five different developments were involved. Tenant management was initiated at the Carr Square and Darst developments in 1973 and at the Peabody and Webb developments in 1974; a church-related neighborhood corporation began managing Cochran Gardens in 1974 in anticipation of conversion to tenant management, which came about in 1976. The initial funds for the tenant management in St. Louis were provided by the Ford Foundation (Wendel 1975).

Ford's involvement in St. Louis led to its joint sponsorship with the U.S. Department of Housing and Urban Development (HUD) of a National Tenant Management Demonstration Program. The demonstration operated between 1976 and 1979 and involved seven public housing sites in six cities—Jersey City, Louisville, New Haven, New Orleans, Oklahoma City, and Rochester. In evaluating the program, the Manpower Demonstration Research Corporation (1981) noted that while at most sites tenant management seemed to have worked as well as housing authority management had, several objective measures, such as rent collections, vacancy rates, and speed of response to maintenance requests, showed no improvement. Resident satisfaction with tenant managers, however, was higher than with housing authority managers.

Manpower also concluded that tenant management was costly. Expenditures were from 13 to 62 percent above conventional management costs, primarily because of training, employment, and technical assistance. Nevertheless, there were benefits from the increased expenditures, including employment for some tenants, a sense of personal development in all aspects of their lives among tenants who actively participated in management, and a greater overall satisfaction with management among all tenants. Noting the additional costs, varying attitudes of housing authorities about tenant management, and the rapid turnover rate of housing authority directors, Manpower suggested it was unlikely that tenant management could be universally successful and recommended against expanding the demonstration program.

Although the program was discontinued, several developments initially remained under tenant control. But when external funds disappeared, so did the interest of the participating housing authorities (Chandler 1991); over time, all but one of the developments reverted to conventional management. By 1989, only the A. Harry Moore development in Jersey City still had some degree of tenant management (Monti 1989). In St. Louis, the Darst, Peabody, and Webb developments, which were not part of the demonstration program, also reverted to housing authority control.[2] An observer in the early 1980s would likely have concluded that tenant management was an idea whose time had come and gone. However, tenant management reemerged in the mid-1980s with a new set of champions, the new name of "resident management," and a new lease on life. Conservatives became attracted to resident management, seeing its self-help focus as a way of both instilling responsibility in residents and reducing, perhaps eliminating, federal involvement in public housing. Taking the lead in promoting resident management was the National Center for Neighborhood Enterprise (NCNE), a Washington, DC, organization headed by Robert Woodson.

The conservative idea of resident management contained a new feature, ownership, which was seen to be a logical outcome of the resident management process. NCNE (1984) claimed that "many residents of public housing . . . believe that once they have made the commitment to turn their developments around . . . they . . . deserve and have the right to maintain and own their homes in those developments" (pp. 7–8). NCNE was instrumental in getting resident management included in the federal Housing and Community Development Act of 1987, which created a formal procedure for establishing resident management corporations (RMCs) and provided up to $100,000 for developing and training them. With the encouragement of the incoming Bush administration, especially its dynamic HUD secretary, Jack Kemp, local housing authorities began promoting resident management groups, and residents, hearing of successes elsewhere, began seeking resident management at their developments. By the end of the decade, RMCs were springing up all over the country.

Despite the emphasis of the Bush administration on resident management, the actual growth in the number of resident-managed developments was modest. By 1992, at the end of the Bush administration, an evaluation of emerging resident management corporations conducted by ICF (1992) for HUD's Office of Policy Development and Research identified nearly 300 resident groups as having received some assistance and 80 groups as having received federal technical assistance grants intended to move them into management. Yet only 27 of the 80 groups receiving grants had actually progressed to some form of management. Only two unidentified groups were carrying out some management functions independently and had a management contract with their housing authority. ICF concluded that the small number of groups achieving management status "strongly suggests that resident management requires a fairly long period of time to implement" (ICF 1993, iii).

When ICF (1992) looked at 11 RMCs incorporated before 1988, it drew conclusions that were similar to those in the earlier Manpower (1981) report. These

RMCs performed well in terms of annual inspections, resident move-outs, resident recertifications, and maintenance and maintenance staffing, but less well with respect to tenant accounts and vacancy rates. Residents of developments where the RMC took responsibility for the majority of the management functions had significantly more positive perceptions of the quality of life than residents at comparison sites, but ICF suggested this was due at least in part to poor perceptions at the comparison sites. Operating costs, based on admittedly limited data, were lower for RMCs.[3]

Resident management has not been promoted as vigorously by the Clinton administration. Based on my conversations with local HUD officials and tenant leaders, this position seems to reflect both a recognition that resident groups need more in-depth training to successfully implement self-management and a policy shift that emphasizes choices rather than a single option. Although HUD's Urban Revitalization Demonstration (HOPE VI), first announced in January 1993 and now being implemented, provides funds for resident programs, it calls for a bold, comprehensive approach to public housing revitalization rather than focusing on a single element such as resident management (Vale 1993). Irene Johnson, tenant leader at Leclaire Courts, has also suggested that finding a way for residents to leave public housing through the purchase of HUD-foreclosed homes may be a better option than the purchase of units at Leclaire (personal communication). Both the demonstration and Johnson's comment suggest a restructuring of public housing that would result in less isolation of poor households, which in many ways is the opposite of the notion of resident management.[4] Thus, during the past 25 years, resident management seems to have experienced a roller-coaster ride of support and popularity, and it seems to be on the verge of heading downhill again. It may be appropriate yet once more to try to appraise its potential. Much of the recent rhetoric about resident management emphasizes the notion of empowerment. This chapter reflects on empowerment and on the assumed link between it and resident management and questions whether empowerment is a realistic expectation of resident management efforts.

Different Meanings of Empowerment

Nearly all advocates of resident management claim it is an empowering act. It is not always clear, however, what they mean by empowerment and just how empowerment occurs when residents become managers. The lack of a clear definition of empowerment allows just about anyone, representing any political persuasion, to use the term and allows others, no matter what their persuasion, to agree.

In my work I have identified three different general meanings of empowerment as it is applied to resident management. Each meaning is associated with a specific political perspective. Purposes, procedures, and expected outcomes of resident management differ markedly from meaning to meaning.

CONSERVATIVE MEANING

Individual freedom and property rights undergird the conservative notion of empowerment. Caprara and Alexander (1989), in a resource guide published by NCNE, contend that public housing residents are powerless because they are dependent on housing authorities. To them, resident management empowers by eliminating dependency and restoring pride. However, only by becoming owners do residents become truly independent.

Conservatives' belief in empowerment through ownership is tied to their notions of the "natural social order" and the role of government in society, which can be traced to the political writings of John Locke. To Locke, property was the inherent right of free men. In the United States, our notions of social order and class have been constructed around the ownership of property. Perin (1977) notes that in American society "the form of tenure—whether a household owns or rents its place of residence—is read as a primary social sign, used in categorizing and evaluating people, in much the same way that race, income, occupation, and education are" (p. 32). Thus, for conservatives resident management is a means to empowerment that is fully realized only when residents attain ownership and thus are elevated to a higher social order. In this individualistic notion of empowerment, community organization is seen only as a mechanism for attaining individual achievement.

LIBERAL MEANING

The liberal definition is drawn from the urban reform movement of the 1960s, which emphasized citizen involvement and participation. Liberals see successful governance of public housing as evolving out of an inclusionary process in which residents are encouraged to participate. In such a situation, both the housing authority and the residents share responsibility for a development, and resident management is thus viewed as a collaborative partnership between the authority and the resident corporation.

Liberals believe the idea that public housing problems can be solved without substantial federal involvement and support is a "cruel hoax" (Rigby 1990). For example, Robert Rigby (former director of the Jersey City Housing Authority), in speaking about how distressed public housing was turned around, argued for "a working partnership with . . . tenant organisations, the organisation of estate[5] and agency management in a fashion that maximize[s] estate-based capacity and sufficient capital improvements or modernisation" (Rigby 1990, 7).

Empowerment thus means bringing residents into the system and giving them a voice in making decisions about the present and planning for the future. The liberal notion of resident management is often expressed through the policy of "dual management." The term "dual management" seems to have first been used in reference to the transitional period of resident management at Leclaire Courts in Chicago, during which the housing authority gradually relinquished management control to the RMC (Peterman 1993).

Subsequently housing authorities, including the Chicago Housing Authority (1989), have also used the term to mean an indefinite period during which residents take on some management activities, leaving others to the housing authority. Housing authorities also use the term "full management," which is said to follow "dual management," to mean everything from residents' assuming all management functions to their assuming only a few (Chicago Housing Authority 1989). When residents chose to perform a limited set of functions under full management, they usually chose site-related activities such as maintenance, rent collection, and tenant screening.

PROGRESSIVE MEANING

Progressives equate empowerment with the notion of community organization and control. To them, the community, not individuals, is the focus of empowerment. Bratt (1989), for example, argues for "a new housing policy built on empowering community groups and low-income households" and providing "more than shelter" (p. 5). Leadership is an outgrowth of community empowerment, and one role for leaders is to take control of management. Resident management is thus not a means of empowerment, but rather a possible outcome of community organization.

Progressives reject the notion that form of tenure (whether a household owns or rents) constitutes a primary determinant of social status (Perin 1977). They view actual ownership of the developments as either irrelevant or problematical. Since ownership schemes tend to emphasize personal empowerment, progressives are likely to view them as antithetical to community building, except for the creation of cooperatives, which is seen as a way of engendering community solidarity.

Since who has power and who is in control are key issues for progressives, they are skeptical about any form of partnership or dual management. Traditionally in community organizing there is always an "enemy," and in the case of public housing, the enemy is the housing authority. Sharing management control with the enemy is undesirable. Progressives argue that the only time an RMC should share management responsibilities with a housing authority is during a period of transition to full control.

Can Resident Management Really Empower Public Housing Residents?

Empowering residents is often seen as an essential element of any workable future public housing policy. Thus it seems an appropriate topic for our discussions. But whose version of empowerment should we consider? Do all versions lead to better public housing? Do any?

Chandler (1991) notes that early resident management efforts, including the National Tenant Management Demonstration Program, neither used the term "empowerment" nor had it as a goal. Instead, resident management was viewed as a "means to decentralize some housing authority responsibilities and to create a bit more stability in the resident population" (Chandler 1991, 137). She points out that the NCNE first suggested a relationship between empowerment and resident management. Liberals and progressives, however, were quick to join their conservative counterparts in claiming that empowerment was also associated with their notions of resident management.

But how are resident management and empowerment linked? Chandler (1991) argues that the link is community organization. This position is echoed by Monti, who, after reviewing 11 resident-managed sites, concluded that successful resident management emerges from the ability of tenants to organize and that "one cannot put the resident management 'cart' before the community organization 'horse'" (Monti 1989, 51). This view strongly suggests that resident management by itself does not empower; if this is true, each of the three versions of resident management may be flawed.

Conservatives acknowledge the importance of organizing as a stepping-stone to resident management (Caprara and Alexander 1989), but they see resident management itself as a stepping-stone to private ownership. Ownership is the real and ultimate empowering act. Thus, community organization[6] creates a temporary form of empowerment, setting the stage for residents to enter into the mainstream of society as owners (Perin 1977).

Can ownership, and thus personal empowerment through ownership, actually be achieved? In their evaluation of HUD's Public Housing Homeownership Demonstration initiated in 1985, Rohe and Stegman (1990) found that selling public housing units to residents, even with the best tenants and the best housing, is difficult. They found that after 50 months of the program, only 320 out of 1,315 units initially targeted had been transferred. Also, 10 to 15 percent of the resident home buyers had experienced late payments or more serious delinquencies within the first 18 months of closing on their homes. A full 30 percent of the purchasers reported that mortgage payments were causing a strain on their budgets.

Resident-owned cooperatives are often suggested as an alternative form of ownership. However, when I was exploring options for management at Leclaire Courts in Chicago, a feasibility analysis showed that converting the development to a resident-owned cooperative would result in monthly charges (rents) that were much higher than residents could afford. Most residents would not be able, without subsidy, to own their development even in the limited sense of cooperative ownership.

Resident management cannot be considered a successful means to homeownership if so few tenants could become owners. This limitation lends credibility to those (e.g., Clay 1990; Silver, McDonald, and Ortiz 1985) who argue that conservative proponents of resident management are more interested in getting the federal government out of the housing business than in helping poor people. It is also likely that any indiscriminate implementation of ownership schemes could result in failures and foreclosures, leaving some housing in worse shape than it was under housing authority ownership. Such was the case in Chicago when Altgeld Gardens was converted to a resident-owned cooperative in the 1970s. The cooperative failed shortly thereafter when extensive roof repairs were needed and reserve funds were not available. Today Altgeld Gardens remains one of the worst of Chicago's garden-style public housing developments.[7]

Whether the liberal shared management notion of resident management results in empowerment is also open to question. Its supporters stress the need for good working relationships between the tenant organization and the housing authority. Both Manpower (1981) and Kolodny (1981), for example, conclude that a cooperative relationship was essential to RMC success in the demonstration project. The more recent ICF evaluation similarly found that "in general, the stronger [the] working relationships were, the better the RMCs tended to perform" (ICF 1992, 9).

These conclusions, however, are contradicted by Monti (1989), who argues that a "creative tension" is essential to resident management success. An RMC's relationship with its housing authority must be neither "too cozy nor too hostile" (Monti 1989). Interest in resident management usually arises when an authority fails to satisfactorily do its job, and this interest becomes focused when residents organize. Relationships between a developing community organization and its housing authority are bound to be strained because the inadequacy of the housing authority is the reason for the change. However, for an RMC to be ultimately effective, it must turn the situation into one of "creative tension," for it must be both a manager and a community leader (Monti 1989).

Proponents of shared management reject the idea of creative tension and instead see community organizing not as a way of building an independent RMC but as a means of building support for the notion of resident management. Organizing, they argue, need not be confrontational because an enlightened authority will favor and support resident efforts. Rigby (1990), for example, argues that while a strong resident organization is needed to rescue a troubled development, it is but a part of a larger effort involving both the residents and the authority.

Shared management most closely corresponds to the "partnership" rung of Arnstein's (1969) ladder of citizen participation. Partnership is the lowest of Arnstein's three rungs of citizen power and two steps below the level of full control at which both the conservative and progressive versions of resident management would be placed. Unless real power is transferred to the RMC, citizen control may be illusory. Arnstein cautions that if a partnership such as shared management is to work, then citizens, in this case the residents or the RMC, have to take power because it is unlikely to be given. She suggests further that an equality of resources (e.g., access to technicians, lawyers, and community organizers) is needed if there is to be real sharing and thus equal participation.

Characteristically, authorities in shared management situations give only site-related powers to RMCs, such as responsibility for maintenance, security, and some clerical tasks. Major decisions about operating policies, redevelopment, and budget are retained by the housing authority. Rather than empowering an RMC, the generally onerous site tasks cause the RMC to become a buffer between the authority and residents, and as such it becomes the target of resident displeasure when something goes wrong. Rather than taking control, the RMC in a shared management situation can find itself in the awkward position of acting as the authority's agent rather than as a representative of the residents.

The dilemma of cooperation versus creative tension is a variation of a common issue faced in most low-income communities. Leaders of community-based advocacy organizations contend that the "establishment" must be confronted if a low-income community's demands are to be met, while leaders of community-based economic and housing development organizations contend that the community must learn to play by establishment rules if the resources needed for redevelopment are to be obtained. Organizers argue that playing by the rules ensures continuing second-class status for a community, but developers respond that confrontation leads to only limited gains (Keating 1989). Shared management seems to adopt the developers' perspective and therefore supports the more modest goal of improving management, which creates a better environment for tenants. Chandler (1991) attributes acceptance of shared management to the original National Tenant Management Demonstration Program rather than to the more expansive process of community empowerment.

Since community empowerment is central to the progressive version of resident management, it is tempting to conclude that this is the appropriate model. But there is a potentially fatal flaw here also. In the progressive model, resident management is a means, not an end. In creating and maintaining an RMC, means and ends often become confused, and in the confusion the lofty goal of community empowerment is lost.

Monti (1989) concludes that community organizing and the creation of a strong board or resident council are more important to the development of an effective RMC than a strong individual leader. But it appears that attention too often becomes focused on a strong leader, while community organization and board development are neglected. This situation results either in a weak organization unable to use the power it has or in an organization dominated by a leader who becomes disconnected from the community.

While it may be possible to correct problems associated with community organizing and board development, it remains questionable whether management is an activity compatible with social control and empowerment. The struggle to improve a troubled development is often realized through community organization, and the promise of resident management can be a powerful organizing tool. Once resident management is established, the resident organization must identify new goals of community empowerment if momentum and community interest are to be retained.

Unfortunately this process is rarely completed because once the organization gains management control, energy and talent must be diverted to the technical task of managing. This diversion can easily sap the energies of the organization, turning its attention from the original goal of community empowerment to the goal of organizational survival.

Even though none of the three versions of resident management seems to be directly related to its version of empowerment, the possibility remains that through the building of resident self-esteem and assurance, resident management—no matter which version—leads to positive outcomes for both residents and communities. Both Manpower (1981) and ICF (1992) report that residents in resident-managed developments are more satisfied with their managers and with their development. Rohe and Stegman (1994) have found that when low-income residents in Baltimore became homeowners, their life satisfaction was greater. But such good feelings do not automatically lead to socioeconomic mobility, and whether increased satisfaction from resident management results in substantial economic and social benefits has yet to be determined.

Should Residents and Others Seek Out Resident Management?

None of the versions of resident management, it appears, is particularly appropriate for empowering public housing residents. Does this mean that resident management is a bad idea that should be abandoned by residents, housing authorities, housing advocates, and policymakers?

Many of the concerns about management by RMCs are similar to concerns about the management of low-income housing in general, whether by nonprofit community-based or private sector organizations. In a recent study, Bratt et al. (1994) identified effective housing management as the key to nonprofit housing organizations' ability to maintain their growing inventory of low-cost housing. The need for nonprofit community development organizations to pay more careful attention to management concerns was also highlighted in a recent United Way of Chicago (1995) community development needs assessment.

Both the Bratt and the United Way studies identify the balancing of the "double bottom line" of financial accountability and social goals as a challenge to good management (Bratt et al. 1994). This same challenge applies to resident management organizations. As a way of balancing the double bottom line, more and more nonprofit organizations are contracting out management services when good outside management agents are available to take on low-income housing. This option may also be appropriate for resident management groups. Contracting for management with a private or even another nonprofit firm might help avoid problems relating to conflicting interests that can arise when boards of directors and their management staffs are all residents and neighbors.

Resident satisfaction should be the basis of any program to improve public housing, argues Stanley Horn (reported in Peterman and Young 1991), former director of the Clarence Darrow Center and a major participant in creating resident management at Chicago's Leclaire Courts.[8] Although supportive of resident management, Horn contends that residents should be less concerned about who is managing than with how good the management is. While resident control may be the only way to ensure good management in some circumstances, the deciding factor should always be whether management provides the basis for a livable, healthy community.

Resident management is attractive because it promises a livable, healthy community and possibilities for individuals to improve themselves. However, several housing experts I interviewed during a 1991 review of alternatives to conventional public housing management (Peterman and Young 1991) believe that such results are too much to expect and that neither community nor personal improvement is necessarily an outcome of managing a development.

Some cynical observers suggest that resident management is a way of diverting attention from the serious state of public housing and from the responsibility of government to provide decent housing for the poor. Rachel Bratt, for example, believes that housing authorities abrogate their responsibilities as landlords when they turn developments over to residents (reported in Peterman and Young 1991). She views this as a kind of second-class tenantry or a form of "lemon socialism," where residents are given the management because housing authorities are no longer willing or able to do the job.

Others, notably professional housing managers, argue that management is a technical task best left to professionals. They believe residents would do better to focus their energies on personal growth issues or on important community concerns such as education, crime, and programs for young people (Peterman and Young 1991).

Resident managers have been able to perform as well as conventional housing authority managers on some evaluation measures and even better on a few others (ICF 1992; Manpower 1981). But resident management seems to require a long period of development involving both community organizing and resident training (ICF 1992; Monti 1989). Residents must be willing to work at becoming managers, often taking years to successfully replace housing authority managers. Housing authorities must allow this to happen and neither totally oppose the development of an RMC nor smother it with support (Monti 1989; Peterman 1994).

Some RMCs have been managing developments for nearly a quarter of a century (e.g., Bromley-Heath in Boston and Carr Square in St. Louis), but others have come and gone in just a few years (e.g., Lakeview Terrace in Cleveland and Iroquois Homes in Louisville). The conditions that seem supportive of resident management do not universally exist in public housing. Little public housing is truly troubled,[9] not all residents are willing or able to struggle to become organized and trained, and not all housing authorities are willing to let resident management develop at its own pace.

The options available are not simply housing authority management or resident management. Management by private management companies may be preferred in some instances (see Vale 1996). While resident management may be a strategy for some public housing, it clearly cannot be indiscriminately applied. Whatever the prospects for successful resident management, the link between it and empowerment is at best weak, no matter which meaning is used. Resident management does not automatically lead to ownership, as its conservative proponents argue; nor does it guarantee personal or community power, as its liberal and progressive proponents argue.

Resident management is sometimes an appropriate form of public housing management. However, simply creating an RMC does little to empower residents, and placing too much concentration on the activities of management can detract residents from more critical issues facing their community. Public housing management policy needs to have a clearer goal, and it should not target resident management as the prime or only option. Instead, it should provide for a variety of management and empowerment strategies.

Notes

1. The 11 (see ICF 1992) with their years of incorporation are Bromley-Heath (Boston, 1971), Carr Square (St. Louis, 1973), Stella Wright (Newark, 1975), Cochran Gardens (St. Louis, 1976), A. Harry Moore (Jersey City, 1978), Montgomery Gardens (Jersey City, 1979), Kenilworth-Parkside (Washington, DC, 1982), Clarksdale (Louisville, 1983), Booker T. Washington (Jersey City, 1986), Lakeview Terrace (Cleveland, 1987), and Leclaire Courts (Chicago, 1987). At least one of these, Lakeview Terrace, has had its contract to manage withdrawn by its housing authority since the ICF study (Chandler 1994).

2. There appears to be no documentation on exactly why the St. Louis developments reverted to conventional management. George Wendel, director of the Urban Studies Program at St. Louis University, states that in each case the original resident leader stepped aside and no other resident was both capable of and interested in assuming the role. Thus the housing authority was forced to reassert its control (personal communication 1985).

3. The finding of lower operating costs would appear to contrast with the findings of Manpower (1981). Kolodny (1983), however, argues that Manpower's findings are misleading: Costs associated with the start-up of resident management were included along with regular operating costs. These start-up costs would disappear over time, leading to lower operating costs than reported.

4. If the internal HUD document, *A Blueprint for Reinventing HUD*, which has been widely circulated since the November 1994 federal election, is an accurate description of the way the Clinton administration intends to restructure the department, then public housing will be drastically changed. It is not at all clear how resident management would fit into a situation in which housing authorities must compete for tenants in an open market as outlined in the blueprint.

5. Rigby uses the British term "estate" when referring to a single housing authority development.

6. The term "community organization" can take on many meanings. With respect to organizing for ownership, it appears to refer to a process of building interest in and support

for resident management and ownership rather than to the more radical notion of organizing the community against forms of power and control.

      7. The experience of selling units to residents in Great Britain is often pointed to as an example of successful conversion to ownership. The situation is different in Great Britain, however. Most of the successful sales have involved houses, not units in larger developments, and the new homeowners are generally more affluent than the typical U.S. public housing resident.

      8. This statement and a subsequent statement by Bratt are taken from a set of semistructured interviews conducted during 1990 as part of a study to assess alternatives to conventional public housing management. The study was funded by the John D. and Catherine T. MacArthur Foundation and reported in Peterman and Young (1991).

      9. According to the *Final Report* of the National Commission on Severely Distressed Public Housing (1992), 6 percent of the nation's public housing stock is severely distressed. Distress of one kind or another is no doubt more extensive, although some factors leading to distress (e.g., economic conditions of families or general environmental conditions in the vicinity of a development) are not easily mitigated by management initiatives (Vale 1993).

References

Arnstein, Sherrie R. 1969. A Ladder of Citizen Participation. *Journal of the American Institute of Planners* 35:216–24.

Bratt, Rachel G. 1989. *Rebuilding a Low-Income Housing Policy.* Philadelphia: Temple University Press.

Bratt, Rachel G., Langley C. Keyes, Alex Schwartz, and Avis C. Vidal. 1994. *Confronting the Management Challenge: Affordable Housing in the Non-Profit Sector.* New York: New School for Social Research, Community Development Research Center.

Caprara, David, and Bruce Alexander. 1989. *Empowering Residents of Public Housing: A Resource Guide for Resident Management.* Washington, DC: National Center for Neighborhood Enterprise.

Chandler, Mittie Olion. 1991. What Have We Learned from Public Housing Resident Management? *Journal of Planning Literature* 6:136–43.

Chandler, Mittie Olion. 1994. Colloquy on Deconcentration of Public and Subsidized Housing Tenants. Paper read at the Urban Affairs Association Annual Meeting, New Orleans.

Chicago Housing Authority, Department of Research and Program Development. 1989. *The Resident Management Model.* Internal document.

Clay, William L. 1990. Don't Sell Public Housing. *Journal of Housing* 47: 189–94.

Hailey, Mildred. 1984. Bromley-Heath Tenant Management Corporation, Jamaica Plains, MA. In *The Grass Is Greener in Public Housing: From Tenant to Resident to Homeowner,* ed. National Center for Neighborhood Enterprise, 28–36. Washington, DC. Report submitted to the U.S. Department of Housing and Urban Development.

ICF. 1992. *Evaluation of Resident Management in Public Housing.* Washington, DC. Prepared for the Office of Policy Development and Research, U.S. Department of Housing and Urban Development.

ICF. 1993. *Report on Emerging Resident Management Corporations in Public Housing.* Prepared for the Office of Policy Development and Research, U.S. Department of Housing and Urban Development.

Keating, W. Dennis. 1989. The Emergence of Community Development Corporations: Their Impact on Housing and Neighborhoods. *Shelterforce* 11(5):8–11.

Kolodny, Robert. 1981. Self-Help Can Be an Effective Tool in Housing the Urban Poor. *Journal of Housing* 38:135–42.

Kolodny, Robert. 1983. *What Happens When Tenants Manage Their Own Public Housing.* Washington, DC. National Association of Housing and Redevelopment Officials study prepared for submission to the Office of Policy Development and Research, U.S. Department of Housing and Urban Development.

Manpower Demonstration Research Corporation. 1981. *Tenant Management: Findings from a Three-Year Experiment in Public Housing.* Cambridge, MA: Ballinger.

Monti, Daniel J. 1989. The Organizational Strengths and Weaknesses of Resident-Managed Public Housing Sites. *Journal of Urban Affairs* 11:39–52.

National Center for Neighborhood Enterprise, ed. 1984. *The Grass Is Greener in Public Housing: From Tenant to Resident to Homeowner.* Washington, DC. Report submitted to the U.S. Department of Housing and Urban Development.

National Commission on Severely Distressed Public Housing. 1992. *The Final Report of the National Commission on Severely Distressed Public Housing.* Washington, DC. Report to the Congress and the Secretary of Housing and Urban Development.

Perin, Constance. 1977. *Everything in Its Place: Social Order and Land Use in America.* Princeton, NJ: Princeton University Press.

Peterman, William. 1993. Resident Management and Other Approaches to Tenant Control of Public Housing. In *Ownership, Control, and the Future of Housing Policy*, ed. R. Allen Hays, 161–76. Westport, CT: Greenwood Press.

Peterman, William. 1994. Public Housing Resident Management: A Good Idea Gone Wrong? *Journal of Housing* 51:3, 10–15.

Peterman, William, and Mary Ann Young. 1991. *Alternatives to Conventional Public Housing Management.* Chicago: University of Illinois at Chicago, Voorhees Center for Neighborhood and Community Improvement.

Rigby, Robert J., Jr. 1990. *Revitalising Distressed Public Housing: A Management Case.* Paper read at the International NAHRO-CHRA-IoH Conference on Housing in the '90s, University of Illinois at Urbana-Champaign.

Rohe, William, and Michael Stegman. 1990. *Public Housing Homeownership Assessment.* Washington, DC: U.S. Department of Housing and Urban Development.

Rohe, William, and Michael Stegman. 1994. The Effects of Homeownership on the Self-Esteem, Perceived Control, and Life Satisfaction of Low-Income People. *Journal of the American Planning Association* 60:173–84.

Silver, Hillary, Judith McDonald, and Ronald J. Ortiz. 1985. Selling Public Housing: The Methods and Motivations. *Journal of Housing* 42:213–28.

United Way of Chicago. 1995. *Assessing Chicago's Human Needs: Community Development Series III.* Chicago.

Vale, Lawrence J. 1993. Beyond the Problem Projects Paradigm: Defining and Revitalizing "Severely Distressed" Public Housing. *Housing Policy Debate* 4(2):147–74.

Vale, Lawrence J. 1996. Public Housing Redevelopment: Seven Kinds of Success. *Housing Policy Debate* 7(3):491–534.

Wendel, George. 1975. *Tenant Management Corporations in St. Louis Public Housing: The Status after Two Years.* St. Louis, MO: St. Louis University, Center for Urban Programs.

LEONARD F. HEUMANN

4 Assisted Living in Public Housing

A Case Study of Mixing Frail Elderly and Younger Persons with Chronic Mental Illness and Substance Abuse Histories

Introduction

This chapter discusses the recent history of mixing younger disabled persons into federally subsidized housing for seniors, the extent of this trend, and how it has been studied to date. It also describes the impact on residents and staff and on the cost and quality of assisted living services.

The effect of this practice is examined in a three-year evaluation of a public housing facility in Decatur, Illinois, that was designed to provide assisted independent living for low-income and frail elderly persons. The facility began to admit younger persons nine months into the rent-up process. The younger residents included physically and mentally disabled persons as well as persons with chronic mental illness (CMI) and substance abuse histories. The case study supports previous research showing that the inclusion of younger persons with CMI and substance abuse histories into senior public housing can severely diminish both quality of life and quality of care for the frail seniors and can complicate facility management. It is clear that this policy has not lived up to expectations.

Policy Background

Under the Rehabilitation Act of 1973 (Section 504) (as amended) and the Fair Housing Act of 1988, all single persons who are income eligible, whether they are over

Reprinted from *Housing Policy Debate* 7, 3 (Washington, D.C.: Fannie Mae Foundation, 1996). This copyrighted material is used with the permission of the Fannie Mae Foundation.

61

age 62 or younger and disabled, are eligible to move into senior subsidized housing. For years, federal and local officials ignored this policy because they felt it would make marketing and management of senior housing more difficult. By the late 1980s, however, senior housing was opened up to younger, single individuals because it made fiscal and political sense.

The federal government had cut back all housing subsidies by 70 percent between 1978 and 1988, and pressure on the existing supply had grown tremendously (Levitan 1990). In contrast, some of the older public housing and Section 8 facilities for the elderly began to experience chronic vacancies. There was an oversupply of these units that had multiple market shortcomings: They were commonly small efficiency apartments (most people wanted at least one bedroom), and often the facilities were poorly designed, poorly maintained, and located in "bad" neighborhoods. The U.S. Department of Housing and Urban Development (HUD) filled these vacancies with younger, income-eligible single persons, addressing both issues of fiscal solvency and the pressing need for permanent affordable housing for younger singles.

By the 1990s, younger people with CMI and substance abuse histories presented the greatest need for housing (U.S. General Accounting Office [GAO] 1992). Once the doors to senior public housing were opened to single persons under age 62, aggressive advocacy by mental health case managers made this population the most popular applicant pool at several housing authorities.[1]

People with CMI have been underserved in federal housing assistance programs, mainly as a result of the court decision that "the Secretary of HUD and the PHAs [public housing authorities] can refuse to integrate CMI individuals in federally assisted developments with other eligible housing assistance recipients without violating the rights of the CMI to equal protection" (Newman and Struyk 1990, 452–53). The reason for the court decision, according to most mental health professionals, is that the support needs and supervision of people with CMI are distinctly different from those of all other groups (Newman and Struyk 1990).

Nevertheless, by 1990 HUD had been requiring for several years that public housing and Section 8 facilities designed for seniors fill prolonged vacancies with any and all income-eligible younger persons. In fact, HUD surveyed its 10 regional offices about whether the number of younger persons being admitted to senior facilities had increased and if this was causing any management problems (HUD 1990). All 10 affirmed an increase in senior facilities with mixed age groups. Nine of the 10 said that PHAs in their region reported increased management problems in senior facilities with younger residents.

In 1992, the GAO took note of growing management problems where younger persons were being mixed into senior housing. A GAO study of over one-third of all PHAs in the country reported that about 9 percent of public housing units for the elderly were occupied by nonelderly persons with CMI (GAO 1992); medium to large PHAs reported that management problems with chronically mentally ill persons had grown. About a third of the mentally disabled younger persons caused moderate or serious problems, according to the housing authority administrators. Findings indicate serious problems ranging from increased management burnout to declining quality of life and care for seniors (GAO 1992). In a 1993 survey by the Illinois Association of Housing Authorities, 29 percent of its membership reported that housing the chronically mentally ill with seniors was a problem for their agency (Crouch 1993). Most of the studies to date argue that, at the very least, mixing age populations in subsidized housing requires careful planning and more comprehensive and sensitive management (Burby and Rohe 1990; Cohen, Bearison, and Muller 1987; Kellam 1992; Massachusetts Department of Mental Health 1994; National Association of Housing and Redevelopment Officials 1989; National Resource Center on Homelessness and Mental Illness 1993; Normoyle 1988; Tanzman 1993).

Some reports suggest that mixing nonelderly persons into senior housing, even persons who have CMI and substance abuse histories, is possible with proper support services, cooperative agreements between health service providers and housing authorities, and full cooperation between senior and mental health case managers (GAO 1992; Highrise Mixed Population Committee 1989; National Resource Center 1993). But this supposition remains largely unverified by the professional managers and service providers in the field. The specific conditions for successful integration are currently unknown. Meanwhile, the number of senior facilities with younger disabled residents has grown over the past decade, and problems for both management and resident care and safety continue to be reported (Bauer 1995).

Current Conditions

The Housing and Community Development Act of 1992 was the first congressional recognition of a problem in mixing younger disabled persons into senior public housing. The Act called for "designated housing" solutions that allow owners and authorities of senior-subsidized housing to separate elderly and younger residents. In April 1994, HUD adopted a new regulation to implement the congressional mandate (HUD 1994); it ended HUD's insistence on mixing younger disabled persons into senior housing as long as local authorities produce a plan to house both groups. Current policy allows all local authorities to separate senior and younger disabled persons currently living in mixed facilities with HUD approval of a designated housing plan. Relaxing the regulations, however, has not solved the problem.

According to HUD records, as of February 1996, only 41 authorities had submitted designated housing plans. Furthermore, only 25 of the 41 plans have been approved, and no new HUD funds exist to build housing to accommodate the separation of senior and younger persons. Of the 25 applications approved, almost all are in large cities that have a large stock of senior high-rises and can therefore designate one or more as younger disabled housing facilities. The voluntary compliance provision has caused a further complication: Persons who are in compliance with their current lease cannot be forcibly relocated. Thus the change will be slow, and most of these housing facilities will continue with mixed populations for some years to come.

The second most popular plan is to target rent voucher certificates so that younger persons leaving senior public housing are given preferential treatment. Once again, this process is voluntary and can be done only in cities that have large certificate programs and the flexibility to allocate them in this way. Moderate to smaller cities with only two or three senior public housing facilities cannot designate an entire building to younger disabled persons and will find it hard to target the available certificates to younger disabled persons if they are in short supply for all needy households.

The problems created by mixing the age groups in senior subsidized housing will remain for many years. The following case study illustrates these problems in more detail. Previous studies have indicated that the problems lie in two major areas: resident quality of life and complex management issues. Presentation of the findings in this case study follows this two-part framework.

The Concord Congregate Care Program

The study, conducted between 1992 and 1994, was originally designed to be an analysis of the quality and effectiveness of a community-based congregate care program. Responding to the combined needs to modernize a facility and provide assisted living options for the most frail and low-income seniors in the city, the Decatur, Illinois, Housing Authority closed its oldest senior housing (the Concord), modernized it with federal funds, and reopened it in 1992 as congregate housing for frail seniors.

This case study reflects major trends in senior public housing, which is recognized as the most affected by mixing populations of all government subsidized housing (Crouch 1993; GAO 1992; HUD 1990). Within the universe of senior public housing, the Concord is near mean size (117 units), has a typical building layout (four-story, elevator-serviced efficiency and one-bedroom units), and is constrained by the same HUD program management regulations and resident eligibility criteria that all senior public housing must follow.

The remodeling of the Concord included a major first-floor addition of common spaces for dining, socializing, medical and daily living services, on-site management, and case-managed support, and won a national award for design and service creativity (Henry 1993). Key support services like congregate meals, housekeeping, transportation, and case management were provided from the start, but services were not designed to reach economies of scale that would be affordable to the residents until the facility was fully occupied.[2]

Table 4.1 shows the components of the community-based congregate care program and the initial subsidies. The combination of a site manager and a half-time case manager was designed to provide leadership for the service managers, who meet

TABLE 4.1

Components of the Concord Congregate Care Program

Position	*Source of Support*
Site manager (live-in, full-time)	Housing authority
Case manager (half-time social worker)	Nonprofit community
Program manager (1/5 time)	Housing authority
Meal service (2 meals/day, 7 days/week)	Private caterer
Medication management (1-1/2 days/week)	Nonprofit community
Homemaker/chore service (hours as needed or by resident request)	Profit and nonprofit community
Van services (5 days/week purchased for the Concord but serves all senior facilities)	Housing authority
Beautician/podiatrist (half-time, 3 days/week)	Private for-profit
Social organizer (half-time, providing arts, crafts, recreation, etc.)	Nonprofit community

Subsidies (initially provided by a two-year grant)

Case management	The cost of each full assessment per resident at three assessments per month.
Meals	$2.00 of each breakfast and $2.50 of each noon meal. This subsidy cuts resident meal costs in half and is the largest subsidy each year.
Van service	The salary of a half-time van driver.
Medication management	The full cost of $35.00 per month for 35 to 45 residents. The need for this service occurs most among very frail residents and is vital if they are to remain out of institutional care.
Housing authority	One-time start-up funds for staffing and equipment.
Evaluator	The full cost of evaluating the program for the first three years.

monthly to assess and coordinate individual resident support cases. These key managers and service providers were interviewed in person at the site in November of each year. The residents were interviewed every six months by mail. Those who could not respond on their own were interviewed in person.[3] A reference group of seniors was also surveyed every year.[4]

Case Study Evaluation Criteria

This case study contributes several new dimensions to the debate on mixing seniors and younger persons. First, this case study is of younger persons introduced into a senior public housing facility designed to provide assisted living for the most frail elderly persons. Even while they are trying to accommodate all eligible single persons in senior housing, many housing authorities are searching for ways to help their frail but healthy seniors "age in place" and avoid a move to institutional care. However, seniors with failing mobility, eyesight, hearing, and the like could be adversely affected by the presence of younger persons. Second, this study is not a single-point-in-time evaluation but follows the history of mixed residency for three years after rent-up began. Finally, the majority of previous studies were limited to a few simple, often open-ended, questions about the problems of mixing age groups. As discussed below, the present study is able to identify and cluster multiple costs and benefits as well as offer immediate management and long-range planning solutions.

The following evaluation is divided into two broad issues: quality of life and management. Quality of life is measured by senior reactions to younger persons, changes in the number of friends and perceived isolation, changes in senior activities, and the problems and benefits of mixing. The management problems include staff burnout, resident incompatibility, failure to reach service cost economies, and high resident turnover and vacancy rates.

Quality of Life Issues

REACTION TO YOUNGER RESIDENTS

Responses from seniors to direct questions about mixing age groups are presented in table 4.2. They show increases in senior disapproval of mixing between the first two surveys and the third, which correlates with a sizable increase in younger residents from around 30 percent to 47 percent of total residents. While the percentage of younger persons as a whole increased in the third year, the proportion of younger persons with CMI and recovering from substance abuse held steady at about 18 percent. However, the absolute number of younger people with CMI and substance abuse histories was increasing as the facility reached full capacity.

The overall satisfaction of seniors with the facility and services is also presented in table 4.2. The seniors' perception that life is easier since moving to the facility or that the facility meets their needs did not change significantly between years. However, responses to specific questions about service provision, staff understanding of needs, whether they would recommend the facility, or if they wanted to stay, revealed significant increases in dissatisfaction in the third year when the younger resident population increased significantly (see table 4.7 discussed below).

TABLE 4.2

Senior Resident Approval of the Concord
(percent)

	After 1 Year	*After 2 Years*	*After 3 Years*	*Chi-square*
Younger residents (percent)	32.8	27.1	47.0	
Senior responses to mixing				
Disapprove of mixing age groups	41.7	31.4	64.5	0.10511
Feel socializing is more difficult	33.2	36.0	58.7	0.06712
Feel safer without younger residents	42.9	37.3	71.1	0.04594
Overall senior satisfaction				
Life is easier since moving here	83.8	76.9	78.2	0.30329
The Concord meets my needs	91.2	98.0	84.1	0.37034
Services are provided when requested	94.1	95.8	80.0	0.05039
Staff understand my needs	91.7	95.9	77.3	0.09344
Would recommend the Concord to friends	100.0	97.8	75.0	0.00163
Don't want to live here	2.8	8.3	19.6	0.09631

FRIENDS AND PERCEIVED ISOLATION

Another measure of quality of life is the number of friends seniors have and whether they feel they are becoming isolated. Friendships and acquaintances were measured four ways (table 4.3). The first three measures are the mean number of neighbors in the facility to whom the residents report saying "hello," the mean number of neighbors in the facility the residents report visiting, and the mean number of friends in the facility reported by each respondent. For all three, the percentage declined as the percentage of younger neighbors increased.

The reference group from other housing authority facilities had lived in their units for seven to nine years on average over the three surveys. When they were asked the same questions, the mean number said "hello" to stayed consistent at 31 percent for all three years. The mean number of visits stayed between 11 and 12 percent. The mean number of friends ranged from 23 to 40 percent. Thus, seniors living at the Concord and those in other facilities reported a similar percentage of friends and contacts until the third year, when the percentage of younger residents at the Concord rose appreciably. At this point at the Concord, the percentage of senior friends and contacts fell and senior isolation appeared to increase.

The fourth statistic in table 4.3 shows responses to a Likert-scaled question that asks if the respondent agrees or disagrees that most of his or her friends are neighbors in the facility. The percentage agreeing was similar for the Concord and the reference group for the first two years. In the third year, however, the reference group reported that only 31.4 percent of their closest friends lived on-site, while the Con-

TABLE 4.3

Friendship and Acquaintance Rates for Seniors at the Concord

	After 1 Year	After 2 Years	After 3 Years
Younger residents (percent)	32.8	27.1	47.0
Mean number of people say "hello" to (percent of facility population)	26.4	33.2	11.2
Mean number of visits among neighbors (percent of facility population)	8.6	10.7	3.6
Mean number of friends in the facility (percent of total friends)	29.6	32.4	26.7
Percent who agree "most of my friends are neighbors who live in this facility"	33.3	32.6	40.0

cord seniors reported 40 percent. Despite a declining percentage of acquaintances and friends on-site, the low-income and frail seniors at the Concord depend on the facility to be a major source of friends, which results in a perceived lower quality of life for these residents.

SENIOR ACTIVITY CHARACTERISTICS: A MANAGEMENT PERSPECTIVE

Recording the social and recreational activities of seniors is a third way to measure quality of life. The thirteen program managers and service providers were asked about the use of common rooms. Only six of the program managers could regularly observe tenant use of the social activities in the common rooms. All six noted the increasing danger to, and isolation of, the seniors as the younger resident population became more dominant.

According to the staff, negative contacts between the age groups increased in the common rooms during the third year. A younger resident slashed upholstered chairs and couches in the main lounge (an event witnessed by seniors), and a videocassette recorder was stolen. Staff reported more incidents of confused and incoherent younger residents disrupting activities in the common rooms. Both the site manager and the case manager reported that many seniors were too scared to participate in organized activities or even to use the common rooms as part of their extended living space. They both felt that seniors were becoming isolated in their apartments.

Responses from seniors about the use of social and recreational services are presented in table 4.4. Knowledge and use of activities decreased over time, although seniors who did participate in the activities rated them highly. The proportion of Concord seniors who reported not knowing about or not using social activities was 5.6 percent after year 1, 15.2 percent after year 2, and 25.0 percent after year 3. The reference group reported 24.6 percent, 23.7 percent, and 20.7 percent in similar time frames. The statistics moved in opposite directions over these three years.[5]

Staff changes at the Concord explain part of this trend. The first social activity director lasted for a year and a half. She was replaced by a less competent person and, for a while, by no one. By the third year, a new social director was in place, but she was quick to note, as were other program directors, that by the third year the Concord had such a diverse population and so many seniors who did not like to socialize in the common rooms that there were not enough people to sustain some activities. The activities the younger people were interested in did not interest the elderly and vice versa. Many of the fully independent seniors and younger people tended to go outside the facility for their group activities and registered no demand at all.

TABLE 4.4

Responses by Concord Seniors on the Use of Social and Recreational Services
(percent)

	After 1 Year	After 2 Years	After 3 Years
Recreational programs			
Don't know of or use it	17.6	26.7	30.2
Rate it poor or fair	11.4	15.5	16.3
Social activities			
Don't know of or use it*	5.6	15.2	25.0
Rate it poor or fair	19.4	17.4	15.9
Arts and crafts			
Don't know of or use it	20.6	26.7	28.6
Rate it poor or fair	11.8	13.3	7.2
Opportunities to worship			
Don't know of or use it	17.6	21.3	20.9
Rate it poor or fair	8.8	12.8	13.9

*$p = 0.05$, chi-square test over time.

PHANTOM AND REAL BENEFITS

The three surveys with the program managers and service providers indicated that mixing younger persons into senior facilities can produce some benefits. One benefit, which seems initially attractive to a housing authority with chronic vacancies or slow rent-up, is that younger residents represent an applicant pool, allowing the facility to fill vacant units and acquire a more manageable rental income stream. The larger rental income stream can, in theory, provide financial flexibility for additional services that benefit the seniors. Unfortunately, screening for compatible younger persons is time consuming. Even with extensive checking with former landlords, a higher probability exists that persons with CMI and substance abuse histories will not have a lengthy, stable, or compatible housing history and will have dysfunctional personalities that can further deteriorate after entering a new facility. Increased rental streams can be quickly absorbed by increased administrative costs, management turnover, and time-consuming eviction proceedings, which may even deplete resources that could have supported the senior population.

All the service providers said that there are real benefits of mixing in younger persons who do *not* have CMI or addiction problems—that is, the physically and mentally disabled, the terminally ill, and normal low-income single persons. The presence of these younger people can often lead to more socially active and engaged seniors as a result of the age integration. The younger people can provide more voluntary support services and even a blending of complementary physical strengths among all age groups.

Another presumed benefit is cooperation across community-based service pools for the younger and older residents. Unfortunately, even this benefit generates costs. At the Concord, problems arose in the early stages between vendors and case managers for the two age groups. While support service cooperation improved over time, potential conflicts should have been resolved before mixing the clients instead of making the Concord the testing and negotiating arena. Even with cooperation, the increased number and variety of client advocates and support staff visiting the site changed the look and atmosphere of independent apartment living.

Management Issues

SITE MANAGEMENT BURNOUT

The site manager is probably the most vital person to the coordination of services, the social bonding of residents, the feeling of security, the sense of trust and confidentiality among residents, and the overall administration of the facility and services. The site manager, more than any other person, sets the tone in a senior housing facility. He or she often serves as a "family surrogate" to the residents (Heumann and Boldy 1983). No other support worker engenders the trust of the residents and maintains the depth and breadth of knowledge about the residents and their ever-shifting support needs. When the younger disabled residents were introduced, the site manager became the primary intermediary and negotiator of all social interactions in the halls and common areas, at nights and on weekends, and when other support staff were off-duty.

Nine months into the rent-up, the housing authority hired a new site manager whom it judged as the best person to handle the influx of younger persons; she had the most experience in housing management and social interaction among tenants. At her first interview, four months after beginning the job, she stated that even without the younger people, a congregate facility meant more emergency calls, closer and more careful observation of changes in individual resident support needs, and more coordination between services and activities (the case manager coordinates most support but relies on the site manager for consultations on changing individual needs).

She stated that the inclusion of younger residents with varied mental capacities and substance dependencies expanded the workload significantly. The mentally ill residents became confused and confrontational; the recovering substance abusers could be moody and even depressed, and they often relapsed or brought in friends who were addicts. Between the fourth and twelfth month of her tenure, she reported that six emergency calls per month had grown to sixteen per month. The increase in calls resulted from actions by younger residents. These interventions were usually tense confrontations with younger residents, resulting in stressful and time-consuming eviction proceedings.

In the first interview, the site manager reported that 40 percent of her time was spent in basic physical management of the building (supervising maintenance, building administration, paperwork), 40 percent in basic tenant interaction (visiting and talking to tenants, addressing tenant needs and complaints), and 20 percent in intense tenant-focused activities (monitoring physical and emotional health, counseling, reviewing and assessing tenants for continued occupancy).

At the twelfth month of the site manager's tenure (in a second interview), she had cut physical management to 20 percent of her time, basic tenant management remained at 40 percent, and intense tenant-focused tasks had increased to 40 percent, all because of the younger tenants. She had to sacrifice care of the building to avoid shortchanging the senior residents. In actuality, the quality of time with frail seniors had been compromised. The twelfth-month interview turned out to be an exit interview. The site manager quit over the issue of managing the younger people. She felt overworked and overwhelmed by the management problems they presented and concluded that "it is a *disaster* to mix younger mentally ill people into a senior complex."[6]

The replacement site manager was a younger, more energetic person, hired so she could relate better to the younger people and take on the heavier workload. This second site manager did beautifully for about the same length of time (one year). Unlike her predecessor, however, she did not read the signs of her own rising stress level, and neither did the housing authority. In October 1994, while we were conducting the final evaluation of residents and service providers, she just walked away from the facility and the community, leaving a note stating she could no longer handle the stress caused by the mix of younger and older residents. Unlike her predecessor, her job performance had fallen dramatically and was reflected in the residents' evaluation of this pivotal management role. The results of the site manager evaluation by senior residents are shown in table 4.5.[7]

Within a month of hiring a third site manager in as many years, the community-based organization that provided the half-time on-site case manager withdrew that person because there were not enough frail seniors to warrant the position. They maintained an off-site case manager on a case-by-case need basis.[8] The loss of this case manager put more pressure on the site manager, who no longer had a professional social worker on site half the week to discuss and evaluate changing needs of the frail senior population. The site manager was left with more responsibilities and stress.

FAILURE TO REACH COST ECONOMIES IN CRITICAL SERVICES

Staff working for the service agencies assumed a certain number of seniors would need high levels of congregate services once the facility filled with frail elderly persons

TABLE 4.5

Ratings of the Site Manager by Seniors at the
Concord and in the Reference Group
(percent)

	After 1 Year	*After 2 Years*	*After 3 Years*
Concord seniors			
The site manager is			
Inefficient*	0.0	0.0	45.1
Unfriendly*	0.0	0.0	21.6
Unresponsive*	0.0	0.0	31.3
Unavailable*	0.0	0.0	45.2
Reference group			
The site manager is			
Inefficient	17.9	5.1	16.7
Unfriendly	5.0	0.0	12.5
Unresponsive	14.7	3.4	16.7
Unavailable	15.3	10.3	23.0

*$p \geq 0.0006$, chi-square test over time.

in need of extremely high levels of support. However, the housing authority applicant pool became dominated by younger disabled people and totally independent seniors who did not need or want congregate services such as meals, housekeeping, transportation, or medication management. The independent seniors had no support needs, while the younger population needed services totally different from those in the congregate care program. Some younger people needed psychological counseling for depression or confusion. Others needed help with job training, job hunting, budget management, substance addiction therapy, and a myriad of other services that were not part of the congregate care program. In fact, the site managers and case managers found that some of the services needed by younger residents did not exist.

Where such special services did exist, many providers were unwilling to coordinate with the delivery of the congregate services the younger people also needed. Eligibility criteria for congregate services that younger residents did need, such as medication management and homemaker services, limited use to persons over age 62. The vendors who were part of the congregate care program were also restricted to care of the seniors. Even basic case management, which younger people with multiple problems clearly need, could not be provided by the congregate care program social worker because she was trained and paid under a state Department on Aging grant to serve only seniors.

Even when seniors and younger persons could use the same services, the variations in demand introduced by the younger people often complicated service delivery and raised service costs. For example, some younger people worked outside the facility and had more requirements for daily bag lunches from the kitchen and rides from the van to different destinations than the seniors. The younger people had different tastes in food, hair care and styles, music, and television shows. The diversity of younger residents introduced more management costs to the Concord rather than creating cost economies and efficiencies.

As problems with the younger disabled persons increased, the housing authority sought to admit any and all senior applicants—even totally independent people who did not require congregate services. This practice further diminished demand for the senior congregate services. The biggest effort to fill the facility with any income-eligible seniors occurred between April and October of 1993. During those six months, the median age of the seniors dropped from 81 to 78. Almost all the new senior residents were younger and independent; the proportion who drove their own cars rose from 21.9 percent to 31.3 percent, and the number who said they made all the most important decisions by themselves increased from 59.5 percent to 75.5 percent.

The combination of independent seniors and younger persons thwarted economies of scale in all the support services when the facility filled up in the third year. Demand for congregate meals, case management, transportation, and housekeeping services declined in absolute numbers even as the relative size of the resident population was increasing.

Congregate meals serve many purposes in this type of facility, despite constituting the single largest congregate cost. Congregate dining operates as the primary social event of each day and remains one of the best ways for staff to check on changes in daily health. Also, congregate dining functions as one of the only ways the most frail residents engage in social activities. Between 525 and 700 meals needed to be served each week in the Concord to lower meal prices and match the facility's initial subsidy (see table 4.1). However, as shown in table 4.6, the number of residents taking congregate meals lagged far below the required economy of scale in the third year with a full facility. The subsidy ran out in the spring of 1995, and scale economies were never achieved. Many of the lowest income and frail seniors could not reasonably afford these meals. The combination of not reaching scale economies on key congregate services and having some key services for the mentally ill and recovering substance abusers not available or not coordinated with the congregate services severely complicated site management. These problems also made the individual support needs of seniors and younger persons more difficult to monitor.

The trend in congregate meals over time (table 4.6) reveals that satisfaction with the meals remained high or went up. So the decline in the quantity of meals served, shown in the top half of the table, was not caused by a decline in their quality.[9] Nevertheless, the average number of meals per tenant and the number of meals served per week (seniors and total residents) all declined even as the total number of residents living at the facility increased (table 4.6).

Another major congregate service element is homemaker/chore provisions. At the end of the first year, 47.2 percent of the seniors used this service; this rose to 51.1 percent at the end of the second year but fell to 50.0 percent at the end of the third year. Average hours of service per week was 4.1 in the first year, hit an all-time high of 5.5 in April 1993, and was down to 3.6 as the facility reached full occupancy. Similar trends can be shown for every other service element in the congregate care program.

APARTMENT VACANCY AND RESIDENT TURNOVER

When the Concord reopened as congregate care for seniors, the facility was expected to be fully occupied in nine months. In actuality, the facility was only 40 percent occupied after one year and only 82 percent occupied after two and a half years. The facility filled after three years, but since then capacity has been hard to maintain because of high turnover. As shown in table 4.7, seniors registered a bare majority by the third year (53 percent), and this residential mix affected the social

TABLE 4.6

Statistics on Congregate Meal Services at the Concord

	After 1 Year	After 2 Years	After 3 Years
Percent of seniors taking no meals	33.3	32.0	42.6
Total senior meals served/week*	162	207	145
Total resident meals served/week*	240	325	230
Average number of meals/week for			
seniors taking congregate meals	6.2	6.1	5.4
total residents	2.7	2.4	1.2
Percent of seniors preparing their own			
meals	44.4	34.8	42.3
Satisfaction with meals (1 = excellent, 5 = poor)			
Taste of the food	2.6	2.4	2.2
Look of the food	3.5	2.3	2.2
Size of the portions	2.1	1.9	2.1
Choice of entrees	2.4	2.3	2.2
Day-to-day variety of menus	2.6	2.3	2.4

*$p = 0.0002$, chi-square test over time.

atmosphere. The high turnover rate of all residents also undermined the social stability of the facility.

The reference group's behavior indicated no unique factors in the Decatur
economy that might cause anomalous patterns in the senior population at the Concord. Past studies of both subsidized and market-rate housing for seniors show a steady
turnover rate of 11 or 12 percent per year (Gayda and Heumann 1989; Heumann
1987), which mirrors the senior turnover rate in the reference group during the study.

Rate of turnover may be higher as a senior facility is renting-up because of un-
certainty about who will occupy unrented units. If resident expectations about "tenant chemistry" are not met as newer residents move in, they may leave before investing
much time in the facility. However, when the residents are very low income and frail
seniors with relatively few affordable housing alternatives, we would not expect the
turnover to be high.

Only a very conservative estimate of total turnover at the Concord during the
three-year study is possible. The Concord was estimated to have a 28.9 percent turnover of seniors between the first and second year and a 36.5 percent turnover of seniors between the second and third year.[10]

The turnover of younger residents is even higher. Many of them did not like living in a senior facility. They found it imposed too many rules and was too quiet.
The rapid turnover of younger persons can be confusing and certainly does not add
to a sense of community for increasingly facility-bound seniors. Between the first
and second years, there was a 69.2 percent turnover of younger residents, and between the second and third years the rate was 46.7 percent.

The senior turnover rate at the Concord reached three times that of the reference
group in the third year, even using the conservative estimate of about 30 percent.
Interviews with the site managers and case manager over the three years indicated
that the high percentage of departures in excess of normal turnover was the result of
two factors. First, the families of many departing seniors wanted them to move because the families did not like the presence of the younger mentally ill and recovering substance abuse tenants or the types of guests these younger residents invited
into the building. They felt the safety of their relative was being compromised.

TABLE 4.7

Rent History of the Concord

	After 1 Year	After 2 Years	After 3 Years
Percent occupied	52	73	100
Percent seniors	67	73	53
Percent younger	33	27	47

Second, many of the departing seniors were totally independent people who were not really candidates for a congregate care facility. The support service managers felt that the housing authority admitted these people to fill the facility with seniors so they would not have to take younger applicants. However, these functionally independent seniors tended to find the facility too restrictive for their independent lifestyles and were uncomfortable living with the younger mentally ill residents. According to the site managers, the independent seniors tended to stay only until they found more conventional affordable housing. Because these seniors were independent, they possessed more housing options than the frail seniors who needed on-site support services.

Summary of Problems

The following problems were identified by the program managers and service providers as the results of mixing younger persons, particularly those with CMI and substance abuse histories, into a housing facility for the elderly. Many of the quality of life issues and management problems clearly belong in both lists; the problems that lower resident quality of life also complicate site management, and complicating site management takes staff time, which can lower resident quality of care.

Quality of Life Issues

1. Resident isolation increased, the residents' sense of community declined, and social cohesion and integration among residents were reduced when seniors retreated to their apartments out of fear of the more volatile younger residents.
2. Socializing opportunities dissolved when the facility became so diversified that there were no longer enough residents with common tastes and interests to provide a threshold for specific activities.
3. The involvement of friends and family visits to the facility (providing voluntary support to residents) declined. Younger persons tended to have less of a private support network than seniors. When residents did have potential support, site staff lacked the time to guide and encourage it. In some cases, families were deterred from visiting the facility because of volatile or unpredictable younger persons.
4. Building safety suffered, mostly from friends the younger residents brought into the facility.
5. There was an increase in resident stress, mostly felt by the seniors, which resulted in increased resident turnover and a less stable population base.

Management Problems

1. Staff stress and turnover increased as a result of problems managing mentally ill and emotionally unstable younger persons.
2. There was a loss in service economies of scale, especially for senior services, because most younger persons did not need congregate support services. The result was higher service costs for low-income seniors who needed the services.
3. The introduction of younger disabled persons created a more diverse support need base and a more institutional atmosphere, with more support providers coming and going in the facility.
4. There was a loss of on-site staff time and attention per resident because younger disabled residents were more likely than seniors to be disoriented, confused, depressed, and antisocial and required a higher rate of stressful evictions.

Conclusions

The Concord does not represent an isolated case, but this single case study cannot tell us if the problems and benefits of mixing uncovered in this study are comprehensive, universally applicable, or more or less severely felt in other settings. The Concord was designed as a congregate care facility for very frail seniors, which added a more severe test of mixing in younger persons and more costly repercussions from resident incompatibility.

Nevertheless, universal lessons can be drawn from this study. The most important stems from the inappropriateness of introducing younger people who have CMI or substance abuse histories into senior housing. These young people have volatile and chronic disabilities; no amount of prescreening can guarantee successful integration with seniors who are losing their physical dexterity, mobility, hearing, eyesight, and other skills necessary to cope with irrational and unreasonable behaviors and actions.

The policy question then becomes, What are we going to do with the facilities where these types of younger persons already live with seniors? The HUD policy of designated housing plans provides no real solution for most subsidized housing owners. Even increased funding for new housing to ease the demand among younger low-income individuals will not help their situations. In the short term, forcibly relocating tenants in good standing from existing mixed facilities is not a legal option. Meanwhile, many housing authorities need to keep their senior facility close to fully rented for financial reasons, but they can no longer attract senior applicants because of problems brought about by earlier mixing in of younger people. Therefore, most subsidized housing managers should look for strategies to minimize the tensions and conflict and improve the quality of life for all residents in these mixed facilities. Some simple management practices can be employed:

1. Improve applicant screening of all persons to eliminate incompatible residents and include younger persons who produce more benefits than costs.
2. In buildings with separate wings and entries, effective plans and programs of residential zoning by lifestyle, functional ability, and support needs can be created to minimize housing vacancies and maximize living conditions.
3. Much more local effort is needed to improve case coordination between mental health and social service agencies that provide exclusive services to either seniors or younger people. Also, federal funding streams should be coordinated to create effective and efficient integrated support programs.
4. Finally, new programs in staff training are clearly needed to teach staff to cope with, and be sensitive to, the diversity in living arrangements, to successfully monitor diverse living patterns, to accurately handle interpersonal relations and group dynamics, to call in the proper support services, and to provide sensitivity training for residents as well as their informal support networks.

The Decatur experience demonstrates that if, and only if, all this can be provided on-site at an affordable cost to all residents will such mixing of age groups be potentially appropriate and beneficial.

Further Research

The methodology needed to accurately test the national impact of mixing elderly and nonelderly persons in federally assisted senior housing will be complex and expensive. Every study published to date has serious limitations. When the samples have been large enough to suggest national trends, the surveys have been targeted to the administrative staff above the site level. The questions asked in these surveys were too basic to detail the scope or scale of site problems and did not provide a quality of service evaluation for new solutions. This study is one of four that have detailed problems and evaluated quality of services, but they have used small, nonrandom samples, making it difficult or dangerous to extrapolate national conditions or trends.[11]

A national random sample of senior public housing and Section 8 housing facilities is needed. It must be large enough to establish the significant independent variables that discriminate between positive and negative mixing of age groups and must classify the facilities on these variables. The list of variables is likely to be large and should include the size of the facility, design layout and zoning options, demographic characteristics of the residents, disability characteristics of the residents, ratio of seniors to younger persons, ratio of staff to residents (especially security and support service staff), types of on-site and community-based services available, and degree of cooperation among mental health, social service, and housing agency staff.

Surveys should include residents, site management staff, and on- and off-site support staff using control groups of mixed and nonmixed senior facilities. To handle such complexity, the study should be staged so that an initial classification clusters facilities into types based on demographic and environmental variables along with types of age mixes, but it should not define positive or negative mixing. Facilities in each class can then be sampled with more detailed and controlled tests of residents and staff. The final stage requires an on-site observation by trained teams of analysts to determine with the greatest assurance and intercomparability which management schemes, support programs, training programs, site characteristics, and population characteristics produce successful age-integrated housing.

Notes

1. This observation is based on conversations the author conducted with six public housing authorities in the Midwest.

2. The housing authority applied for and received a grant from the Retirement Research Foundation to fund start-up and initial operating costs for two years. This study was a portion of the Retirement Research Foundation grant set aside to monitor and evaluate the congregate care program and appears in other papers (Heumann 1994a, 1994b).

3. To simplify the data tables and provide a clearer picture of changes and trends, the resident data are shown for every year, rather than every six months. Also, this case study focuses on senior resident responses (1992, $n = 39$; 1993, $n = 50$; 1994, $n = 47$) rather than total resident responses. The younger residents were surveyed, but more of them had severe mental disabilities, resulting in a high percentage who were unable to participate in the survey in a meaningful way (in 1994, 18 percent of the younger residents ($n = 10$) were not competent to participate compared with only 6 percent of the seniors ($n = 3$)). For each year cross-sectional data are presented for each point in time. Because the Concord was still renting up throughout the study period, and because of a high turnover of residents of all ages (discussed in greater detail below), the size of the constant resident population was too small for longitudinal statistical analysis (of the 117 residents in the last year, 1994, only 21 seniors and 3 younger persons had lived in the facility for all three years). Finally, many seniors who might have grown unhappy with the mixed living or quality of life at the Concord moved with no exit interview, and the new group of recent residents comprises a sizable portion of each cross-sectional survey.

4. This reference group was composed of seniors in other high-rise public housing facilities in Decatur who had a similar age and income profile but had no pressing need or desire for the congregate services provided at the Concord (1992, $n = 80$; 1993, $n = 49$; 1994, $n = 43$). They are used as a point of reference with which changes in the Concord senior population can be compared.

5. The reference group does not always have equivalent social services or spaces in their buildings to accommodate these activities. Answers about the use of social activities in general, however, should be comparable.

6. Because her specific problems were so like those found by her replacement and all the other service managers, they will be summarized in the final section.

7. The first time period represents the evaluation of the first manager; the second and third time periods represent the evaluations of the second manager.

8. This is one example of service economies lost as a result of the large number of younger persons ineligible for this support service; other examples follow in the next section.

9. This observation is reinforced by the service managers and providers who occasionally ate in the dining room and reported that meals were very good.

10. This estimate covers population changes between annual surveys, even though there is evidence that some persons were admitted and then left between surveys without ever being counted in the study. This level of transiency was observed during the one month at the site when semiannual surveys of residents were being collected.

11. For other examples, see National Resource Center (1993), Massachusetts (1994), and Hornig (1990).

References

Bauer, Stephen. 1995. Seniors Leaving County High-Rises: Exodus Spurred by Blending Age Groups. *The Champaign-Urbana (Illinois) News Gazette*, February 28, pp. A1 and A14.

Burby, Raymond J., and William M. Rohe. 1990. Providing for the Housing Needs of the Elderly. *Journal of the American Planning Association* 56(Summer):324–40.

Cohen, Frances, David J. Bearison, and Charlotte Muller. 1987. Interpersonal Understanding in the Elderly: The Influence of Age-Integrated and Age-Segregated Housing. *Research on Aging* 9(March):79–100.

Crouch, Beth. 1993. *Annual Public Housing Authority Survey: 1993*. Bloomington, IL: Illinois Association of Housing Authorities.

Gayda, Kathy S., and Leonard F. Heumann. 1989. *The 1988 National Survey of Section 202 Housing for the Elderly and Handicapped*. Committee Publication No. 101–736 for the House Subcommittee on Housing and Consumer Interests of the Select Committee on Aging. Washington, DC: U.S. Government Printing Office.

Henry, J. Marilyn. 1993. The 1992 NAHRO Awards of Excellence. *Journal of Housing* 50(1):10–20.

Heumann, Leonard F. 1987. *The Retention and Transfer of Frail Elderly Living in Independent Housing*. Chicago: Illinois Housing Development Authority, Illinois Department of Public Aid, Illinois Department on Aging.

Heumann, Leonard F. 1994a. Assisted Living in Public Housing: The Use of Community Based Case Managed Support Services. Paper presented at Future Visions of Urban Public Housing: An International Forum, November 17–20. Cincinnati, OH.

Heumann, Leonard F. 1994b. *Final Evaluation: The Concord Congregate Care Program*. Champaign, IL: The Housing Research and Development Program.

Heumann, Leonard F., and Duncan P. Boldy. 1983. *Housing for the Elderly: Planning and Policy Formulation in Western Europe and North America*. New York: St. Martin's Press.

Highrise Mixed Population Committee. 1989. *Highrise Mixed Population Report*. Seattle: Housing Authority of the City of Seattle.

Hornig, Christopher W. 1990. *Legal Analysis of Standards Governing Public Housing Authorities*

with Regard to People with Mental Disabilities. Washington, DC: Reno, Cavanaugh and
Hornig, Attorneys at Law.

Kellam, Susan. 1992. The Mixed Bag to Success: Mixed Housing Compromise Provides Equitable Way of Mixing Aged and Disabled in Public Housing. *Congressional Quarterly
Weekly Report* 50(August 8):2359.

Levitan, Sar A. 1990. *Programs in Aid of the Poor.* 6th ed. Baltimore: Johns Hopkins Press.

Massachusetts Department of Mental Health, Housing and Support Services. 1994. *Massachusetts State Comprehensive Housing Affordability Strategy 1994–1998.* Boston.

National Association of Housing and Redevelopment Officials. 1989. *Mixing Elderly and Non-
Elderly Population: Deinstitutionalization Survey.* Washington, DC.

National Resource Center on Homelessness and Mental Illness. 1993. *Creating Community:
Integrating Elderly and Severely Mentally Ill Persons in Public Housing.* Delmar, NY: Policy
Research Association, Inc.

Newman, Sandra J., and Raymond J. Struyk. 1990. Housing and Support Services: Federal
Policy for the Frail Elderly and Chronically Mentally Ill. In *Building Foundations: Housing and Federal Policy,* ed. Dennis DiPasquale and Langley C. Keys, 435–64. Philadelphia: University of Pennsylvania Press.

Normoyle, Janice B. 1988. The Defensible Space Model of Fear and Elderly Public Housing
Residents. *Environment and Behavior* 20(January):50–74.

Tanzman, Beth. 1993. An Overview of Surveys of Mental Health Consumers' Preferences for
Housing and Support Services. *Hospital and Community Psychiatry* 34(5):450–55.

U.S. Department of Housing and Urban Development. 1990. *Report to Congress: Housing Mentally Disabled Persons in Public Housing Projects for the Elderly.* Washington, DC.

U.S. Department of Housing and Urban Development, Office of Assistant Secretary for Public
and Indian Housing. 1994. Designated Housing: Public Housing Designated for Occupancy by Disabled Elderly or Disabled and Elderly Families. *Federal Register* 59, no.
71, pp. 17652–68.

U.S. General Accounting Office. 1992. *Public Housing: Housing Persons with Mental Disabilities with the Elderly.* Gaithersburg, MD.

PART III

Design Issues

KAREN A. FRANCK

5 Changing Values in U.S. Public Housing Policy and Design

Introduction

Public housing, as a particular kind of built environment, can be viewed as a building or place type. As with other types, it is a cultural *invention,* possessing physical characteristics, meanings, and uses that define it and that may change over time (Schneekloth and Franck 1994). The choice of which characteristics a type should possess is based largely on values, that is, on prescriptive beliefs about what circumstances and conditions are desirable (Rokeach 1973). Values act as guides for ongoing behavior; they give expression to human needs and, as such, motivate us to strive for the goals implied by the values. Since values underlie and direct attitudes and actions, they are particularly important when there is a judgment to be reached, a choice to be made, or a conflict to be resolved, all frequent occurrences in policy making and architectural design.

Just as values guide what we believe and what we build, they also allow us to evaluate what has already been built. As these values change, so do our views of what is good or important. The changes in values can be so profound that the buildings, spaces, and programs that were once deemed appropriate may subsequently be derided as misguided, even after only a short period of time. It is, in part, the values that are dominant at a given time that allow us to identify certain design features as being problems. Without these values to highlight those characteristics, we might not see or define them as problems at all. And, given different values, we would likely identify other features as problems.

This has been the situation in public housing policy and design in the United States and in the United Kingdom as well. Housing schemes that were once seen as fine achievements, socially and architecturally, are now thoroughly rejected and the related programs and policies are seen, like the buildings and outdoor spaces, as having created as many problems as they solved. Many of the criticisms we now make of

85

the extremely large developments that house only low-income families, with few if any services or facilities, are indeed valid criticisms. But they also raise the question, "Why did anyone ever think they would work in the first place?"

The answer to that question lies in the beliefs that were held at the time the projects were built. So when we criticize earlier buildings and programs, often quite harshly, we must also uncover and critique the values that shaped them. Discovering the earlier values allows us to see that those decisions were not arbitrary, thought-less, or fragmented, but part of a larger, often well-considered social and architec-tural view of the world and of what was needed to improve the conditions of cities and housing. Identifying earlier values also helps to clarify our current perspectives and to recognize how they shape current decisions and directions. As we discuss cur-rent values, it is useful to consider how they might be more fully realized and what obstacles need to be overcome in that effort.

Of course, values are not the only forces that shape the creation or modifications of a place type. A great many other conditions and events also contributed to the changes in building and site design identified in this chapter, including political, eco-nomic, and technological changes in society, as well as changes in demographics and lifestyle. Identifying the more hidden influences is not meant to deny the impor-tance of other conditions, nor is it meant to explain in full why these changes in design have occurred. The intention is, instead, to reveal how changes in values have had a significant impact on design and policy decisions. Developing policy and de-signing buildings are not simply technical or practical matters; they are also matters of belief.

Changing Values

OPEN/CLOSED, UNIVERSAL/PARTICULAR

The site and building design of public housing for families with children in the United States has gone through three general stages over its sixty-year history: (1) semi-enclosed courts with walk-up buildings in the 1930s and early 1940s; (2) open space between lines of row houses and walk-up buildings, or around widely spaced elevator buildings, starting in the 1940s and extending into the 1960s; and (3) pri-vate yards and semi-enclosed or fully enclosed courts for row houses and other low-rise buildings in the late 1970s, 1980s, and 1990s (Franck and Mostoller 1995). The relationship of buildings to city streets has also changed: from buildings aligned with streets but with entries largely from the interior of the site in Stage 1; to the closing of streets and the placement of buildings at an angle to neighborhood streets in Stage 2; to the reintroduction of streets and the fronting of buildings and building entries onto them in Stage 3. This chapter focuses on the shift from Stage 2 to Stage 3. Although examples are taken from public housing in Newark, New Jersey, this shift has occurred in the design of new public housing and the redesign of existing public housing in many other cities as well, including New York, Boston, and San Francisco (Franck and Mostoller 1995; Gelfand and Dev 1994; Marcuse et al. 1994; Schnee 1994; Vale 1995).

The shift from Stage 2 to Stage 3 has been dramatic in regard to both the characteristics of sites and the attitude toward outdoor space adopted by planners and architects. In Stage 2, extensive "open space" unencumbered by buildings or other structures was highly valued, even though there was very little program for this space. Low coverage of land by buildings was a frequent measure of the good attributes of a site. At Christopher Columbus Homes in Newark, built in 1955, for example, only 19 percent of the land was occupied by buildings (figure 5.1).

Even more important than low coverage, however, was the visualization of openness. Government design guidelines preceding the building of housing in Stage 2 emphasized this point: " . . . not only must a large percentage of the land remain unoccupied but in addition to this the buildings have to be placed to emphasize this

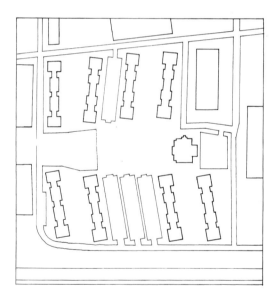

FIGURE 5.1
Site plan of Christopher Columbus Homes, Newark, New Jersey: Example of Stage 2 housing development, 1955. Thirteen-story elevator buildings in superblock. Four buildings were demolished in 1994; four buildings were demolished in 1995. To be replaced by row house dwellings fronting streets and enclosing courts.

fact" (U.S. Federal Emergency Administration of Public Works 1935). The site was to *appear* open. Long vistas, lack of spatial endings and closures, and wide spacing were all used to give a site a "feeling of openness." The enclosure of land by buildings, fences, or through streets was to be avoided since that would reduce the feeling of openness. Even when the building type was a series of row houses with private front and back entrances, as at Stephen Crane Village in Newark, the open space was not divided by fences or other barriers (figure 5.2).

The open space schemes of Stage 2 were generated by a desire for universality. By creating spaces outdoors and indoors (lobbies, elevators, hallways) that were both symbolically and physically open to all, architects envisioned an all-inclusive and unrestricted "community" extending beyond the actual site, no longer contained or constrained by physical location or by physical barriers. Buildings and site would be open to all—to view and to enter.

Similarly, there were no visible architectural distinctions between one dwelling and another, either in terms of facade treatment or treatment of outdoor space in high-rise or row house schemes. Both the identity of individual households and any communal character were downplayed as much as possible in the treatment of buildings and grounds. This preoccupation with the universal, rather than with the individual or the community, suited housing policy perfectly after the 1949 Housing Act. After 1949, the "public" and bureaucratized character of public housing, the clearance of "blighted areas," and the emphasis on cost, efficiency, and the production of large numbers of units supplanted the more experimental and communitarian orientation of the 1930s and the public works employment orientation of the 1937 Housing Act.

In Stage 3, the idea of universality has been vociferously rejected: the accessibility of spaces to anyone and everyone, and the lack of individual (or even group) identity of dwellings, have been decried. The wide expanses are no longer called "open areas" but, in some places, referred to as "asphalt wastelands" (Newark Redevelopment and Housing Authority 1984). Building and site designs of Stage 1 and Stage 2 are often criticized for their anonymity, lack of transitions, and lack of sufficiently defined uses for outdoor spaces (Epp Associates et al. 1990; Newman 1972, 1975).

It is the very *openness*, so prized earlier, that is now seen as a severe problem. So, the opposite imperative is adopted: Individuality of households is to be stressed with private entrances to the outdoors for each dwelling in housing for families whenever possible, opening onto streets and with private outdoor spaces that are separated from each other. Shared spaces are to have clearly defined uses, located in close relationship to building entries, and are not to be easily accessible to nonresidents. Swaths of wide-open, undefined space are to be avoided and in many cases, entire closure of the site is sought through the configuration of buildings or with fences (figure 5.3). Openness is replaced with definition and closure. The site is not to be *any* place, but as much as possible a *particular* place, and made up of a series of smaller *particular* spaces. Distinguishing fronts from backs through treatment of facades and

FIGURE 5.2

"Tending the Lawn." Photograph of Stephen Crane Village in Newark in 1940s shows unenclosed yards and standardized appearance of dwellings.

Source: A Study of the Social Effects of Public Housing in Newark, New Jersey. Housing Authority of the City of Newark 1944. Courtesy of Newark Public Library.

outdoor space and locating entrances on streets with street addresses also embody particularity and individuality, as in the infill public housing built in Newark in the 1980s (figure 5.4).

The actual closing up of the outdoor space of public housing by enclosing private and shared spaces is part of the movement toward individualization and particularization, toward defining and reinforcing the point that the site is a particular place, made of particular, clearly distinct spaces. This movement can be taken quite far. In many cities, housing authorities and nonprofit housing developers are building fences that completely enclose existing projects, and new projects are being built where the buildings themselves enclose the site completely so that the only way to reach the interior of the site is through the dwellings. These are understandable and often valid responses to problems of crime and violence. They show, nonetheless,

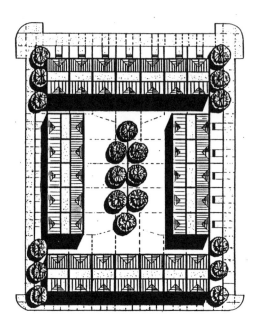

FIGURE 5.3
Diagrammatic site plan for new public housing, Newark, New Jersey.
"Townhouses have private front and rear yards. Where semi-private courts
are provided, they are completely surrounded by housing and have only one
or two entry points; this maximizes resident control of the interior of site."

Source: Public Housing Master Plan, Newark Redevelopment and Housing Authority
1984, 31.

how much the earlier orientation toward open and universal has changed to closed
and particular.

The question may be asked whether the movement toward enclosing and priva-
tizing is too extreme and too automatic a response. In some cities, there is a desire
to assign all outdoor space to individual units, leaving none to be shared. This leaves
little space for children of school age to play, since private yards are not sufficient
for their activities. It also undermines any potential, whether symbolic or actual, for
residents to meet and socialize in nonprivate space. An exclusive emphasis on the
individual realm rather than the universal realm bypasses the middle ground of the
collective realm—of a local community within the development. The push toward
spatial privatization is reflected, and taken further, in the push toward privatization

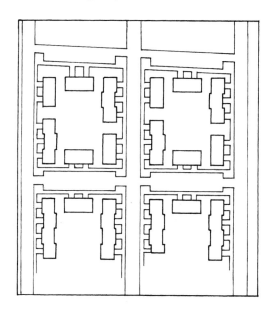

FIGURE 5.4
West Side Villa, Newark: Example of Stage 3 housing development, 1985.
Two-story row houses on streets.

of tenure—in proposals for homeownership by tenants (see chapter 3 in this volume for a detailed discussion of this issue).

The danger of adopting new values so completely, as a reaction (and possibly an overreaction) to the previous values, is that other intermediate or mediating values and conditions may be overlooked. Today we are likely to believe that in enclosing the site completely and in creating only private yards and no collective outdoor space, we will reduce as much as possible opportunities for criminal activities. In many cases we have good reason to believe this. But, at the same time, we will also reduce opportunities for other pursuits, including children's group play or adult group activities. Deciding that these opportunities are worth sacrificing for the possibility of increasing security is a value judgment, both at the level of particular design features and conditions and at the level of larger value orientations.

SEPARATED/CONNECTED

Another imperative behind the site and building design of Stage 2 public housing was to separate the site from the surrounding neighborhood. Just as it was important to modern architects that architecture be different from its context, so it was important to housing policymakers and planners that public housing break with the adjacent "slums." Differences in the form and the arrangement of buildings and the absence of streets and courts did not just symbolize for residents a break from their past lives. It was also believed that the architectural differences would separate and protect residents from their surroundings. Architectural differences, as well as the large size of projects, would "protect" the project from "blight." James Ford (1936) advocated large-scale projects because size "helps the project to dominate the neighborhood and discourage regression to slum life." Elizabeth Wood, director of the Chicago Housing Authority, made a similar argument: "On the basis of experience with large urban redevelopments, we know that if blighted areas are not rebuilt on the protected superblocks, all expenditures will be wasted; the project will decay" (1946, 14).

Everything the "slums" possessed was rejected, including playing in or near streets, sitting on stoops, and standing on street corners. Separation from such activities was to be achieved only through visual and spatial differences between the new housing and the surrounding neighborhood, and through the absence of through streets. That people could easily walk into the site and bring their habits and activities with them from the adjacent areas was not an issue (except, of course, there were no streets to play on, no stoops to sit on, and no street corners to stand on). Actual barriers in the form of buildings or fences were not considered as ways of creating separation. Indeed, such physical separations would have undermined the idea of universality. Exactly how residents would remain independent of adjacent areas while meeting everyday needs and pursuing activities was not analyzed.

The projects in Stage 2, built in very large superblocks, were by no means self-sufficient, since they contained practically no facilities or services. The contradiction is still striking: Large size, absence of through streets, and a distinctively different design of outdoor space were all incorporated to ensure separation and a kind of immunity to the surrounding areas, but no functional provisions, other than schools, were made to support a community. The idea of separation was an abstraction. Nonetheless, like other abstractions, it fueled the planning and design of the largest proportion of public housing units ever built in the United States.

In Stage 3, the exact opposite imperative has been adopted: Public housing is to be integrated into the surrounding neighborhood. Its separation is now seen as isolation and as a contributor both to problems within the site and in the surrounding neighborhood. Rather than serving as an inoculation against social problems, size and separation are seen to have bred more "disease." Thus, it is commonly observed that large housing projects have contributed to the crime and vandalism in nearby areas (National Commission on Severely Distressed Public Housing 1992a; Newark Redevelopment and Housing Authority 1984).

Instead of protecting residents from the "slum" conditions of adjacent neighborhoods, or from the neighborhoods that the projects replaced, large superblocks are now seen to have exacerbated those conditions. A new responsibility is now to be undertaken by housing authorities: to help improve neighborhood conditions outside the confines of the project by improving conditions inside the project (National Commission on Severely Distressed Public Housing 1992a).

In Stage 3, neighborhood and project are seen as unavoidably, and potentially beneficially, connected. The desired and attempted social separation between neighborhood and project in Stage 2, which posited them as opponents, is not only not sought, it is recognized as being socially and functionally impossible. The report by the National Commission on Severely Distressed Public Housing (1992a; ch. 1, 6) states: "Public housing developments do not exist as entities separate from other city neighborhoods; they are an integrated element of the surrounding community." One way of becoming more integrated is by adopting an architectural style and site design that does not make public housing stand out from its context. Often, this means reintroducing city streets into public housing sites and placing building entrances on the street. This approach, advocated by the Newark Housing Authority in 1984 (figure 5.5), is being adopted in the row houses that will replace the demolished high-rise buildings at Christopher Columbus and that have already replaced the demolished buildings at Scudder Homes. It is very difficult, however, to strengthen the relationship between housing development and neighborhood, physically or socially, when the housing developments are extremely large, when several exist next to each other and there is virtually no surrounding neighborhood left, or when the housing was built on such an isolated site that there was none to begin with.

How public housing can be designed, or redesigned, to improve the quality of life in urban neighborhoods, and not just within the housing complexes themselves, remains a very important question, requiring an enlarged responsibility on the part of public housing policy and program developers and the coordination of efforts by local authorities with other local organizations. The National Commission on Severely Distressed Public Housing (1992b; ch. 1, 7) stresses the revitalization of neighborhoods and projects: " . . . economic development incentives for commercial activity in surrounding neighborhoods would help provide jobs for residents. Increased commercial activity, in turn, would likely lead to improved infrastructure conditions, decreases in criminal activity and a general improvement in the community's image."

The Commission recommends close coordination with neighborhood representatives in planning the revitalization of public housing (1992b). Funds allocated to severely distressed public housing developments under the Urban Revitalization Demonstration (URD) Program, started in 1992, are to be used in part to support such efforts. A second URD program, URD Plus, subtitled "A Tool for Neighborhood Revitalization," has as its goal ending the isolation of public housing. However, while closer social and economic connections with the neighborhood are now being envisioned, recent site design changes posit a new and unprecedented kind of separation: the enclosure of the outdoor space of the development and, hence, its *physical* separation from the adjacent neighborhood, as a security measure. Courtyards and

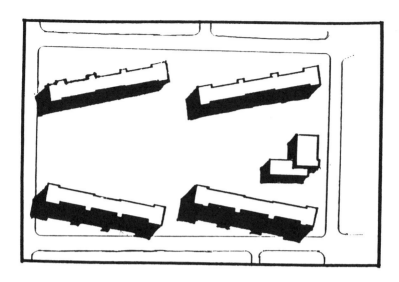

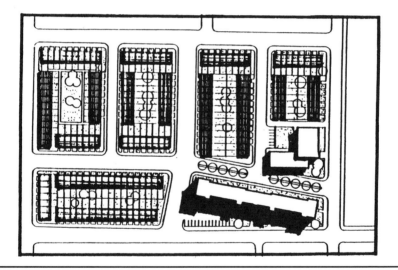

FIGURE 5.5
Previous and proposed schemes for portion of Scudder Homes, Newark.
"Overpowering institutional structures in high-density superblocks are
replaced with lower-density housing built at human scale. The units face
residential streets, as does most private housing in Newark."

Source: Public Housing Master Plan. Newark Redevelopment and Housing Authority
1984, 28.

private backyards are now sometimes completely closed off from neighborhood streets and are accessible only from the interior of buildings, or fences with locked gates are sometimes installed around the entire site.

Even though complete social separation, if not complete independence, of the project from the neighborhood was the goal in Stage 2, sites were designed to be completely open and physically accessible to all. Now, mutually beneficial relationships between project and neighborhood are being envisioned, but physical separations of various kinds are being adopted. In some cases, the contradictory quality of the latter circumstance is offset by community facilities that will be shared with the surrounding neighborhood, or by the fact that adjacent housing developments are similarly enclosed.

Recognition of the necessarily reciprocal relationship between project and neighborhood and the need to strengthen both—not one at the expense of the other—is a complete reversal from the Stage 2 approach of trying to make the project large enough and strong enough to overcome any negative influences the neighborhood might exert. After sixty years, the obligation to provide housing *and* more economically vital neighborhoods with services and amenities where the housing is located is being recognized as part of the purview of public housing. How to build or revitalize that enlarged community, comprised of housing developments and the surrounding neighborhoods, while also improving the security of the development itself, is a significant challenge.

The value being placed on connections extends to social aspects of housing as well. During Stage 2 and until very recently, housing needs were separated from other needs, such as those for education, day care, job training, employment opportunities, and other commercial and social services. The purpose of public housing was seen as providing housing only—not as being concerned with these other needs, not even to see how they might be related to housing requirements, or to the success of meeting those requirements. This segregation of housing from other aspects of daily life was physically manifested and enforced by the mandated absence of commercial establishments of any kind within projects. One could say that public housing in many ways mirrored the land-use separations so central to suburban life in the United States, albeit for very different reasons.

The URD program has adopted a much more integrative view with suggestions for services, facilities, and opportunities to be developed in the neighborhood *and* on-site. It is a rare program—one that has removed regulatory requirements that fostered the kind of separations it seeks to change. The program allows up to 20 percent of the funds allocated to URD sites to be used for community services, job training, economic development, and education and employment services. Housing is finally being seen in connection to other needs, and the success of the housing is recognized as dependent on fulfilling other requirements of daily life.

The final bastion of separation that is being questioned is the division between income groups. One of the key defining (and regulated) features of public housing for families in the United States is that the housing is only for poor families—a feature that, particularly in large projects, separates these families from all others. That these families are usually minority, single-parent families with welfare as their sole source of income creates additional separation. URD Plus has recommended the creation of mixed-income neighborhoods both on public housing sites and in adjacent areas.

Compared to the earlier ideas of what public housing is and what it should be allowed to be, the development of services and the integration of income groups represent tremendous changes. They require significant modifications of federal statutes and regulations and call for imagination, creativity, and coordination locally in developing the possibilities.

This movement toward viewing public housing as part of a neighborhood where mixtures of activities can occur and mixtures of people can live is a welcome change. However, this view must not lead anyone to overlook the many current and future low-income residents of public housing. By focusing on "neighborhoods," "revitalizing neighborhoods," and "economic development," it can become all too easy to lose sight of those people who do not fit into the stereotyped picture of a completely revitalized urban neighborhood, namely those who are very poor and may have many other problems. The one good thing that could be said about separate housing intended exclusively for the poor is that, however deteriorated and dangerous it became, it did provide some kind of shelter. By mixing the goal of improved housing with so many other goals, will its importance be lessened, or, under future administrations, lost?

Another reason for closing existing streets to create superblocks in Stage 2 was to remove sources of noise, danger, and harmful fumes by removing through traffic, thus creating places for children to play that were safer than the neighborhood streets the housing had replaced (figure 5.6). Such reasoning was consistent with the more general orientation of separating housing sites from their immediate surroundings. The value-based decisions may seem exceedingly plausible and indeed laudable at the time they are made. Yet, those design choices that seem so obviously good and right at one time may be viewed as much less significant at a later time. Traffic is still dangerous today, perhaps more so; however, because of the value now placed on connecting public housing to surrounding neighborhoods, through streets are being reinstated. In recognition of the potential safety problems, physical features are often included to reduce the speed of cars, such as speed bumps or necked-down entrances.

STANDARDIZED/VARIED, UNIVERSAL/LOCAL

Public housing built during Stage 2 is remarkably similar throughout the country. Two fairly uniform site-design schemes were employed: swaths of open space were placed either between rows or around freestanding buildings, with few if any through streets. Today, many of these developments remain remarkably similar to each other in site design, building form, and other material attributes, thereby making them stand out as "public housing." While there were many reasons for this uniformity, two significant factors were federal design guidelines and the expectations and demands of local authorities. As in many areas of design, a few, indeed very few, solutions were seen to be the best ones, with the reasons given in only very curt and undeveloped terms in the design guidelines (U.S. Federal Emergency Administration of Public Works 1935; U.S. Housing Authority 1939; U.S. National Housing Agency 1946). Experimentation with different solutions, even in the form of proposals or schematic design, was not encouraged under the design guidelines; standards and regulations, either as written or as interpreted by local officials, constrained alternatives and variety even further. Standardization, uniformity, and a rather institutional appearance were also consistent with the attempt to make public housing palatable to a public that questioned its cost.

Variety within a given site was also discouraged. Differences of any kind between buildings in a single development were not only unacceptable to the bureaucracy that built and managed public housing, they were also aesthetically unappealing to architects in the 1950s and 1960s. In New York, for example, the middle-income housing developments of Co-op City and LeFrak City possess the same uniformity.

The move toward uniformity, standardization, and order is apparent in the design guidelines published immediately prior to this period. "Order," not mentioned in the 1935 public housing design guide, was emphasized in the 1940s (U.S. Federal Emergency Administration of Public Works 1935; U.S. National Housing Agency 1946). In 1946, the guidelines in *Public Housing Design: A Review of Experience in Low-Rent Housing* encouraged straight or curved rows (over courts) because they have "uniform orientation" and a "quality of good order." This same set of guidelines criticized the U-shaped court plan for "inconvenience of circulation, inefficiency of service drives, difficult use of land at the exterior corners" (U.S. National Housing Agency 1946, 30).

The tendency to adopt a very few solutions and to apply them across the board because they seem to be the best, if not the *only*, solutions, is now being resisted. In many of the recent and ongoing redesign efforts, particular local conditions are being respected and solutions tailored to those conditions (Epp 1994; Rosenthal 1994). In order to realize fully the values being promoted in Stage 3, particular site characteristics, the specific physical and social relationships of that site to the surrounding neighborhood, and the history of the individual project as recounted by current residents all need to be considered and accommodated in redevelopment efforts. Circumstances specific to a particular site may suggest that the complete enclosure of private spaces or the reestablishment of through streets is not the best solution for that site (Rosenthal 1994). This approach requires attention to *local, particular* opportunities and constraints, not allegiance to some vision of universal conditions, and requires attention to detailed, concrete information, not generalized, abstract information.

Attending to and accommodating the specific and the variable is not something bureaucracies like housing authorities are set up to do. At the same time, if the value of the particular, and not the universal, is to be truly embraced, local conditions and differences demand attention and support. The URD program encourages innovation and the exploration of alternatives; it asks for creativity and imagination at the local level.

After such a very long period of standardization, regulation, and constraint, this switch can be very hard to make. Fortunately, in redeveloping existing buildings some degree of variety between sites is unavoidable. When existing buildings are kept, the different types—row houses, walk-up buildings, elevator buildings—require different methods of enclosing open space and "re-fronting" the buildings onto streets. In addition, various methods of ensuring that dwellings have private entries, even in walk-up buildings, are being adopted. For example, in San Francisco, external stairs have been built to ensure that all apartment entrances in a walk-up building are visible from the street; in Boston, walk-up buildings have been converted to single-story flats and duplexes to meet the same objective. Not only does this variation help to meet the stated objective of making public housing less identifiable and less "institutional," it also offers the opportunity to respond to local conditions and local context.

Variety is also pertinent to the design of units, particularly in recognition of the variety of household types and cultural backgrounds of residents. The present focus on families with children or on the elderly ignores other possible combinations, including intergenerational households, grandparents caring for grandchildren, and several single people living in the same unit. Making the regulatory standards for unit size and layout more flexible would accommodate a greater range of alternatives. Katrin Adam's proposed design for Neighborhood Women Renaissance Housing in Brooklyn, while not an example of public housing, does offer some illustrative examples (Franck 1994). Again, variety could be translated into a range of particular, detailed circumstances rather than remain an abstract concept.

STABLE/CHANGING

Public housing in the United States was originally envisioned as providing temporary accommodations—to house working-class families while they accumulated the resources to buy or rent market-rate housing. For a while that did happen, but eventually, starting in the 1960s, public housing became the permanent accommodations for poor and very poor families who were unable to afford market-rate housing. And in today's public housing, several generations may live in the same development. Thus, although it was originally expected that the housing would remain the same and the population would change, instead, it is the housing that has been changed, while most of the population remains.

Can possibilities for *future* change be built into new or remodeled buildings? This may be the most surprising and most difficult goal to achieve: that in redesign or new construction, we build for future modifications to the size, layout, and configuration of units and outdoor spaces. Even in middle- and upper-income housing in the United States, this is only very rarely done. The changes could be quite minor, such as making two units independent of each other at one point and connected at a later point, or allowing a space for a bedroom that can be converted to a work space or home office at another point. Katrin Adam's proposed design for Neighborhood Women Renaissance Housing incorporates the former arrangement (Franck 1994). Site design might also incorporate opportunities for the future expansion of row house units to include an efficiency unit, another bedroom, or a space where wage work can be conducted. While we have the opportunity to redefine public housing, the possibility for *change* merits the same kind of concern that is being given to particularity and connectedness.

Such changes in the design of units could respond to changes in the population composition of developments or to changing needs of individual households who remain in the development for long periods of time. While the latter has been the case in public housing, the circumstance has never been embraced or supported by policy or design. Intending to have households remain, and making the housing attractive for them to do so, even when they can afford to move to other housing, would help create the kind of stable, mixed-income communities being envisioned. But such an intention alters fundamentally the earlier goal of providing housing for families in transition. This change in goals, from providing transitional housing to creating long-term stable communities, has not yet been sufficiently acknowledged or the ramifications explored. Local conditions in different cities and variations in kinds of redevelopment efforts will likely lead to different approaches in this regard as well.

Conclusion

Values are beliefs about preferred states or conditions. The changes in values apparent in U.S. public housing policy and design reveal how much beliefs have changed, and very importantly, are still changing. The programs and policies adopted, the buildings and sites constructed and reconstructed, and the services provided are enactments of beliefs, not merely technical or practical means to solve problems, although they are that also. It is possible to view the values described in this chapter as characteristics of an image, even a dream, of what public housing should be. The photographs and diagrams from the Newark Housing Authority's promotional literature

FIGURE 5.6
"A Safe Place to Play." Photograph of Newark public housing in 1940s shows semi-enclosed shared space used for children's playground.

Source: A Study of the Social Effects of Public Housing in Newark, New Jersey. Housing Authority of the City of Newark 1944. Courtesy of Newark Public Library.

depict changes in that image, particularly figures 5.6 and 5.7. While we do draw upon empirical knowledge in devising policies and programs and in advocating certain kinds of building and site designs, we also base decisions on beliefs, and relatedly on images, that may not be and often cannot be fully justified by empirical knowledge.

The modification and transformation of public housing in various cities is significant not only because many discrete changes are being made, but also because we are reconceiving what the social/architectural type called public housing *is*. A type is a built form of beliefs (Schneekloth and Franck 1994). By creating small housing developments, adopting individual street addresses in place of project names, integrating public housing into the surrounding community, and integrating income groups within the same street block or housing development, we are beginning to dismantle both the idea and, eventually, the reality of the type called "the projects" as separate, homogeneous, and monolithic enclaves.

As we recognize the connections that can exist between "project" and surrounding "neighborhood," both as ideas and as material places, we are also exploring how

FIGURE 5.7
Drawing of an imaginary backyard in 1980s shows enclosure of yards and some differences between dwellings. "Elements in meeting the goal for housing families with children include private entrances and yards for the larger units."

Source: Public Housing Master Plan, Newark Redevelopment and Housing Authority 1984, 11.

public housing, in many new architectural and social forms, can constitute and contribute to economically and socially vital *neighborhoods.* The types called "housing," "project," and even "development" as they were once viewed, defined, and regulated in public housing in Stages 1 and 2 did not capture the rich variety of activities and people that "neighborhoods" comprise. As Stage 3 proceeds, the characteristics of neighborhoods continue to offer fertile ground for redefining the mandate of public housing in the United States and for exploring how this mandate can best be met.

Notes

This chapter is based in part on research conducted under a grant from the National Endowment for the Arts, with the author and Michael Mostoller as co-principal investigators.

A more complete description of the research appears in Karen A. Franck and Michael Mostoller, "From Courts to Open Space to Streets: Changes in the Site Design of U.S. Public Housing," *Journal of Architecture and Planning Research*, special issue on public housing (Autumn 1995). The author appreciates comments from Gayle Epp on an earlier draft.

References

Epp, Gayle. 1994. Urban Public Housing in the United States: Evidence of Distress and Strategies for Revitalizing Communities. In Wolfgang F. E. Preiser, David P. Varady, and Francis P. Russell, eds., *Future Visions of Urban Public Housing*. Proceedings of "Future Visions of Urban Public Housing: An International Forum," held at the University of Cincinnati, Cincinnati, Ohio, November 17–20.

Epp Associates, TAMS Consultants, and Swander Associates. 1990. *Redevelopment Handbook: Procedures and Design Guidelines for Redeveloping Public Housing*. Boston, MA: Bureau of Modernization and Redevelopment.

Ford, James R. 1936. *Slums and Housing*. Cambridge: Harvard University Press.

Franck, Karen A. 1994. Questioning the American Dream: Recent Housing Innovations in the United States. In *Housing Women*, eds. Rose Gilroy and Roberta Woods. London: Routledge.

Franck, Karen A., and Michael Mostoller. 1995. From Court to Open Space to Street: A History of Site Design of U.S. Public Housing. *Journal of Architecture and Planning Research* 12(3).

Gelfand, Lisa, and Gita Dev. 1994. Typology as Policy. In Wolfgang F. E. Preiser, David P. Varady, and Francis P. Russell, eds., *Future Visions of Urban Public Housing*. Proceedings of "Future Visions of Urban Public Housing: An International Forum," held at the University of Cincinnati, Cincinnati, Ohio, November 17–20.

Marcuse, Peter; David Burney; and Efithia Tsitiridis. 1994. New York City: Historical Perspectives, Current Policy and Future Planning. In Wolfgang F. E. Preiser, David P. Varady, and Francis P. Russell, eds., *Future Visions of Urban Public Housing*. Proceedings of "Future Visions of Urban Public Housing: An International Forum," held at the University of Cincinnati, Cincinnati, Ohio, November 17–20.

National Commission on Severely Distressed Public Housing. 1992a. *Final Report of the National Commission on Severely Distressed Public Housing: A Report to the Congress and the Secretary of Housing and Urban Development*. Washington, DC: U.S. Government Printing Office.

National Commission on Severely Distressed Public Housing. 1992b. *Case Study and Site Examination Reports*. Washington, DC: U.S. Government Printing Office.

Newark Redevelopment and Housing Authority. 1984. *Public Housing Master Plan*. Newark, NJ.

Newman, Oscar. 1972. *Defensible Space*. New York: Macmillan.

Newman, Oscar. 1975. *Design Guidelines for Creating Defensible Space*. Washington, DC: U.S. Government Printing Office.

Rokeach, Milton. 1973. *The Nature of Human Values*. New York: The Free Press.

Rosenthal, Gilbert A. 1994. Renovate or Replace: The Policies, Politics, and Technology of Public Housing Redevelopment. In Wolfgang F. E. Preiser, David P. Varady, and Francis

P. Russell, eds., *Future Visions of Urban Public Housing.* Proceedings of "Future Visions of Urban Public Housing: An International Forum," held at the University of Cincinnati, Cincinnati, Ohio, November 17–20.

Scarry, Elaine. 1985. *The Body in Pain: The Making and Unmaking of the World.* New York: Oxford University Press.

Schnee, David. 1994. An Evaluation of Robert Pitts Plaza. In Wolfgang F. E. Preiser, David P. Varady, and Francis P. Russell, eds., *Future Visions of Urban Public Housing.* Proceedings of "Future Visions of Urban Public Housing: An International Forum," held at the University of Cincinnati, Cincinnati, Ohio, November 17–20.

Schneekloth, Lynda H., and Karen A. Franck. 1994. Types: Prison or Promise? In *Ordering Space: Types in Architecture and Design,* eds. Karen A. Franck and Lynda H. Schneekloth. New York: Van Nostrand Reinhold.

U.S. Federal Emergency Administration of Public Works. 1935. *Site Plans.* Washington, DC.

U.S. Housing Authority. 1939. *Planning the Site.* Washington DC: U.S. Government Printing Office.

U.S. National Housing Agency, Federal Public Housing Authority. 1946. *Public Housing Design: A Review of Experience in Low-Rent Housing.* Washington, DC: U.S. Government Printing Office.

Vale, Lawrence J. 1995. Transforming Public Housing: The Social and Physical Redevelopment of Boston's West Broadway Development. *Journal of Architecture and Planning Research* 12(3).

Wood, Elizabeth. 1946. Realities of Urban Development. *Journal of Housing* 3.

DAVID M. SCHNEE

6 An Evaluation of Robert Pitts Plaza

A Post-Occupancy Evaluation of New Public Housing in San Francisco

Introduction

The creation of Robert Pitts Plaza in San Francisco was originally intended to be a modernization of a dilapidated tower complex. But concerns over the appropriateness of high-rise buildings for family occupancy, combined with projected costs that exceeded those for new construction, led to the decision to demolish the towers and build a new low-rise complex. The completed new development (figure 6.1) is one of the first examples of a new trend in the reconstruction of public housing and serves as a case study of current approaches to modernization and redevelopment design.

The design of this development was supported by significant research and programming efforts; a series of project-specific design guidelines was formulated, discussed, and implemented. These guidelines, and the design decisions made to implement them, are the focus of this evaluation. The guidelines address building height; unit access and orientation; secure, shared open spaces and their uses; and overall project image.

The study reveals discrepancies between the intended image of the project and residents' perceptions of it, and between the intended activity and the actual use of the structures and areas designed to achieve that activity. Parking areas, for example, considered a liability by the architects, in fact became an important social amenity and a surprising benefit to the general ratings of security.

This project also provides evidence that demolition followed by new construction may be more advantageous and cost-effective than modernization of older structures. The application of social design objectives such as defensible space, resident privacy, and the provision of social and recreational opportunities for people of all ages required such extensive physical change that new construction was less expen-

104

FIGURE 6.1
View of Robert Pitts Plaza

sive. A focus on social design issues, the participatory establishment of design guidelines, and the implementation via specific design solutions make this project an excellent model for other urban public housing redevelopments.

Modernization

The history of Robert Pitts Plaza had an important impact on the final design and is relevant to discussions about modernization versus demolition and new construction (table 6.1).

In 1956, on the current site of Robert Pitts Plaza, 332 units of housing were constructed and dedicated as Yerba Buena Plaza West (figures 6.2 and 6.3). The original buildings were a combination of two familiar public housing prototypes, consisting of three-story walk-ups[1] and ten-story towers. The towers were set back from the street and reached by walking across a parking lot and passing through an unsecured open-air elevator lobby. The walk-ups also had unsecured lobbies that, like the towers, provided direct and free access through the building and to all residential floors.

This arrangement was to a great degree responsible for the acute security problems that developed later. By the early 1980s, the project was plagued with criminal

TABLE 6.1

Project Chronology

Original towers constructed	1956
Modernization process begun	1982
Bids received; project stopped	1984
New construction redesign begun	1986
Towers demolished	1989
New construction completed	1991

activity, including frequent thefts and muggings in hallways, squatting in vacant apartments, and the use of the buildings as escape routes for criminals fleeing police. Vandalism, much of which was attributed to nonresidents, led to frequent elevator breakdowns that forced tower residents to negotiate as many as ten flights of stairs on foot.

Parking lots became dumps for abandoned and burned-out cars. The shadowed asphalt area between the buildings, intended for children's play, was instead used by adults as a place to drink, and was typically littered with broken glass. Conditions

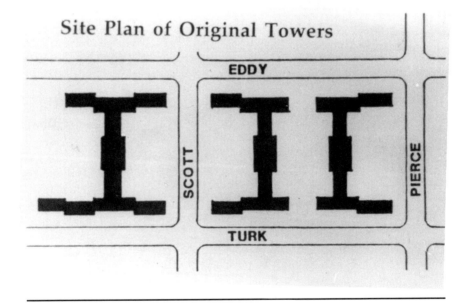

FIGURE 6.2
Plan of Yerba Buena Plaza West

FIGURE 6.3
View of Yerba Buena Plaza West

Source: Photograph by Sara Ishikawa

became so deplorable that the project attracted the attention of local newspapers, which described it as "prison-like" and "unfit for human habitation."

In 1982 the San Francisco Housing Authority (SFHA) hired the architectural firms of Community Design Collaborative (CDC) and ED2 International (ED2I) to design the renovation of the 25-year-old "severely distressed"[2] complex. The design effort started with a detailed analysis of existing physical and social conditions by ED2I. CDC, in collaboration with Clare Cooper Marcus, a social research consultant, reviewed issues in other high-rise public housing. Members of the design team also observed and mapped resident-use patterns and interviewed key staff members, management, and residents.

This effort led the design team to conclude that "high-rises are, in general, not suitable for families" (CDC/ED2I 1986). At that time, HUD's Comprehensive Improvement Assistance Program (CIAP) policies did not allow for the construction of new units, so demolition and reconstruction did not appear to be an option. As a result, the designers aimed to make the site and buildings "work as well as possible for families."

TABLE 6.2

Modernization Design Guidelines

- Parking in small lots
- Terraces between low-rise buildings and streets
- Gathering places for different age groups
- Visible playgrounds near entrances
- Four-story walk-ups in towers
- Defined entrances
- Enlarged lobbies in towers
- Use of ground-floor space for apartments
- Improvements to living room, kitchen, bath, and bedroom

The predesign effort addressed issues related to the number of units and what qualities they should have. In response to an increased demand for large-family units, an architectural program was developed that proposed the elimination of one-bedroom apartments and the addition of three- and four-bedroom apartments. Issues related to design quality were addressed by guidelines developed through a participatory process that involved residents and management. Through this process, the design team developed nine modernization design guidelines, as shown in table 6.2.

These aspects of the architectural program clearly required extensive renovation of the existing buildings. The lower floors of the towers were redesigned to have private entries from semiprivate exterior stairs. Upper floors were redesigned with new elevators in each wing serving four apartments per elevator lobby. This arrangement permitted the elimination of all semipublic hallways. Ground-floor entries were redesigned to be enclosed; parking areas were to be smaller, and play areas were to be located in more observable locations. The proposed renovations would have resulted in an 8 percent reduction in the number of bedrooms.[3]

These proposals were approved and developed into construction documents that were publicly bid. The low bid of $22.1 million greatly exceeded CIAP cost guidelines. Considering the design team's feelings that "towers were not suitable for families," the wisdom of continuing as planned seemed dubious, and the project was stopped.

Reconstruction

Both the design team and the Housing Authority believed that new construction could create a more satisfactory outcome for less money. SFHA's director of design circulated a drawing of a new scheme showing dozens of new three-story buildings. Local political pressure and a grant of nearly $3 million from the City of San Fran-

TABLE 6.3

New Construction Design Guidelines

- Nonstigmatizing image
- Three-story walk-ups/private yards
- Unit entries facing street
- Private entrances off common stair and front porch
- Parking in small lots open to the street
- Secure, common, open spaces
- Outdoor areas for different age groups
- Visible tot lots

cisco brought the project back to life. The design guidelines previously developed for the modernization phase became, with slight modification, the basis for the new design. Table 6.3 shows these guidelines.

This time the approval process went smoothly. The project was successfully constructed at a cost of $18 million—more than $4 million, or nearly 20 percent, less than what had been projected for the modernization design.

The completed project (figures 6.1 and 6.4) comprises thirty-seven two- and three-story wood-frame buildings that enclose common courtyards in the center of each block. Approximately half of the buildings face the public sidewalk; the other half are set back around small parking areas located at the middle of each block. These setbacks divide the central courtyard into five distinct but interconnected areas in an X pattern. The four ends of the X each contain seating, raised garden beds, and a "tot lot" with a climbing structure in a sand area. In the central areas are larger play structures, a grass lawn, and a half-length basketball court.

Every apartment has a private front entrance facing the street or parking lot, and a back entrance leading to the play and garden areas. All first-floor apartments have private front and rear yards. Upper-level apartments can be reached by an exterior stairway that leads to a second-floor front porch shared by either two or four units. From this porch, third-floor apartments are reached by an internal, private stairway. A three-level exterior stairway serves as a rear "porch" and the second means of egress from each apartment. There are no interior public or semipublic hallways or stairs anywhere in the development.

Post-Occupancy Evaluation Methodology

This study was designed to evaluate how well the project met the eight new-construction design guidelines listed in table 6.3. Research was begun approximately six

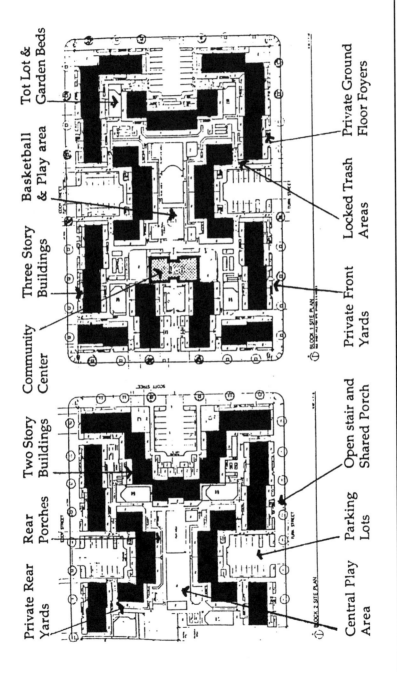

FIGURE 6.4
Plan of Robert Pitts Plaza

months after occupancy and continued through a four-month period ending in May 1992. Thorough site inspections were conducted on six different occasions to observe patterns of resident use of the outdoor spaces. A behavior-trace survey recorded all observable uses of the private, semiprivate, and public exterior spaces. A 102-question, multiple-choice, resident survey was delivered to all households; forty-three of these (21 percent) were returned. To gather more detailed responses, nine of the forty-three households were interviewed directly. Additional interviews were conducted with the architects, the director of planning and design at the SFHA, the on-site property manager, and the president of the resident council. The survey included questions asked to residents of the original development as part of the modernization design research.

Design Guidelines, Design Translations, and Evaluations

The design guidelines were developed in the form of patterns, similar to those found in *A Pattern Language,* co-authored by Sara Ishikawa, one of the architects from CDC (Alexander et al. 1977). Each project guideline contained a title,[4] a concise description of a significant design problem, a brief design solution, and a sketch diagram. The guidelines also described benefits to be realized if the patterns were followed. Taken together, these guidelines form a succinct statement of the designer's assumptions and offer a window into the often hidden world of design reasoning. Each of the design guidelines is summarized below, its translation into physical form described, and a summary of the findings of the evaluation presented.

GUIDELINE 1: THREE-STORY HEIGHT LIMIT

The problem statement, written during the modernization phase, asserted that "high-rise buildings are not appropriate for family housing because they put children too far from the ground." It argued that direct and immediate access to ground-level areas encourages children's outdoor play. The final design follows this guideline. Two- and three-bedroom units are located in three-story walk-ups, and four-bedroom units are located in two-story townhouses (see figures 6.1 and 6.4).

Research by Cooper Marcus (CDC/ED2I 1986) conducted in the original tower complex found that in 1982 only 10 percent of residents surveyed indicated that their children went to play outside as much as they would have liked. At Robert Pitts, 70 percent of respondents expressed satisfaction with the amount of their children's outdoor play.

Moreover, this project provides evidence that lower building height does not necessarily mean a sizable loss of housing. The new design represents a 15 percent reduction in the number of bedrooms from the original complex but only an 8 percent reduction from the original modernization design. This modest loss could be a worthwhile trade-off if it helps to accomplish other project goals. In fact, given the high vacancy rate of the original buildings, there was an actual increase in the number of people housed.

GUIDELINE 2: UNITS FACING THE STREET
GUIDELINE 3: PRIVATE EXTERIOR-UNIT ENTRIES

These two guidelines were developed with security and maintenance in mind. The architects argued that streets with lots of activity are more desirable and are perceived to be safer than quiet areas. They also argued that private entries in clear view are safer than interior hallways.

The architects, thus, tried to balance two opposing concerns: keeping the street active and under the surveillance of residents while trying to provide residents with reasonable privacy. They struck a balance by orienting a majority of unit entries and living rooms toward the street and providing yards and porches as buffers (see figures 6.1 and 6.4). Residents reach first-floor units through a small fenced and gated private yard, or via a covered, gated, exterior vestibule tucked under the second-floor porch. Again, upper units are reached by an open stairway and porch shared by either two or four units. The apartments are then entered through private exterior doors; third-floor apartments have private internal stairways.

Residents reported feeling equally secure on the streets and by their front doors during the day. By contrast, at night they felt safer by their doors. This suggests an important transitional safety zone provided by proximity to their doors, and by the presence of porches.

The other objective, that of fostering a rich street life, was less successfully realized. The architects had spoken of the stairs and yards as places for people to congregate. However, mapping of resident use patterns revealed that only 13 percent of the front yards showed any signs of use such as plantings, the presence of furniture, storage of toys, or visible wear. Moreover, in the course of six site visits—which included two evening visits and one weekend visit of at least two hours—only once did the author observe anyone using a front yard.

Similarly, residents did not use the porches as much as the architects had hoped. Except for brief stops when entering or exiting apartments, in fact, the porches were seldom used at all. Teenagers would occasionally "hang out" on them while watching the street scene below, but the porches are too narrow for anything other than such short-term use. There is no room for chairs or other personal items, and the stairway is too narrow to sit on and allow others to pass at the same time.

Another way narrow porch width works against the designers' intentions is by making it difficult to personalize unit entries. Whereas nearly half of all ground-floor households had doormats or other personal items outside their doors (typically in the gated vestibule), less than one-tenth of second- and third-floor households had personalized their entries in any way. Such personalization is often considered a positive expression of a sense of ownership that is critical to creating defensible space.

GUIDELINE 4: PARKING IN SMALL LOTS

The architects argued that "large parking lots seem like no-man's lands and are unpleasant and feel unsafe to park in or walk through." They also argued that "lots will feel and be safer if they are small and visible from the street so that the entire area can be seen by passing cars and police"(CDC/ED2I 1986). Although a traffic study showed that less than 5 percent of the original tower residents owned cars, the city required that parking be provided for 40 percent of the apartments. Even at an average of five residents per apartment, the city requirement was nearly double the need.

Originally, the architects suggested that lots be limited to no more than seven cars. In the final design, the lots averaged fourteen spaces (see figure 6.4). Prior to occupancy, the architects expressed concern that the lots were too large and would detract from resident perceptions of security.

However, results of the resident survey may suggest the opposite (figure 6.5). Residents who lived around the parking lots reported somewhat greater feelings of security near their front doors than their neighbors who faced the street. If parking lots actually contributed to residents' feelings of security, an explanation may be that the lots served as a buffer zone from the street; the street was often described in resident comments in a negative light.

In addition to contributing to higher perceptions of security, the parking areas provided important social and recreational amenities, giving residents a place for automotive maintenance, ball playing, bicycling, and casual socializing.

GUIDELINE 5: SECURE COMMON OUTDOOR SPACES

The architects argued that "tenants do not want outside teenagers, children, or others using their shared outdoor areas," and that "the common spaces should be made completely private for the exclusive use of the tenants" (CDC/ED2I 1986). As a result, the most dramatic feature of the site design is the complete control of access to the common outdoor areas in the courtyard at the center of each block (figure 6.4). The buildings form a nearly continuous site perimeter that encloses common outdoor areas and rear private yards. The only gaps in this perimeter are small spaces used for garbage collection that have nine-foot-high double gates, with the outside gate openable only by the garbage service. With this arrangement, there is essentially no access to the common outdoor areas except via the apartments.

It was observed that these common spaces were heavily used by preteens who spent

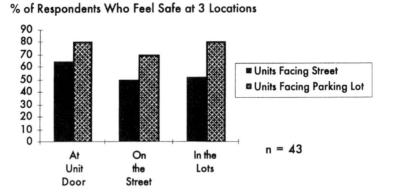

FIGURE 6.5
Perceptions of safety at night by unit location

most of their outdoor play time in the shared central courtyard. Resident comments suggest that the architects' guideline statement was appropriate. One resident said, "It's okay for my kids to play in the back, because it's safe from kids who come over from other places to fight them." Another said, "I don't let my kids play on the sidewalks because the back is better."

GUIDELINE 6: DIFFERENT RECREATION AREAS FOR DIFFERENT AGE GROUPS

The architects argued that different age groups tend to congregate with their peers and need defined "turf" to do so. "Preschool children," they suggested, "need to play in areas within view of their units, teenagers need a place to hang out and a place to play basketball, [elementary] school-aged children need separate play areas, and adults and the elderly need sitting spaces perhaps near some gardens or near the community center" (CDC/ED2I 1986).

More than a dozen different recreation areas were provided in the final design. Prefabricated, painted-metal climbing-swing structures are located in the central areas of each block, along with an adjacent lawn. Other recreation areas contain a half-court basketball area, a patio next to the community room in the community building, numerous benches, sitting walls, and other sitting areas (see figure 6.4).

Observers confirmed that the play areas were heavily used, but not necessarily by the expected age groups. Indeed, the children rarely confined their play to the formal play structure and sand area, but extended it throughout the site, including the ramps for handicap access, rails, stairs, benches, and planted areas. The ramps were perfect for rolling balls, tricycling, and skateboarding. The metal stair rails and guard rails provided an environment for mazes, chases, and other games. The rear fire stair/porches were also used by children for more private outdoor play.

Interviews with the architects and staff at the SFHA revealed concern about conflicts between teens and younger children and a subsequent desire to limit teen time spent in the shared play areas. During site observations, no teens above the age of 14 were seen in the central courtyard areas; rather, they were seen only on occasion on the street side of the development. This was not surprising given that the design designated no teen recreation areas, with the exception of the half-length basketball court. Teenagers' needs in public housing, and their effect on play areas shared by younger children, require further study to determine whether other designs could have more adequately served them.

GUIDELINE 7: TOT LOTS SHOULD BE VISIBLE FROM THE UNITS

This guideline was one of the simplest to achieve and most successful. The architects argued that young children would get to play outside more, and in the company of other children, if they could do so in a secure place where a parent or guardian could monitor them from within the building. To this end, all units were designed so that the kitchens faced the rear; 170 of the 203 units have a direct view of a tot lot (see figure 6.4).

On each site visit, observers saw groups of young children playing on one or more of the play structures. During the day, young children were the primary users, and surprisingly, only about half played under the direct supervision of a parent or guardian. On two of six occasions, children between the ages of three and six were observed playing in a tot lot while actively supervised by a parent in an upper-story unit. This allowed the adult to do other things simultaneously, such as cooking, chores, or talking on the phone. This pattern seemed successful for several reasons: parents perceived the play areas as safe, adults could directly supervise while engaged in other activities, and there were sufficient play possibilities within the space to keep young children busy.

GUIDELINE 8: NONSTIGMATIZING PROJECT IMAGE

Evaluating this guideline produced some of the most interesting findings. The architects argued that "one of the worst aspects of public housing is that it looks like public housing, and that tenants feel stigmatized." They recommended that public housing projects should resemble other housing in surrounding neighborhoods.

The neighborhood around Robert Pitts Plaza is architecturally diverse. The architects chose nearby Victorian row houses as the image they wanted to reflect and

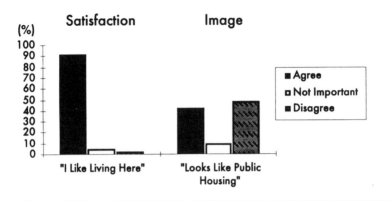

FIGURE 6.6
Resident opinions on project satisfaction and image at Robert Pitts Plaza

designed the project to incorporate major features of such houses, including exterior stairs and porches, projecting bays in the living rooms, and vertical rectangular windows. This image was further enhanced by the use of wood siding, an articulated frieze and cornice, and metal picket fences. These elements give a simplified and updated quasi-Victorian feel. The buildings are handsome. But the question remains: Does this design eliminate the stigma of public housing?

The findings revealed that, even though residents were overwhelmingly satisfied with living at the development, they were split in their response to the statement: "Robert Pitts Plaza looks like public housing" (figure 6.6). Most of those who disagreed with this statement (i.e., those that thought the project did not resemble public housing), had previously lived in public housing. One woman said, "It looks like condos." Another said, "It looks different, like paradise to people from Chicago or down South; it's beautiful." Conversely, most of those who agreed with the statement were new to public housing. Comments from such first-time residents show that the stigma of public housing remains for many. One said, "It looks like public housing because of the people who live here, but it doesn't look like the projects." A neighbor had a similar and quite succinct view: "A rose is a rose. It's still public housing."

These comments show that the characteristics of the resident population were important predictors of people's image of the development. From this, it may be concluded that in relation to other public housing, Robert Pitts looked better. But in comparison to market housing, the image of public housing remained. This, in turn, raises the question of whether the essence of a building's image is contained in its appearance or in its use. Further research would be helpful to establish the ability of design to overcome a negative image presented by a socially stigmatized use.

Conclusions

This chapter was greatly facilitated by the architects' careful documentation of their design process, which allows us to consider the reasoning behind their decisions and examine their decisions in the light of future applications. The findings show that the design of secure private and common spaces was successful in creating safe areas for a variety of play activities. The design of the street faces, while objectively sound, was less successful. Porches and first-floor entrances were properly oriented but too small to support activities that encouraged street life. Contrary to the architects' assumptions, the parking lots contributed to the social, recreational, and security needs of the development.

The high level of satisfaction with Robert Pitts Plaza expressed by residents, designers, and administrators supports the conclusion that the project is successful at many levels. The design guidelines reveal a realistic concern about security. The history of crime and violence in the original towers, and in other public housing developments, clearly played a significant role in shaping the new construction. But instead of creating defensible space through the design of a fortress, the design team restricted nonresident access in a simple and nonintimidating way through building placement. Instead of abandoning shared amenities, the design team promoted the active use of public and semipublic spaces by placing shared recreational areas and unit entries under the informal surveillance of residents. The design team further worked to create a humane and richly satisfying environment through the promotion of a sense of ownership by residents.

This study also found that there is a considerable question about what role architectural style or building form can play in influencing negative perceptions based on type of use (i.e., the public housing stigma). These findings may be a caution to architects, housing authorities, and policymakers to avoid the deterministic thinking that the stigma of public housing can be removed by making a development appear like its noninstitutional neighbors. Making handsome buildings that fit their neighborhoods, while worthwhile goals in their own right, may not be enough to change the perceptions of some residents.

Within the context of redevelopment of original public housing sites at near-original densities, Robert Pitts Plaza offers many valuable lessons in site and building design, and demonstrates that new construction can be cheaper and more effective than modernization. But in a larger context, this study begins to show the limitations of design in overcoming such larger community concerns as the concentration of the poor in a single development. Some public housing developments are plagued by other community-scale problems as well, such as physical isolation and a lack of nearby transportation and commercial services. If public housing continues to be examined only at the level of the unit, the building, or the development, it may continue to fail. Social design guidelines should be extended to include community planning and design. Only then can we be confident that our future visions of safe, humane, and nonstigmatizing public housing will be realized.

Acknowledgments

The author wishes to thank Clare Cooper Marcus for her guidance in the design and execution of this study.

Notes

1. A walk-up is an apartment building that has stacked single-level units, each of which is accessed by a stair, and has no elevator.

2. The term "severely distressed" was used later by the National Commission on Severely Distressed Public Housing. Robert Pitts Plaza was used as a case study in that report, which looked at management, operational, and resident service components, and to some extent design. See National Commission on Severely Distressed Public Housing, *Case Study and Site Examination Reports* (Washington, DC: U.S. Government Printing Office, 1992).

3. Throughout this chapter, residential density is measured by the number of bedrooms or bedrooms/acre. This measure, as opposed to units/acre, more closely reflects the number of people living at the development.

4. Pattern names in this chapter have been modified from the original to make for clearer reading.

References

Alexander, C., et al. 1977. *A Pattern Language: Towns, Buildings, Construction.* New York: Oxford University Press.
Community Design Collaborative and ED2 International (CDC/ED2I). 1986. Programming Report: Yerba Buena Plaza West. Unpublished report submitted to the San Francisco Housing Authority, Resident Council, and U.S. Department of Housing and Urban Development by the architects.

PART IV

Comprehensive Approaches to Public Housing Revitalization

GAYLE EPP

7 Emerging Strategies for Revitalizing Public Housing Communities

Introduction

Recurring themes in public housing revitalization under the Urban Revitalization Demonstration (URD) program of the U.S. Department of Housing and Urban Development (HUD) include integrating the public housing development into the surrounding neighborhood, income mixing, promoting family self-sufficiency through comprehensive support services, and leveraging federal funds to stimulate neighborhood redevelopment. The unique flexibility of the URD program, along with the increasing deregulation of the public housing program overall, requires public housing authorities (PHAs) to develop their own local programs based on identified needs and opportunities. There is no industry standard to guide income-mixing policies, so PHAs are developing their own development-specific strategies based on resident demographics, local housing market forces, site location issues, and financial feasibility. Little definitive research exists to indicate which approaches, and in which combination, will ensure the long-term sustainability of these revitalized communities. This chapter reviews what little research there is, examines emerging practitioner experience through two case studies, and argues for a continued need to evaluate the URD efforts so that future housing policies are more informed.

Reprinted from *Housing Policy Debate* 7, 3 (Washington, D.C.: Fannie Mae Foundation, 1996). This copyrighted material is used with the permission of the Fannie Mae Foundation.

121

Recent Public Housing History

The 1.3 million units of public housing, which account for about 5 percent of rental units in the United States, are an important source of affordable low-income housing. These public housing units, whose estimated real estate value has been reported at $90 billion, take on greater importance in large urban areas, where they represent an even higher percentage of the affordable housing stock.[1] The severe distress in many of the large, urban public housing developments, graphically illustrated in numerous journalistic accounts, has become the vivid symbol of our public housing program. Even though most units are reportedly in good physical condition (Abt Associates 1988), the commonly held image of public housing is one of deteriorated buildings and asphalt-paved sites devoid of function and use, occupied by single-female-headed households on welfare and riddled with gangs, drugs, and criminal activity. Most large urban areas in America have one or more developments that reinforce this image of a public housing program in distress.[2]

While the awareness of serious distress in public housing may be relatively recent for the public at large, those in the housing industry have acknowledged simmering problems for almost two decades. In the late 1970s, Meehan (1979) published a detailed critique of the federal public housing program. Using St. Louis as a case study, Meehan essentially argued that ambiguous policies and uncertain target populations made it difficult to evaluate the public housing program, to learn from identified mistakes, and to improve the program accordingly.

Over the decades, public housing has been targeted at various times to serve different populations in need of affordable housing, including the temporarily unemployed, the working poor, worst-case households on welfare, the homeless, and the disabled (Meehan 1979; Spence 1993; Welfeld 1994). Such tinkering has not led to any clear vision or purpose for the public housing program. Rather, these interventions have made it difficult to evaluate any significant outcomes associated with different policy directives.

At the same time Meehan was analyzing the St. Louis disaster of Pruitt-Igoe within the context of federal housing policies, HUD funded a study of problems affecting public housing projects (Jones, Kaminsky, and Roanhouse 1979). The study focused on the "troubled" portion of the inventory—projects with a high incidence of serious problems or judged by a "public housing specialist" to be in "bad" or "very bad" condition. It estimated that 7 percent of public housing developments, which accounted for 15 percent of the units, were troubled along four problem dimensions: social, physical, financial, and managerial. The social problems identified as the most important "involve the various social needs of a tenant population composed predominantly of very low income, single parent households with public welfare as a primary income source" (Jones, Kaminsky, and Roanhouse 1979, 9). At the same time, Newman (1980) raised similar concerns about the concentration of female-headed welfare families in public housing developments in New York. Clearly, red flags were raised early on, prompting concern about occupancy policies that concentrated the neediest families in public housing.

In the mid-1980s, with minimal federal investment in expanding the nation's public housing stock,[3] national efforts focused more on preserving the existing public housing inventory. A HUD-funded study (Abt Associates 1988) indicated that the vast majority of the public housing stock was in good condition, requiring only minor modernization. Given the size of the stock, however, the overall estimate for addressing the modernization needs of all developments was $22 billion. By 1992, ICF (1992) estimated that this need had increased to $29 billion. With annual funding of modernization improvements under the Comprehensive Improvement Assistance Program (CIAP) and the Comprehensive Grant Program (CGP) running between $2 billion and $3 billion, it would take more than a decade to fund 1992 modernization needs, without even addressing the needs that would be accruing after 1992 as the buildings continued to age. Moreover, these estimates were only for physical improvements, and no funding was included for resident programs and services or management enhancements, which drew funding under separate targeted program initiatives.

According to the Abt Associates study (1988), although the bulk of the public housing stock was in good condition, a small percentage (5 to 8 percent) was in need of substantial renovation—and redesign—because of physical deterioration. While HUD and housing advocates debated the study's methods and the amount of money needed to address the problem, the deteriorated developments—and the low-income families living in them—became increasingly distressed. The same problems plaguing America's cities in general were present, and often more severe, at many public housing sites in aging urban centers.

National Commission on Severely Distressed Public Housing

In 1989, Congress established the National Commission on Severely Distressed Public Housing (NCSDPH) to explore the factors contributing to distress, to identify strategies for remediation, and to develop a national action plan to eliminate distressed conditions nationwide. This was the first comprehensive public housing study undertaken in more than a decade. NCSDPH looked not only at the physical and social conditions of public housing but also at the regulatory obstacles that have become increasingly burdensome in recent years. Through public hearings, site visits, case studies, and reviews of studies and evaluations, a picture emerged of the characteristics of severely distressed developments: physical deterioration and uninhabitable living conditions, increasing levels of poverty, inadequate and fragmented services reaching only a portion of the residents, institutional abandonment, and locations in neighborhoods often as blighted as the developments themselves (NCSDPH 1992a). It became clear that existing programs, funding sources, and strategies were inadequate to address the systemic failure evidenced in these dysfunctional urban environments.

The NCSDPH's *Final Report* emphasized throughout the multidimensional nature of "distressed conditions," including physical, social, and economic indicators. Charged with developing a definition and a rating system for PHAs to use to evaluate their developments, the commission identified four primary indicators: families living in distress, rates of serious crimes in the development or the surrounding neighborhood, barriers to managing the environment, and physical deterioration of buildings (NCSDPH 1992a). Lack of data at the PHA level for several of these indicators, and the lack of comparability of data between PHAs, made the measurement of "severe distress" problematic. Two key indicators, however, deserve further elaboration: families living in distress and physical deterioration of buildings.

FAMILIES LIVING IN DISTRESS

The NCSDPH's research and analysis clearly highlighted that the problems identified more than 10 years before, including the increasing numbers of families headed by single females on welfare (Jones, Kaminsky, and Roanhouse 1979; Newman 1980), had now reached new levels of severity:

> Public housing was not initially designed to house the poorest of the poor, and the rules governing the selection of public housing residents have changed over the years, with the households residing in public housing changing most dramatically since the early 1980's. There has been an especially marked increase in public housing households that have incomes below 10 percent of local median, a key indicator of extreme economic disadvantage. In 1981, this group constituted only about 2.5 percent of the total public housing population, but by 1991, this figure had increased to almost 20 percent. (NCSDPH 1992a, 48; see also Vale 1992)

There are other indicators of increasing poverty in public housing: More than 80 percent of family (nonelderly) households live below the poverty threshold, most households have incomes below 20 percent of the local median, and the overwhelming majority of households with dependent children are headed by single women (Lane 1995).

Many of the demographic changes are a direct result of federal tenant selection policies that give priority to those who often have the greatest need—homeless persons, households paying more than 50 percent of their income for housing, and those displaced or living in substandard housing.[4] Such large concentrations of persons in need, with very little access to services and supports, create islands of poverty and despair in many large cities. Most surprising is the extent to which these communities of need have been "abandoned by the very institutions that exist to serve the overwhelming needs of low-income families" (NCSDPH 1992a, 48). Institutional abandonment of such basic services as police and fire protection, health care, education and training, employment, and youth programs is a common thread running through severely distressed communities—whether they are public housing developments or the deteriorated neighborhoods where public housing too often is found.

PHYSICAL DETERIORATION OF BUILDINGS

In addition to the shifts in occupancy characteristics, there are similarities in the physical condition of distressed public housing developments. Historically, their modernization needs have been underfunded. At the federal level, "triage" often results in targeting scarce modernization dollars to developments with only minor needs. According to ICF (1992) figures, between 1985 and 1991 severely distressed developments with high modernization needs[5] accounted for almost 20 percent of the national needs but received only 7.6 percent of the total modernization funding. At the same time, the developments with minimal needs, which also represented 20 percent of the total stock, received almost 40 percent of the modernization funding. While it can be argued that this triage approach maintains the most successful developments in good condition, the neglect of the more distressed developments leads to rapid deterioration, complete systems failures, and uninhabitable conditions at many large urban developments (ICF 1992). Escalating vacancy rates exacerbated by these deteriorated conditions, lack of funding for repairs and replacement, and refusal of applicants to move into such conditions regardless of their current housing status were typical in city after city visited by the NCSDPH (1992b).

Poor physical condition alone cannot account for the level of dysfunction encountered during visits to many sites around the country; inappropriate design has also contributed. Originally designed 40 to 50 years ago as housing for families temporarily residing in public housing, many developments do not meet the needs of today's households.[6] To modernize developments without remedying the original poor design of units, buildings, and sites may be shortsighted, given the current movement toward tenant-based assistance. Under tenant-based assistance, where the resident rather than the public housing development receives the subsidy, residents are no longer captives of their environment but can seek alternative housing in the general market. In such a system, public housing developments must be market-competitive to attract subsidies; meeting contemporary design standards is therefore an economic necessity.

The NCSDPH found that most severely distressed public housing developments exhibited similar, and numerous, design deficiencies, including poor site location, excessive scale or density, poor site design, inadequate building and unit design, difficulties associated with the use of high-rises for families with children,[7] use of inappropriate materials and inadequate construction standards, and lack of facilities for resident services and programs (Epp and Lane 1992). Poor original site and building design that cannot easily be remedied through renovation argues for demolition and new construction, in many instances, as the only means for ensuring the "marketability" of public housing.

In addition to identifying the many factors that contribute to severely distressed public housing conditions, the NCSDPH collected information on strategies for remedying the various causes of distress. Case studies (NCSDPH 1992b) were prepared of three redevelopment efforts—in Boston, Albany, and San Francisco—to illustrate the types of interventions PHAs used to turn around troubled public housing. These interventions include programs and methods for resident involvement, provision of community facilities, coordinated service delivery programs, and alternative forms of management. Many of these components of success are difficult to measure and rather subjective (see Vale 1996).

While the NCSDPH's *Final Report* has been well received, particularly the research and analysis that document the increasing levels of social and physical distress in public housing communities, it has several shortcomings. As Vale (1993) has carefully argued, the commission's identification of a defined set of severely distressed units—estimated at 86,000, or roughly 6 percent of the total inventory—belies the true nature of the problem, which is symptomatic of the entire public housing program and not confined to selected developments. Focusing only on worst-case developments draws attention and resources away from systemwide reforms. Rebuttals by Gentry (1993) and Lines (1993) refute Vale's claim, indicating that the special nature of severely distressed properties calls for unique, project-specific, nontraditional approaches that are best achieved through special demonstration programs (such as the URD program described below). Vale also raises justified concerns about the definition of "severe distress," which includes most of the public housing stock, and he argues for more reliable databases with improved measures of social and economic factors to complement existing data on physical needs.

Urban Revitalization Demonstration Program

In the fall of 1992, partly in response to the work of the NCSDPH and the concerted lobbying efforts of numerous public housing professionals and advocates, Congress created the URD program. Also known as HOPE VI, this program provides a comprehensive approach to revitalizing distressed urban communities (HUD 1993). The overarching goals of the URD program are (1) to transform public housing communities from islands of despair and poverty into a vital and integral part of larger neighborhoods and (2) to create an environment that encourages and supports individual and family movement toward self-sufficiency. Many of the NCSDPH's recommendations have been incorporated into this demonstration program.

As outlined in the notice of funding availability (HUD 1993), 40 of the largest housing authorities were eligible to apply for the special program; all but 1 applied. In the first two years of the URD program (fiscal 1993 and 1994), Congress authorized more than $1.2 billion, which was allocated to 32 PHAs across the country.[8] In 1995, another $500 million was authorized for both planning and implementation efforts. Each housing authority could apply for implementation grants of up to $50 million for no more than 500 units. The URD program guidelines call for at least 80 percent of the funds to be used for capital costs for physical improvements, certificates for replacement housing, management improvements for the reconstructed development, and planning and technical assistance. The remaining 20 percent can be used for community service programs, supportive services, job training, economic development costs, and services related to education and employment. In 1996, approximately $480 million was appropriated in the URD program, with an emphasis on demolition, replacement housing that lessens the concentrations of very low income families, and Section 8 tenant-based assistance. All public housing authorities are eligible to apply for 1996 funding (HUD 1996).

The level of funding and its flexibility in use for physical, social, and operational change provide a demonstration program that encourages innovation and new solutions and expands capacity well beyond the scope of earlier funding programs. Once limited only to renovation of existing structures, housing authorities now have the flexibility to renovate, selectively demolish and build new additions, or completely demolish a development and construct new housing on the original site or elsewhere, depending on local political and market conditions, and to mix market-rate with publicly supported units.

The flexibility of the URD program and the emphasis on local planning generate substantial challenges for housing authorities. Too often constrained by the oppressive regulatory environment of the 1980s, many PHAs struggle to be expansive in their vision and inclusive in their planning process. Most invest their own time and money in developing a thorough and comprehensive planning effort that brings new participants and partners to the decision-making table.[9]

Efforts at comprehensive planning for the revitalization of severely distressed public housing parallel similar efforts across the country in neighborhood renewal initiated by the community-based development sector. These initiatives, exemplified by the Enterprise Foundation's Community Building Partnership effort in Baltimore and New York's South Bronx Comprehensive Revitalization Project, are described by Walker (1993, 405):

> Two features, in particular, distinguish these initiatives from past efforts: (1) they purport to shape community strategies that cross-cut human service, health, economic development, housing, and community-building policy domains, and (2) they strongly emphasize community participation in policy formulation and program implementation.

The recent empowerment zone program is yet another example of the growing trend toward local strategic planning and community involvement in policy formulation and program implementation.

URD revitalization efforts, given the flexibility of the program, can respond to community constraints and opportunities and build on available local resources and talent. Some URD sites have market potential and lend themselves to new mixed-income communities with private-sector participation. Other developments, in more distressed neighborhoods, focus on density reduction and creating partnerships with community development corporations (CDCs) to develop replacement housing (typically focusing on homeownership) in the surrounding neighborhood.

While each URD plan is unique, URD recipients share several goals: comprehensive and coordinated support services; strong, decentralized management, regardless of the management entity (authority, private management firm, or resident management corporation); and resident participation in planning and implementation. More recently, URD efforts increasingly emphasize physically and economically integrating the public housing development into the surrounding neighborhood and leveraging URD funds to stimulate neighborhood reinvestment and produce additional housing units. More and more PHAs are considering the development of public housing communities that serve the needs of a broad range of income groups.

Development of Mixed-Income Communities

There is growing acceptance of the politically charged policy directive to move public housing away from "housing of last resort" and toward communities that reflect a broader range of incomes. While some still argue that limited housing resources should be targeted to worst-case needs (Nelson and Khadduri 1992), increasing numbers of housing professionals are calling for increased economic diversity in public housing communities (Cavanaugh 1992; Spence 1993). In his review of the NCSDPH's *Final Report*, Spence (1993), former receiver of the Boston Housing Authority and receiver of the city of Chelsea, Massachusetts, argues that while the commission accurately assessed that the high concentrations of extremely poor female-headed households are a key factor in the distressed conditions in public housing, it failed to aggressively call for changes in public housing occupancy policies:

> Instead, to avoid confronting directly the tenant selection policies that define a disastrous social role for public housing, the commission holds to a naive optimism about the possibilities of altering the condition of community in distressed developments through social service and economic development initiatives. . . .
>
> If severely distressed developments represent aggregations of severely distressed and isolated people, then two courses are open to us: We might alter our admissions policies to reduce the aggregations of severe distress and thereby relieve isolation, or we might focus interventions on these aggregations of human distress, in the hope of relieving it.
>
> The commission chose the latter approach, however wanting in credibility, because the former is so politically daunting. (pp. 362–63)

The concentration of households headed by unemployed single women in public housing, which results from occupancy policies that give preference to worst-case families, has a parallel in ghetto neighborhoods studied by Wilson (1987) that have experienced an out-migration of working families. In both environments, the lack of employed role models takes a toll on the social fabric of the community:

> Thus, in a neighborhood with a paucity of regularly employed families and with the overwhelming majority of families having spells of long-term joblessness, people experience a social isolation that excludes them from the job network system that permeates other neighborhoods and that is so important in learning about or being recommended for jobs that become available in various parts of the city. And as the prospects for employment diminish, other alternatives such as welfare and the underground economy are not only increasingly relied on, they come to be seen as a way of life. (p. 57)

Such an analysis argues not only for increased access to jobs in these disadvantaged communities, but also for encouraging the integration of working households. The New York City Housing Authority recently announced that it will give preference to working people over welfare recipients in filling vacant units, in an effort to "restore economic and social stability to projects" (Kennedy 1995). To increase the number of working families on the waiting list, the authority will advertise and recruit potential residents at their workplaces (New York City Housing Authority 1995).

Proposed federal housing legislation also acknowledges the advantage of increasing the number of working families throughout public housing, not only in the more distressed developments. The recent proposed housing bill calls for a broader range of household incomes in public housing. Under current rules, public housing built before October 1981 can have up to 25 percent of households earning between 50 and 80 percent of area median family income; public housing constructed after October 1981 has been limited to no more than 5 percent of households in that income range. The current House bill (H.R. 240) calls for at least 35 percent of public housing households to be at or below 30 percent of area median income; the Senate bill (S. 1260) requires at least 40 percent of annual admissions to be families with incomes less than 30 percent of area median, and at least 75 percent to be families earning less than 60 percent of area median. Either proposal would lead to a much broader range of incomes in public housing developments, since the current median income of nonelderly public housing households is 16 percent of area median (Lane 1995). Such income mixing is believed to result in more manageable housing sites, public housing residents who are less isolated from the economic mainstream of the surrounding community, and reduced operating subsidies because of the admission and retention of higher income and rent-paying households.

"Planned" mixed-income housing is not a new concept.[10] Mixed-income developments have been constructed around the country for more than 25 years; as of

1987, state housing finance agencies had developed 25,000 units of mixed-income rental housing under tax-exempt bond programs (Mulroy 1991). There are also several examples of troubled public housing that have been transformed into mixed-income communities.

Two severely distressed public housing sites in Massachusetts—King's Lynne in Lynn and Harbor Point[11] in Boston—have become models for the transformation of abandoned, isolated public housing developments into diverse and multiracial communities that can compete with market-rate developments in attracting residents. While evaluations of early stages of occupancy at both developments indicated that residents were generally pleased with their new communities, the developments are not without the typical problems associated with community living, such as teens hanging out on street corners and noisy neighbors (Pader and Breitbart 1993; Upshur, Epp, and Werby 1981).

King's Lynne and Harbor Point are mixed-income communities that include very low income families and market-rate households, but other models are also available for study, including Lake Parc Place in Chicago. Lake Parc Place is a demonstration program under the Mixed Income New Community Strategy in the 1990 National Affordable Housing Act, with half the units designated for families with incomes below 50 percent of area median and the remaining half designated for families with incomes between 50 and 80 percent of area median, or the working poor (NCSDPH 1992b).

Lane (1995) reports early indicators of success with this demonstration: There have been no major crimes, vandalism, or graffiti since reopening, and 20 percent of the households who started on welfare now have heads with full-time jobs. Current policy development and planning efforts, particularly around the mix of income levels, would benefit from systematic postoccupancy evaluations of these different types of mixed-income communities. The evaluation should focus not only on community issues and resident satisfaction but also on such key operational factors as marketability, turnover rates, maintenance costs, and need for supportive services.

Mixed-income communities are clearly a bold approach to mitigating the overconcentration of very poor families, but one that can be implemented only when the local housing market and site location are appropriate. To encourage housing authorities to consider housing options that promote communities of economic diversity, Kevin Marchman, acting assistant secretary at the HUD Office of Public and Indian Housing, issued a memorandum to all URD grantees in February 1994 that describes "URD Plus: A Tool for Neighborhood Revitalization." Under this scenario, housing authorities are encouraged to use the flexibility in the URD program to leverage URD funds in three ways (Marchman 1994):

1. In conjunction with Community Development Block Grant, HOME, state, and private financing, to produce more housing than could be constructed by using the URD funds only for capital costs of public housing improvements

2. To replace some of the units in the surrounding neighborhood to encourage broader neighborhood revitalization
3. To combine URD funds with other subsidies and loan funds to generate mixed-income developments on the public housing site as well as on other sites

While specific details of how public housing funds can be leveraged have not been finalized, several housing authorities incorporate the concept into their revitalization plans.

Creating a new mixed-income community might be feasible in those cities with strong housing markets and with URD sites in neighborhoods that can attract households with different incomes. Participants in the URD program have pointed out that not all sites have income-mixing potential between 60 and 80 percent of area median and that even fewer sites can attract market-rate families (with incomes greater than 95 percent of area median). Many URD planning efforts include exploring a range of income-mixing options, including income tiering within public housing regulations. As noted earlier, public housing can serve households with up to 80 percent of area median income; however, partly because of federal preferences, most households now living in URD developments fall below 50 percent of area median income.[12] To provide a broader income range within current public housing regulations, some housing authorities are considering "income tiering," in which applicant waiting lists are organized by income tiers and placement in public housing developments is based on maintaining a predetermined mix of income ranges.

In many cities, it will take a concerted effort to attract working families back to public housing, given its perception as the housing of last resort. Market studies that identify the type of households likely to be attracted to a revitalized housing community, the rent levels that can be attained, and the types of unit amenities that must be provided are being undertaken as part of the URD planning effort in many cities. Some URD sites are believed to have full market potential (e.g., Holly Park in Seattle and Techwood in Atlanta), while others may only be able to attract families below 60 percent of area median (e.g., Concord Village in Indianapolis).

Financing sources also play a role in the income-mixing strategy. The use of low-income housing tax credit (LIHTC) funds, which are the proposed leveraging vehicle in many URD Plus efforts, limits occupancy to households below 60 percent of area median family income. Social goals for new public housing communities are very much tied to local market conditions and available financing tools.

The income-mixing approach deals with the concentration of very poor families by increasing economic diversity and by offering several presumed benefits to residents:

1. Employed persons will provide role models for children and the unemployed.
2. Communities will likely be more stable because a family can remain in the

unit even if the head loses a job, becomes employed, or gets a raise (rents could be adjusted).

3. Resident services and programs are more likely to be acknowledged as critical components of successful communities, and therefore their funding is often built into the development's operating budget.

4. Institutions, public agencies, and commercial businesses are more likely to invest in, rather than abandon, a mixed-income neighborhood.

As Gordon Cavanaugh (1992, 75) has aptly concluded, "the only way to serve the poor properly is by hitching their needs to those of a more influential population." These assertions of the benefits of income mixing will need to be studied and evaluated as these new communities unfold over the next decade.

Family Economic Self-sufficiency

In addition to the income-mixing strategy, many URD efforts include the development of a family economic self-sufficiency program to assist very low-income households in becoming less dependent on federal subsidies. Since a housing authority can spend up to 20 percent of its URD grant (which translates into $10 million for a full $50 million grant) for supportive and community services, as well as economic development initiatives (HUD 1993), the level of URD funding currently flowing into self-sufficiency efforts is sizable. It is essential that these moneys be allocated to a comprehensive and coordinated array of programs and services that most effectively help acutely poor families gain economic self-sufficiency.

Recent research on family self-sufficiency programs indicates that there is long-range promise for decreasing economic dependence among acutely poor households, but the short-term results report little measurable success (Shlay 1993; Shlay and Holupka 1992). One of the most studied demonstration programs is the Family Development Center (FDC) in Baltimore (Shlay and Holupka 1992). Opened in the summer of 1987, this demonstration program provides comprehensive and coordinated services to the residents of Lafayette Courts, Baltimore's large public housing development. Every family enrolled in the program is assigned a case manager who determines the needs of each resident and then identifies specific programs for mandatory resident participation.

The progress of the initial families enrolled in the program has been carefully tracked over a multiyear period, and this research resulted in several key findings:

1. The FDC was successful in getting families to participate in the program.
2. Participants reported increased educational aspirations, enhanced self-esteem, and a greater sense of control over their lives.

3. Participants spent more time in other neighborhoods and less time doing nothing.
4. The economic circumstances of families were not altered by participating in the FDC in its early years. In fact, employment rates appeared to decrease slightly because of participation in education and training programs.

The evaluation research indicates that "the FDC is neither a quick fix to either fighting poverty or reducing families' reliance on welfare" (Shlay and Holupka 1992, 531). It may be too optimistic to expect short-term positive results from the self-sufficiency programs developed under the URD efforts; a longer time frame for measuring successful outcomes may be necessary. However, this should not diminish the importance of these programs in a comprehensive community revitalization effort.

Homeownership is often a desired outcome of a self-sufficiency program (along with higher education and business development), but recent studies indicate that it is difficult to achieve for many public housing residents. Rohe (1995) has evaluated Charlotte's Gateway Families Program, which focuses on enhancing labor market skills so that residents can afford to purchase their own homes. Preliminary findings indicate that it was difficult to attract qualified applicants, the dropout rate from the program was high, remedial skills took longer to develop than originally anticipated, and residents preferred to be clustered in homes near one another. Rohe concluded that homeownership should not be a primary goal for most public housing residents and that providing a variety of remedial job training activities is essential.

Homeownership, family self-sufficiency programs, and income mixing are only some of the components of many of the URD revitalization efforts. To illustrate the variety of tools that housing authorities are employing and the difficulties they face revitalizing and integrating public housing properties and their surrounding neighborhoods, a summary of two different URD plans in Seattle and Indianapolis follows.

Holly Park: A New Mixed-income Community

Holly Park in Seattle provides an interesting case study of the magnitude of change and innovation that is possible through HUD's URD program (Seattle Housing Authority 1994). Holly Park is a 900-unit public housing development on a 110-acre site in southeast Seattle. Unlike many of the cities on the East Coast, Seattle is growing; 60,000 new households are expected by 2000. The city has embarked on an extensive planning effort that proposes to manage this growth through the development of a series of "urban villages," each having a commercial core, transportation loop, and residential development of different densities and scales.

The Seattle Housing Authority worked closely with the city to have the Holly Park site designated as part of a new "residential urban village." The housing authority also established a planning process with steering and advisory committees consisting of representatives from various city agencies, the private development community, local service providers, the state, and the residents to develop a shared vision and mission for transforming the distressed development. Resident involvement has been particularly challenging at Holly Park because all written and oral communication is translated into at least six languages[13] to deal with the ethnic diversity of the residents.

Although the 110-acre Holly Park site is not spatially dense (nine units per acre), the concentration of 900 very low income families is considered by the housing authority and larger Seattle community to be problematic. As part of an urban village, the site can support the proposed higher residential densities called for in the city's 20-year plan. As a result, the revitalization plan for Holly Park calls for demolishing the 900 units of public housing and constructing a 1,200-unit mixed-income development on the cleared site. As proposed, the plan includes 400 units of public housing, 400 units of housing for moderate-income families (the working poor), and 400 units of market-rate housing.[14] Although the development is primarily planned as a rental community, up to 20 percent of the units will be targeted for homeownership to help stabilize the community and provide opportunities for much-needed affordable housing in southeast Seattle. The homeownership component will include affordable units for households earning between 50 and 95 percent of area median.

The new mixed-income community will be supported by substantial neighborhood investments, including a major expansion of the existing community center and ball fields, the construction of a satellite public library, and the development of a new neighborhood resource center to serve the needs of all residents throughout southeast Seattle. The implementation of a new transportation link system, proposed as part of the urban village strategy, will also be pursued.

A family self-sufficiency program is also planned for Holly Park, in conjunction with a ceiling rent policy to encourage working families to remain in the revitalized community. The URD budget includes funding of a full-time program coordinator, who will be responsible for the daily administration and oversight of a resource fund (also funded through URD) to ensure the continuation of the program. The Seattle Housing Authority has been administering a family self-sufficiency program, as mandated by HUD for new Section 8 certificates, and the lack of funding for program administration and service coordination has been problematic (Kustina 1994). This problem can be addressed with URD funds.

In addition to the 1,200 on-site units, 500 units of off-site replacement housing are planned, in smaller developments scattered throughout other neighborhoods in Seattle. This will provide an opportunity for the housing authority to form partnerships with experienced local nonprofit groups to develop and manage housing for low-income and very low-income persons. The URD funds are a possible source of "gap" financing for affordable housing developed by these nonprofits; another financing source being explored is the transfer of public housing operating subsidies to off-site replacement units.

The estimated cost of the new 1,200-unit mixed-income community substantially exceeds the $47 million URD implementation grant awarded the authority. Additional funding will be provided by state and local public and private entities; possible sources include the use of tax-exempt bonds, LIHTC funds, and a city contribution for new infrastructure. Given the complexity of the proposed financing models, the housing authority seeks the involvement of consultants experienced in financial analysis, program management, and relocation. The authority also wants to involve the private sector in developing and managing the new community. There will be built-in assurances, through a land lease and operating agreement, that the long-range needs of low-income and very low-income families will be met, regardless of the ownership and management structure. In addition, residents will be involved in key decisions, through the establishment of a governing board, as well as in the day-to-day operations of the new community. Holly Park represents a new approach to providing housing options for low-income families—in economically integrated and supportive environments that promote self-sufficiency and community living.

Indianapolis: Revitalization of the Near Westside

The Indianapolis Public Housing Agency (IPHA) is currently implementing one of its URD revitalization plans for two public housing communities in the Near Westside neighborhood (Tise, Hurwitz & Diamond, and Clyde E. Woods & Associates 1995). Unlike the program in Seattle, where the revitalization plan focuses primarily on the site, the IPHA URD plan involves a neighborhoodwide revitalization strategy that encompasses 200 public housing units at Concord Village and 110 at Eaglecreek Village. IPHA, in cooperation with the city and the neighborhood, has used the URD funds to contract with a program manager to oversee the entire revitalization effort in the larger community.

Unlike Seattle, Indianapolis is not experiencing a noticeable increase in population and has an abundant stock of affordable housing. Since much of the housing is in substandard condition, the city does not have a sound source of safe and sanitary housing for very low-income families. The proposed plan, which has the support of residents and the neighborhood, calls for demolishing a total of 310 units on both sites, building 170 units on these sites at a lower density, and blending a new street system into the existing neighborhood. The new units, in contrast to the existing clustered row houses, will be side-by-side duplex units, similar in scale and design to the surrounding neighborhood's bungalows. The primary goal of this plan's physical component is to weave the public housing site back into the neighborhood's fabric to make it indistinguishable from the larger community.

IPHA and the planning consultants agreed early on that this neighborhood likely could not attract market-level rents to cover debt service and operating costs. A financial consultant had preliminary indications that rental units in the neighborhood would appeal to households with incomes no greater than 50 to 60 percent of area median family income.[15] As a result, income tiering will occur within the current regulatory framework for income mixing below 80 percent of area median. Ninety percent of current residents and waiting list applicants have incomes below 30 percent of area median, so attracting even the working poor to these new sites will require a substantial outreach and marketing effort.

The revitalization plan also calls for constructing 70 units for homeownership in the immediate neighborhood. Retaining all these replacement units in the Near Westside is viewed as critical to reinforcing the city's plans for redevelopment of this area. A neighborhood inventory of potential sites for replacement housing identified more than 200 vacant lots or dilapidated structures near the public housing sites. These abandoned sites have become havens for drug dealers and crack users. The lots' redevelopment is viewed as key to reducing the high crime rates in the Near Westside.

The scattered-site replacement units will be set aside for households who participate in a family self-sufficiency program that requires them to enter into a formal contract, with specified goals and participation requirements, leading toward self-sufficiency and, in many cases, homeownership. It is projected that through job training programs, access to employment opportunities, and a ceiling rent program, many public housing families will become homeowners. Fifteen- and 5-year lease-purchase programs are being explored, with the knowledge that homeownership is a long-term goal rather than an immediate one. The off-site replacement units will be constructed on vacant lots that the city conveys to IPHA in small packages to encourage the involvement of small, local contractors. Eighteen of the 70 off-site units will be developed by IPHA in partnership with the local CDC (Westside CDC), with support from the Indianapolis Neighborhood Housing Partnership. Westside CDC recently received a tax credit allocation for the project.

One of the more interesting initiatives in the Indianapolis plan involves supportive services and the establishment of an endowment fund. Many organizations in the Near Westside are providing services now; there is a multiservice center within several blocks of the public housing sites. The current plan calls for the construction of a neighborhood youth center to meet the needs of all children in the larger community. Lack of transportation has been identified as a key impediment to accessing services in the area, and a resident-operated shuttle van service is in the planning stages. To ensure that the service needs of the residents are provided for beyond the term of the five-year implementation grant, IPHA and the residents are seeking to establish a "permanent" community endowment fund with some of the URD funds for supportive services. Funds would be professionally invested and managed in conjunction with an established foundation or philanthropic entity. A limited amount of funding would then be available each year for supportive service priority areas as determined by a board composed of residents, IPHA, and neighborhood representatives. This approach provides for an ongoing source of service funding and greater flexibility in the annual targeting of service needs. It also ensures that public housing residents will have some leverage in determining what services are provided in the neighborhood.

Conclusion

The problems facing severely distressed public housing communities and the transformation required to address the isolation of very low-income families will require significant investment of time, energy, commitment, and money. There are no quick fixes in communities where institutional abandonment and hopelessness have prevailed for years.

While the vast majority of the 1.3 million public housing units are in good condition and remain an important housing resource for low-income households, clearly the most severely distressed developments require remediation of some form. Not all can or should be demolished; not all can or should be revitalized. How do we make these critical decisions? Should a site be abandoned if long-term viability—or marketability—cannot be assured? How can we be sensitive to residents who desire to remain in their communities? When are community ties to distressed neighborhoods stronger than society's goals of economic or racial integration? Are worst-case families on welfare, in need of a comprehensive support network, best served in scattered-site units distant from friends and family who may be their only source of support and assistance?

There are no evaluations, no studies, and no data to definitively answer many of these questions. The research reviewed in this chapter remains far from conclusive. In the meantime, revitalization is proceeding with a multifaceted strategy, combining income mixing, family self-sufficiency programs, homeownership, and other components. While the debate continues over the purpose of public housing and the goal of its revitalization, URD efforts can be designed with a dual purpose: as a stepping-stone on the way to self-sufficiency and as mixed-income communities that promote support and stability. In the end, a combination of these approaches may be the most useful.

Given the current political climate and decreasing financial resources, we cannot afford to waste URD funds by thinking too small, by not encouraging resident self-sufficiency and economic advancement, or by not involving other private and public institutions in the much-needed provision of affordable housing. The success of this unique public housing initiative, which seeks to reintegrate very low-income families into the fabric of our urban communities, must be measured by how much it improves the lives of residents, not just the buildings.

Acknowledgments

The author thanks the anonymous reviewers of this article, as well as Wolfgang Preiser, David Varady, and Francis Russell, editors of *Future Visions of Urban Public Housing: An International Forum*, where an earlier version was first published. The author also acknowledges the contribution of her URD colleagues in the formulation of many of the ideas. Particular appreciation is extended to Jeffrey Lines of TAG Associates and to Stephen Tise and Merrill Diamond of Tise, Hurwitz & Diamond, Inc.

Notes

1. In cities such as Boston, Atlanta, and Cleveland, the public housing share of all rental units is 10 percent or more (Struyk 1980).
2. This list includes such infamous sites as Pruitt-Igoe in St. Louis, Columbia Point in Boston, Robert Taylor Homes and Cabrini Green in Chicago, Desire in New Orleans, and Allen Parkway Village in Houston.
3. Only 11 percent of the public housing stock (less than 200,000 units) was constructed after 1980, and most new development units were replacements for units lost through demolition (National Association of Housing and Redevelopment Officials 1990).
4. HUD introduced these federal preferences in 1980.
5. Those with modernization costs exceeding 60 percent of HUD's total development cost guidelines.
6. As-built units average 20 to 30 percent smaller than current standards for unit size, so storage space is inadequate, kitchens are too small for a dining table to seat all family members, and bedrooms do not accommodate double occupancy (Epp Associates, TAMS Consultants, and Swander Associates 1990).
7. Note that buildings with elevators constitute only 12 percent of the severely distressed public housing stock, as measured by rehabilitation costs in excess of 60 percent of total development costs (Schnare 1991).
8. Initially, 24 housing authorities received only implementation grants, 6 received only planning grants, and 2 received both a planning and an implementation grant for different developments.
9. Of the 32 PHAs that received initial funding based on hastily prepared plans, 26 invested more than $500,000 and six months to revise their plans and to include other parties in the planning effort (HUD 1995).
10. "Mixed-income housing" is used to describe a variety of income-mixing approaches; no industry standard exists. Within public housing, it refers to mixing families with various incomes below 80 percent of median income, which includes both working and nonworking families. State housing finance agencies include market-rate households in their definition of mixed-income communities. When discussed, specific income ranges should be defined.
11. For a detailed discussion of the Harbor Point redevelopment effort and a preliminary assessment of resident satisfaction with mixed-income living, see Pader and Breitbart (1993).
12. At Elm Haven in New Haven, 86 percent of current households have incomes below 50 percent of area median family income. At Jeffries Homes in Detroit, 93 percent of

households have incomes below 50 percent of area median, with the vast majority below 30 percent of area median.

13. Resident surveys indicated that English is the predominant language spoken in slightly less than half the respondent households; the remaining households at Holly Park use a language other than English, including Vietnamese, Cambodian, Laotian, Tigrinya, Oromo, and Somali.

14. A market study was contracted during the planning effort to assess the market demand and to identify specific qualities of a residential community that would enhance its marketability to this income group.

15. Discussions regarding the feasibility of income mixing have included Milan Ozdinac, from HUD's Office of Public Housing Investments; Joni Brooks of Hamilton, Rabinowitz and Alschuler, Inc., development consultants; and Linda Cappello, former planning director of the New York City Housing Authority.

References

Abt Associates. 1988. *Study of the Modernization Needs of the Public and Indian Housing Stock—National, Regional, and Field Office Estimates: Backlog of Modernization Needs.* Washington, DC: U.S. Department of Housing and Urban Development.

Cavanaugh, Gordon. 1992. Comment on Kathryn P. Nelson and Jill Khadduri's "To Whom Should Limited Housing Resources Be Directed?" *Housing Policy Debate* 3(1):67–75.

Epp Associates, TAMS Consultants, Inc., and Swander Associates. 1990. *Redevelopment Handbook: Procedures and Design Guidelines for Redeveloping Public Housing.* Prepared for the Massachusetts Executive Office of Communities and Development. Boston.

Epp, Gayle, and Jonathan Lane. 1992. Capital Improvement Programs and the Physical Condition of Public Housing. In *Working Papers on Identifying and Addressing Severely Distressed Public Housing*, National Commission on Severely Distressed Public Housing, 5–1–5–55. Washington, DC: U.S. Department of Housing and Urban Development.

Gentry, Richard C. 1993. Comment on Lawrence J. Vale's "Beyond the Problem Projects Paradigm: Defining and Revitalizing 'Severely Distressed' Public Housing." *Housing Policy Debate* 4(2):175–82.

ICF, Inc. 1992. The Modernization Needs of Severely Distressed Public Housing. In *Working Papers on Identifying and Addressing Severely Distressed Public Housing*, National Commission on Severely Distressed Public Housing, B–1–B–24. Washington, DC: U.S. Department of Housing and Urban Development.

Jones, Ronald, David Kaminsky, and Michael Roanhouse. 1979. *Problems Affecting Low Rent Public Housing Projects.* Washington, DC: U.S. Department of Housing and Urban Development, Office of Policy Development and Research.

Kennedy, Shawn G. 1995. Working People to Have Priority for City Housing. *New York Times*, February 4.

Kustina, Rick. 1994. Seattle Housing Authority's Experience with the Family Self-Sufficiency Program. In *Future Visions of Urban Public Housing: An International Forum*, ed. Wolfgang F. E. Preiser, David P. Varady, and Francis P. Russell, 244–49. Cincinnati: University of Cincinnati.

Lane, Vincent. 1995. Best Management Practices in U.S. Public Housing. *Housing Policy Debate* 6(4):867–904.

Lines, Jeffrey K. 1993. Comment on Lawrence J. Vale's "Beyond the Problem Projects Paradigm: Defining and Revitalizing 'Severely Distressed' Public Housing." *Housing Policy Debate* 4(2):183–98.

Marchman, Kevin. 1994. Memorandum on URD Plus: A Tool for Neighborhood Revitalization. Distributed to all URD awardees. February 14. U.S. Department of Housing and Urban Development.

Meehan, Eugene J. 1979. *The Quality of Federal Policymaking: Programmed Failure in Public Housing.* Columbia, MO: University of Missouri Press.

Mulroy, Elizabeth A. 1991. Mixed-Income Housing in Action. *Urban Land,* May, pp. 2–7.

National Association of Housing and Redevelopment Officials. 1990. *The Many Faces of Public Housing.* Washington, DC.

National Commission on Severely Distressed Public Housing. 1992a. *The Final Report of the National Commission on Severely Distressed Public Housing.* Washington, DC: U.S. Government Printing Office.

National Commission on Severely Distressed Public Housing. 1992b. *Case Study and Site Examination Reports.* Washington, DC: U.S. Government Printing Office.

Nelson, Kathryn P., and Jill Khadduri. 1992. To Whom Should Limited Housing Resources Be Directed? *Housing Policy Debate* 3(1):1–55.

New York City Housing Authority. 1995. *Revitalization Plan: Beach 41st Street Houses, HOPE VI Urban Revitalization Demonstration Program.* November 15. New York.

Newman, Oscar. 1980. *Community of Interest.* New York: Anchor/Doubleday.

Pader, Ellen J., and Myrna Margulies Breitbart. 1993. Transforming Public Housing: Conflicting Visions for Harbor Point. *Places* 8(4):34–41.

Rohe, William M. 1995. Assisting Residents of Public Housing Achieve Self-Sufficiency: An Evaluation of Charlotte's Gateway Families Program. *Journal of Architectural and Planning Research* 12(3):259–77.

Schnare, Ann B. 1991. The Preservation Needs of Public Housing. *Housing Policy Debate* 2(2):289–318.

Seattle Housing Authority. 1994. *Holly Park Redevelopment: HOPE VI Urban Revitalization Demonstration Plan.* Seattle.

Shlay, Anne B. 1993. Family Self-Sufficiency and Housing. *Housing Policy Debate* 4(3):457–95.

Shlay, Anne B., and C. Scott Holupka. 1992. Steps toward Independence: Evaluating an Integrated Service Program for Public Housing Residents. *Evaluation Review* 5:505–33.

Spence, Lewis H. 1993. Rethinking the Social Role of Public Housing. *Housing Policy Debate* 4(3):355–68.

Struyk, Raymond J. 1980. *A New System for Public Housing.* Washington, DC: The Urban Institute.

Tise, Hurwitz & Diamond, Inc., and Clyde E. Woods & Associates, Inc. 1995. *Concord Village–Eaglecreek Revitalization Plan for the Urban Revitalization Demonstration (URD) Program.* Final plan submitted to the Indianapolis Public Housing Agency. Brookline, MA.

U.S. Department of Housing and Urban Development. 1993. Revised Notice of Funding Availability (NOFA) for the Urban Revitalization Demonstration Program: Revised Procedures to Reduce Burdens on Applicants. *Federal Register,* March 29, 16590–605.

U.S. Department of Housing and Urban Development. 1995. Impact on Progress. Facsimile received from the Office of Distressed and Troubled Housing Recovery by the Housing Research Foundation, dated October 6.

U.S. Department of Housing and Urban Development. 1996. Notice of Funding Availability (NOFA) for Public Housing Demolition, Site Revitalization, and Replacement Housing Grants (HOPE VI). *Federal Register,* July 22.

Upshur, Carole, Gayle Epp, and Elaine Werby. 1981. Social Service Programs Essential for Mixed Income Housing. *Journal of Housing* 38(5):262–69.

Vale, Lawrence J. 1992. Occupancy Issues in Distressed Public Housing: An Outline of Impacts on Design, Management, and Service Delivery. In *Working Papers on Identifying and Addressing Severely Distressed Public Housing,* National Commission on Severely Distressed Public Housing, A-1–A-60. Washington, DC: U.S. Department of Housing and Urban Development.

Vale, Lawrence J. 1993. Beyond the Problem Projects Paradigm: Defining and Revitalizing "Severely Distressed" Public Housing. *Housing Policy Debate* 4(2):147–74.

Vale, Lawrence J. 1996. Public Housing Redevelopment: Seven Kinds of Success. *Housing Policy Debate* 7(3):491–534.

Walker, Christopher. 1993. Nonprofit Housing Development: Status, Trends, and Prospects. *Housing Policy Debate* 4(3):369–414.

Welfeld, Irving. 1994. Public Housing: The Need for a New Framework. In *Future Visions of Urban Public Housing: An International Forum,* ed. Wolfgang F. E. Preiser, David P. Varady, and Francis P. Russell, 118–34. Cincinnati: University of Cincinnati.

Wilson, William Julius. 1987. *The Truly Disadvantaged: The Inner City, the Underclass, and Public Policy.* Chicago: University of Chicago Press.

LAWRENCE J. VALE

8 Public Housing Redevelopment: Seven Kinds of Success

From Devastation to Redevelopment

Most of the research and writing about public housing in the United States has stressed the intractability of its problems (Bauman 1994) yet has frequently focused on the search for a solution that emphasizes the transformative power of a single factor. For some, a key variable is architectural design (Coleman 1985; Cooper 1975; Newman 1972, 1980); for others, it is management reform (Kell 1978, 1979; Kolodny 1979; Sadacca et al. 1974), service provision and family self-sufficiency programs (Shlay 1993), drug prevention (Keyes 1992), resident satisfaction (Francescato et al. 1979), or public policy initiatives such as economic mixing (Spence 1993), resident management (Chandler 1991; Peterman 1993), homeownership programs (Rohe and Stegman 1992), or housing vouchers (Schill 1993).

Clearly, as the needs of public housing residents and public housing authorities have expanded, more and more specialists have been called in for consultation. Their prognosis, almost always dire, is further complicated by disagreements about the best course of treatment. It has long been clear that no single form of intervention is sufficient, and most who struggle to support or reform public housing (whether as residents, managers, designers, or policymakers) are only too well aware that the challenges come in many interlinked categories.

With signs of success in urban public housing so hard to come by, it is not surprising that most who attempt to build or redevelop low-income housing will look for indications of partial victories. These narrow successes are important, but it is also important to remember that success can be measured in many ways. Public housing redevelopment efforts today are necessarily partnerships among a variety of pro-

Reprinted from *Housing Policy Debate* 7, 3 (Washington, D.C.: Fannie Mae Foundation, 1996). This copyrighted material is used with the permission of the Fannie Mae Foundation.

fessionals and nonprofessionals who often have different agendas and priorities. The research reported here is part of an attempt to look across many possible criteria for success and to apply them to actual cases of public housing redevelopment. It represents a continuation of the author's efforts to link the socioeconomic changes affecting public housing residents to the prospects for comprehensive redevelopment (Vale 1993).

It is commonly recognized that the problems of severely distressed housing—often thought of as a matter of ill-conceived and deteriorating buildings—are also fully entwined with the socioeconomic problems of severely distressed public housing residents (Vale 1992). Eighty percent of the nonelderly public housing population lives below the poverty line, and a majority of households in big-city public housing developments are headed by unemployed single parents and report incomes below 20 percent of the local median. If public housing redevelopment efforts are to contribute to sustained improvement in the lives of such residents, their promoters will need to pursue and achieve success across multiple dimensions simultaneously.

As public housing authorities around the United States attempt to implement large grants received under the Urban Revitalization Demonstration (HOPE VI) program of the U.S. Department of Housing and Urban Development (HUD), it seems pertinent to consider the history of comprehensive attempts to revitalize severely distressed public housing.[1] In 1992, when the National Commission on Severely Distressed Public Housing (NCSDPH) assembled its *Case Studies and Site Examination Reports* (NCSDPH 1992b), it devoted chapters to four "turnaround" efforts thought worthy of special commendation; one of these was Boston's Commonwealth development, built in 1951 and redeveloped between 1979 and 1985.[2] Of the four redevelopment programs touted by the commission, only Commonwealth's was accomplished without total demolition of the site or wholesale restructuring of occupancy.[3]

What follows is an attempt to dissect and assess the reasons for Commonwealth's widely praised success by setting this redevelopment effort in the context of the other two Boston Housing Authority (BHA) redevelopment efforts—at West Broadway and Franklin Field—that were carried out at the same time. It is hoped that the experiences of the BHA may be seen as both seminal and instructive.

COMPARING PUBLIC HOUSING REDEVELOPMENT POTENTIAL

Close examination of the three major redevelopment efforts reveals characteristics that seem to contribute to success as well as features that seem to stymie all efforts to implement positive change. Drawing on data from 265 interviews with a broad spectrum of residents about the process of redevelopment and current conditions,[4] as well as on other documents and interviews with designers, community organizers, managers, and housing authority officials, this chapter describes and compares the effectiveness of each redevelopment effort by examining its successes and limitations from the point of view of those most affected.[5] It attempts to explain the reasons for differential success and to explore which parts of the redevelopment efforts were most important to residents.

Given that these redevelopment efforts were centered on improvements to the physical environments of each place, this article examines how these environmental transformations are related to other kinds of necessary changes. Taking note of the extremely high costs of this sort of redevelopment effort (approximately $100,000 per unit in today's dollars), it concludes by exploring the benefits that such expenditures can bring, while noting the ways that design-centered redevelopment approaches can fall short of the comprehensive social and economic package of change that is necessary to meet the full range of needs of an increasingly disadvantaged public housing population.

There are many ways that one might compare the three redeveloped Boston housing projects under study. Franklin Field, West Broadway, and Commonwealth were built during the same period (in fact, as part of the same state-funded veterans' housing program) and were redeveloped during the same period, but they also differ in key ways that may help explain some of the difference in their redevelopment experiences (see table 8.1). There are differences in racial and ethnic makeup, size, building type, and form of post-redevelopment management. Moreover, each place exists in its own highly individual neighborhood context and has its own internal dynamic (figures 8.1 and 8.2). All of these factors can play some role in interpreting the trajectories of redevelopment, often in ways that are all too predictable but sometimes in ways that are counterintuitive.

In December 1979, the BHA Planning Department produced a report on *Site Selection Criteria for Substantial Rehabilitation* (BHA 1979b) to identify the places where investing large amounts of money was most likely to yield success. The report compared the 10 most troubled BHA family developments (including Commonwealth, West Broadway, and Franklin Field) in terms of site accessibility, physical design, neighborhood characteristics, and tenant characteristics, and it assessed BHA redevelopment priorities and prospects in relation to the research findings contained in HUD's national study of "troubled" public housing (Jones et al. 1979).

In terms of site accessibility, the BHA planners hypothesized that redevelopment was more likely to be successful in cases where the site was better served by transportation, shopping, recreation, and health care facilities. In terms of design, they felt more confident in the ability to effect a turnaround in cases where a development was small, lacked high-rise units, had ample parking, featured buildings with identifiable fronts and backs, was of relatively low density, and was amenable to greater territorial control by residents.

In terms of neighborhood characteristics, they stressed the hypothetical advantages of rising residential market values, a high percentage of owner-occupied units, a low percentage of subsidized units, low unemployment rates, and high ongoing public and private neighborhood investment. Finally, in terms of tenant characteristics,

TABLE 8.1

Three Boston Public Housing Developments

	Franklin Field	*West Broadway*	*Commonwealth*
Year constructed	1954	1949	1951
Dates of redevelopment	1977–87	1977–91	1979–85
No. of units (as built)	504	972	648
No. of apts. occupied (1993)	348	649	392
Building type	3-story walk-up	3-story walk-up	3-story walk-up 6-story midrises
Racial/ethnic makeup (1993)	80% black 20% Latino	65% white 15% Latino 10% black 10% Asian	40% white 38% black 15% Latino 7% Asian
Form of management (1993)	BHA	BHA	Private

Note: BHA = Boston Housing Authority.

they hypothesized that redevelopment success would be best ensured in places with a lower percentage of female-headed households, a higher percentage of working adults, and a lower percentage of minors. No judgments were made about the racial or ethnic composition of a development, though in Boston—where the BHA has faced 30 years of desegregation pressures—this remains a highly contentious issue. The BHA's assessment of the pre-redevelopment situation at Commonwealth, West Broadway, and Franklin Field relative to BHA averages for all of the above categories reveals no clear pattern (see table 8.2). Moreover, the assessment suggests that each of the three developments had distinctive strengths and weaknesses relative to the other two; out of 18 categories of assessment, there is not one for which all three developments are in the same place relative to the BHA average. That said, if one weighs all 18 categories equally,[6] the composite scores show that Commonwealth (+4) ranked better than average, West Broadway scored about average (–1), and Franklin Field (–4) lagged behind BHA averages, with a score brought down by the intensity of its residents' poverty and by the perceived limitations of its neighborhood.[7] Reflecting this, the BHA's own weighted scores for the 10 developments based on these 18 categories ranked Commonwealth second, West Broadway fifth, and Franklin Field dead last.

By the time of the BHA study, however, redevelopment efforts at West Broad-

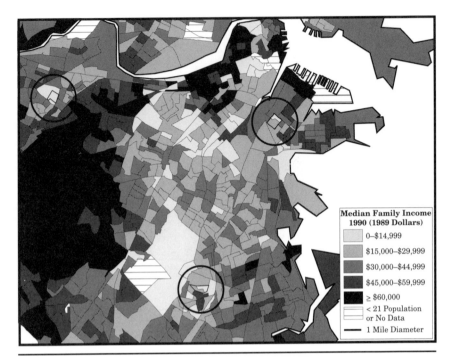

FIGURE 8.1
Neighborhood Location

Note: This map of Boston (the portion north of the river at the top is part of Cambridge, and some of the wealthiest area at far left is part of Brookline) shows the location of Commonwealth (at center of top left circle) in Brighton, West Broadway (top right) in South Boston, and Franklin Field (bottom) in Dorchester. The map shows that, in each case, there is a mix of incomes within a half-mile radius of the development. However, only Commonwealth is close to predominantly middle-class residential areas. By contrast, Franklin Field, despite a pocket of higher income residents just south of the development, is near other areas of extreme poverty, and West Broadway's neighborhood may be characterized as more uniformly working class.

Source: Created from block group data, 1990 U.S. census.

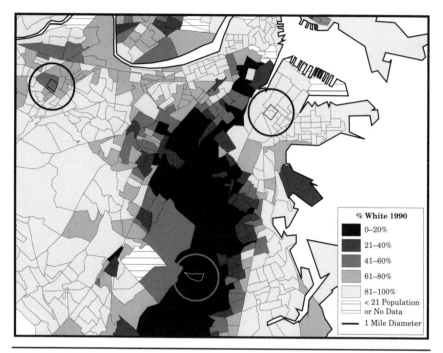

FIGURE 8.2
Neighborhood Racial Composition

Note: This map of Boston shows the extreme racial polarization of the city. West Broadway (top right) is located in overwhelmingly white South Boston; Franklin Field (bottom) is located in a predominantly nonwhite swath of the city; while Commonwealth (top left) is located in a mixed-race and multiethnic part of the city. Comparable maps from 1980 (not included here) reveal similar racial compositions in the three neighborhoods immediately surrounding the housing projects during the time immediately preceding redevelopment.

The Franklin Field neighborhood underwent a rapid and highly contentious white-to-black transition between 1968 and 1975, and the West Broadway project, briefly integrated by the BHA between 1965 and 1975, reverted to all white until after redevelopment because of racial harassment, when it was again integrated by the BHA during the early 1990s. The Commonwealth neighborhood, though still predominantly white, has become increasingly diversified during the last 30 years.

Source: Created from block group data, 1990 U.S. census.

TABLE 8.2

Pre-Redevelopment Characteristics of Three
Developments Relative to BHA Average

	Franklin Field	West Broadway	Common-wealth
Site accessibility			
Transportation	−	+	+
Shopping	−	+	0
Recreation	0	+	0
Health care	0	0	+
Physical design			
Total no. of units	0	−	0
High-rise vs. low-rise units	0	0	−
Parking	+	−	+
Fronts and backs	+	0	0
Low density	+	0	0
Defensible edges	0	−	+
Neighborhood characteristics			
Increase in residential market values	−	0	0
High percentage of owner-occupied units	+	0	+
Low percentage of subsidized units	0	−	0
Low unemployment rate	−	0	+
Public and private investment	−	−	0
Tenant characteristics			
Female-headed households	−	0	−
Adults working	−	0	0
Low percentage of minors	−	+	0
Total (if given equal weight)	−4	−1	+4

Note: BHA = Boston Housing Authority.
+ denotes that the development ranks well ahead of the authoritywide average.
− denotes that the development ranks well behind the authoritywide average.
0 denotes that the development approximates the authoritywide average.
Source: Adapted from BHA 1979b.

way and Franklin Field were already under way and politically irreversible. There is no evidence that the housing authority regarded this one internal study as sufficient to warrant reconsidering its allocation of funds. Still, the BHA study may be seen as implying that Commonwealth was the development where comprehensive redevelopment would have the greatest impact as well as the greatest likelihood of success (BHA 1979b).

The BHA did not define success, however, and the factors that might condition it—neighborhood economic health, design attributes, tenant characteristics, and the like—were thoroughly conflated in the aggregate development scores. Moreover, as the BHA planning department itself realized, many crucial aspects of comparative advantage and disadvantage at individual developments were highly subjective and interlinked and did not lend themselves easily to quantitative assessment. In addition to the 18 categories mentioned above, the BHA recognized other mitigating factors such as the presence of a strong tenant organization, evidence of influential outside neighborhood support, a record of previous or ongoing revitalization efforts, the relative availability of state (versus federal) funds for certain developments, limitations imposed by HUD regulations on renovating certain building types, and the relative urgency of a development's physical needs.

This analysis sorts out the elements of success in public housing redevelopment and relates them to the characteristics of specific housing developments, neighborhoods, and planning processes. However, any comparative study of public housing projects is constrained by the fact that every development differs from every other in multiple ways. This study—through its careful selection of developments and its openness to the presence of multiple explanatory variables—attempts to maximize the grounds for making valid comparisons. Despite the manifold differences among Franklin Field, West Broadway, and Commonwealth, many characteristics of their baseline pre-redevelopment conditions and the subsequent approaches to redevelopment seem similar enough to make a comparative study plausible. The three each received approximately $30 million[8] that was spent primarily on enlarging and upgrading apartments, reconfiguring buildings, and relandscaping and restructuring the site. A central goal of these revitalization efforts, though not always explicitly stated, was to eliminate the institutional features that had worked to stigmatize these places (see Vale 1996a, 1996b).

CONDITIONS BEFORE REDEVELOPMENT

Fifteen years ago, when work on the redevelopment got under way, the tasks seemed as overwhelming as those facing housing authorities today. In 1979, by anyone's definition, these developments were "severely distressed," characterized by rapidly escalating vacancy rates and plagued by vandalism and violence.[9] By the time redevelopment efforts started, Franklin Field, West Broadway (then known as D

Street), and Commonwealth (then known as Fidelis Way) all had vacancy rates of between 30 and 50 percent, involving scattered unusable apartments and abandonment of entire buildings (Carr, Lynch Associates and Wallace, Floyd Associates 1982; Community Planning and Research 1979; Lane, Frenchman, & Associates and Goody, Clancy, & Associates 1981).

Moreover, the conditions at individual developments were a product of a system in disarray. Even after tenant-initiated lawsuits had finally resulted in assignment of a court-appointed master to oversee the operations of the BHA after 1975, the pattern of institutional corruption continued unabated despite the master's best efforts. In 1979, the BHA was put into court-ordered receivership, seen as a last desperate measure to gain some relief for the tenant plaintiffs (Schneiderman 1982). As the judge who ordered the receivership observed, the failures of management entailed horrific consequences for Boston's public housing tenants:

> The conditions in the BHA's family developments are depressingly similar irrespective of the deterioration or absence of deterioration in the surrounding neighborhoods. Those tenants [including residents of Commonwealth, West Broadway, and Franklin Field] who testified did so concerning the physical conditions of their apartments and of their developments generally. Their testimony, again incontroverted, of leaky ceilings, of frequent cessation of such basic services as heat, hot water and electricity, of windows which do not open in hot weather and which cannot be closed in cold weather, of infestation of rodents and insects, of mounds of rubbish and trash, of packs of wild dogs and of much more remind one of casualty lists in wartime. One's sensibilities become saturated until one realizes that each and every name on the casualty list represents a human tragedy. In recent years it seems that if the media requires a housing horror story to fill air time or newspaper space, one is guaranteed such a story by trekking to almost any of the BHA's family developments and to many of its elderly developments. (Garrity 1979, 102)

What followed during the next five years, under the celebrated leadership of receiver Harry Spence (Cohen 1981; Lovinger 1981; Pynoos 1986), was an attempt to tackle three of the more egregious failures of this system by allocating substantial and disproportionate resources to the redevelopment efforts at Commonwealth, West Broadway, and Franklin Field.[10]

APPROACHING COMPREHENSIVE REDEVELOPMENT

The physical redevelopment goals at all three sites, though carried out by different teams of designers, shared many principles. At the level of the apartment design (which was the primary concern of most residents, at least at the beginning), there were several goals, nearly all of which were carried out to some extent at all three housing developments. Apartments were enlarged[11] and reconfigured to match family size, using both vertical and horizontal breakthroughs. Dining areas were increased to accommodate all family members eating at once, and a separate entrance vestibule with closet was added to provide privacy for the living room. Second bathrooms were added to larger apartments, and individual washer and dryer hookups were provided in many cases. At a more conceptual level, apartments were given a clearly defined front and rear, with living rooms facing the front and more service-oriented rooms facing the rear, and new semiprivate front stoops and back yards were added to encourage families to regard more of their environment as being under their own control and management.

At the level of individual buildings, there were also attempts to make public housing resemble more closely the private housing stock. Many of the multibedroom apartments were reconfigured into two-story or three-story pseudo row-houses, allowing for larger apartments and clearer division between sleeping and living areas. In this process, common stairwells, seen as overcrowded and unsupervisable, were substantially eliminated, as was free access to roofs from stair landings, which had been a security risk. The new reconfiguration into apartments resembling town houses allowed for many units to gain private entrances and direct ground floor access through both front and back doors. At West Broadway, the accommodation of middle-class building imagery even entailed the construction of pitched roofs on both the row-houses and suburbanesque village community centers.

Finally, at the level of urban design and site planning, the designers also attempted to reduce the stigma associated with the housing developments as separate enclaves. In each case, this was done by decreasing overall density. The number of units was reduced both by reconfiguring them into fewer, larger apartments and by replacing some buildings or apartments with nonresidential community facilities. In contrast to the goals of some housing authorities to reinforce the separateness of the development by constructing perimeter fencing, the Boston plans all involved greater inclusion of the surrounding streets instead of continued reliance on a superblock. This feature was combined with concerted efforts to control and direct the presence of cars by separating them from pedestrians and providing parking near dwelling entrances, thereby allowing vehicle surveillance and easy access. Extensive relandscaping was done to extend residents' control over space outside their apartments by providing a variety of traversable, semitraversable, and nontraversable barriers. Play areas were delineated for different age groups, including hard and soft surfaces, with paved areas for above-ground tenant-owned wading pools, wide sidewalks, and other kinds of less obviously "purpose-built" places.

At all levels of design, then, the shapers of these redevelopment efforts seem to have drawn on many of the "defensible space" principles first articulated by Oscar Newman and others (Chermayeff and Alexander 1965; Coleman 1985; Jacobs 1961; Newman 1972, 1980).[12] This was no accident. In 1980, just as the planning efforts for Commonwealth, Franklin Field, and West Broadway were gearing up, BHA design consultant Gayle Epp was commissioned to write a thorough overview of this emerging literature. Harry Spence set up an environment of thoughtful, careful decision making, Epp recalls, marveling that "this very academic piece . . . was the subject of a whole senior staff meeting" (Epp 1994). What Oscar Newman had proposed, the BHA—using a variety of experienced architecture and urban design firms—chose to extend and apply.[13]

Measuring and Explaining Seven Kinds of Success

As already noted, success in redevelopment efforts may be measured in many ways and may be an indication of many different things. It is not only that individuals and groups involved in these ventures may use widely differing criteria for evaluation; it is also that these criteria and goals for redevelopment efforts seem rarely to be set out explicitly. As a consequence, even when there is a consensus that a redevelopment effort has been a success or a failure, there is often less consensus about how or why this is so. The range of definitions of success is accompanied by a range of attempts to explain it. Interviews with a wide range of individuals associated with each of these redevelopment efforts, including tenants, managers, designers, housing authority officials, service providers, and community organizers, suggest at least seven kinds of success:

1. Smooth implementation
2. Recognized design quality
3. Improved tenant organization capacity
4. Enhanced maintenance and management performance
5. Improved security
6. Progress on socioeconomic development
7. Resident satisfaction

Certainly, some individuals judge success by many of these measures rather than only one, yet personal and professional identities often dictate the lens through which the redevelopment is seen. Moreover, the reasons that individuals give to explain success according to one or more of these measures are closely linked to such personal stakes and institutional affiliations. Each of these measures exists as a continuum, and evidence of progress—in almost every case—is rarely collected or assessed.[14] In the end, however, true institutional learning—the capacity to fix problems in midstream and to do better next time—depends on such reflective assessment and on a consolidated and holistic view of success. Each of these forms of success matters.

What follows is an articulation of the seven measures of success as applied to the redevelopment efforts at Commonwealth, West Broadway, and Franklin Field.

Smooth Implementation

For many housing authority officials, particularly those in a construction management division, the overriding challenge is to get the job done, and the key measure
of success is adherence to budgets and timetables. Success means coping with strict
budgetary constraints and managing the complex processes of construction and resident relocation. Anything resembling a full account of the three redevelopment implementation processes at Commonwealth, West Broadway, and Franklin Field is far
too involved for inclusion here, though a few key points may be set out. All three
redevelopment efforts experienced costly delays and were compromised by the limitations of their budgets.

At West Broadway, the redevelopment was carried out in phases. It was clear from
the beginning that the initial funding was insufficient to carry out a comprehensive
redevelopment of the whole 972-unit state-owned project. Rather than scale back
the intervention by eliminating the dramatic reconfiguration of the buildings, the
BHA chose to work intensively on limited areas of the project at a time. Predictably,
perhaps, the money needed to complete the last phase of the redevelopment has not
been forthcoming. Nearly 15 years after it began, approximately 80 percent of West
Broadway has been redeveloped, but the remainder (mostly still inhabited) still looks
as it did during the late 1970s (see figures 8.3 and 8.4). The result has been not
only a physical problem but a severe social problem: The obvious inequities were
exacerbated by the mid-redevelopment attempt to integrate this previously all-white
project, during which some white long-term residents still living in the old part have
had to watch as new, nonwhite arrivals have been given renovated apartments in the
redeveloped sections. In short, failure to find funds to complete the redevelopment
has compromised its success.

At Commonwealth, too, there were delays and cost overruns, and all parties con-
cede that the private developer, John M. Corcoran & Company, lost money on this
turnkey venture.[15] Nonetheless, all concur that this was still the redevelopment effort that proceeded most smoothly. In fact, all the key players in the Commonwealth
redevelopment effort seem to regard it as a high point in their professional careers.
By contrast, the redevelopment effort at Franklin Field was the one that suffered the
most setbacks, including the bankruptcy of the major contractor. There were tensions over the budget from the beginning, and tenants frequently mentioned ways
that their raised expectations were frustrated by the elimination of favored amenities
and by shoddy construction. Here, even though nearly a decade has passed since the
redevelopment was finished, most long-term residents and others who were interviewed still feel bitter. Tenants who were frustrated veterans of the redevelopment
wars complained about a low level of resident influence, while interviews with several of the redevelopment planners invariably turned to a discussion of what went
wrong; no one attempted to defend either the process or the end product.

Interviews with key players reveal diverse explanations for the wide variation of

FIGURE 8.3
Site conditions at the West Broadway Development prior to redevelopment
(c. 1981)

Note: This view shows the deterioration of the landscaping, in which all outdoor space is
fully public and automobiles move freely across the project.
Source: Stephen E. Tise, A.I.A.

quality in the three redevelopment processes. Some stress the relative strength of
political connections, which clearly favored West Broadway and Commonwealth.
Local newspaper accounts provide some insight into the ways that powerful neighborhood politicians in South Boston championed West Broadway as a candidate for
redevelopment, just as they had influenced early decisions to site a disproportionate
share of Boston's public housing in their neighborhood when that housing was first
built and was seen as a desirable amenity. Moreover, the court-appointed master, Robert Whittlesey, went out of his way to tout the redevelopment potential of West Broadway (as well as Commonwealth) in his July 1976 report (Whittlesey 1976), and the
West Broadway tenants' association engaged excellent outside community development and design consultants, who initially worked pro bono.

In 1977, armed with an arsenal of connections and a clearly demonstrable need,
West Broadway was awarded an initial $6.5 million pilot modernization grant from
the Massachusetts Executive Office of Communities and Development. This gave it

FIGURE 8.4
West Broadway transformed

Note: The imagery of the renovated buildings attempts to eliminate the institutional features of the original structures.

a head start in the competition for redevelopment funds when Spence launched the BHA's full-scale efforts in 1980. However, because West Broadway was located in an overwhelmingly white neighborhood in the city, there was pressure to award money also to a housing development serving a primarily nonwhite community. This, according to several sources, is why Franklin Field (now approximately 80 percent African American and 20 percent Latino) received a pilot grant. And, in turn, the pilot grant was the main reason Franklin Field was chosen for large-scale redevelopment, even though it had ranked last according to the BHA planning department's *Site Selection Criteria for Substantial Rehabilitation* (BHA 1976b). In this context, while it is not clear whether one should interpret Franklin Field's inclusion in the redevelopment program as evidence of political strength or political weakness, it seems important to reiterate that the BHA *began* the Franklin Field redevelopment process with the recognition that it was the least likely to succeed.

Commonwealth's relative political clout seems to have come about less because of state house connections (although these were ample) than because of its location on a highly desirable parcel of land. Before the BHA's decision to seek substantial funding for its redevelopment, Commonwealth not only had Whittlesey's attention and blessing but was already the subject of two lengthy planning reports funded by a state grant. One of these focused on financial issues and confirmed that Commonwealth, unlike other public housing projects, has excellent real estate redevelopment potential by virtue of its hilltop location, its surrounding middle-class residential and institutional community, and its proximity to transit (Walsh & Associates 1979).

Just after these reports were completed, a large parcel of land adjacent to Commonwealth was proposed for sale, and the Boston Redevelopment Authority established a task force to assist it with coordinating all planning and development in the area known as Monastery Hill, including Commonwealth. Though this task force ultimately did not get to plan the future of Monastery Hill as a whole, it did serve as a major catalyst for the Commonwealth redevelopment. Its diverse membership, bringing together representatives from all the city and state planning, funding, and regulatory agencies and a broad array of neighborhood agencies and groups—including representatives from both the Commonwealth Tenants Association and the project-based Commonwealth Health Improvement Program—provided a highly public platform for discussing the needs of the development and its residents, a forum unparalleled and unprecedented in the city (see Vale 1996a). As a result, by the time the BHA was ready to commence its three large redevelopment efforts, Commonwealth had emerged as a clear priority, especially since—in stark contrast to Franklin Field—it ranked as most likely to succeed in the BHA's own internal judgment.

There is, however, another persuasive explanation for the success of Commonwealth's redevelopment process. Some key players (even in the BHA itself) attribute the superior performance of the Commonwealth process to the presence of an outside private developer who, under the turnkey process, was able to bypass some of the constraints associated with the usual public bidding process. But the act of privatization of the development process is not the only issue. Through the extremely fine detail included in its *Commonwealth Developer's Kit* (BHA 1981) and through the careful process by which six creditable proposals from developers were scrutinized and evaluated, the BHA served as a highly active player throughout the process. Delegation to the private sector did not entail abrogation of responsibility.

While local political influence is surely central to getting redevelopment projects launched, and while the ability to employ a private developer for Commonwealth seems to have been important, some key players in the redevelopment efforts attribute the success of Commonwealth to less tangible factors. Several participants in the Commonwealth redevelopment effort spoke of it as a kind of "confluence of personalities," one that was not matched elsewhere. It is not fully clear how to interpret this, since the confluence may well be a result of other successful aspects of the process, rather than the cause. The relative quality of the relationship among the various parties during the process does seem to be a key indicator of problems. During the course of the Franklin Field redevelopment, especially, there were many open conflicts about how to proceed and an undesirably large number of turnovers of leadership among on-site management, tenant organizers, BHA redevelopment staff, and resident leaders. Part of this "confluence of personalities" explanation also seems rooted in the presence of specific strong leaders—whether tenants, consultants, or housing authority personnel.

Clearly, successful project management during planning and construction is one kind of success, and it may well be a good predictor of others. Yet, while it does expedite completion, this form of success does not necessarily lead to sustainable positive change. Because the research reported here continued for a decade after post-redevelopment reoccupancy, it is possible to go beyond analysis of implementation to examine how well the redevelopment efforts have been received and sustained.

Recognized Design Quality

In addition to the central concerns about the time and money involved in a redevelopment process, almost everyone in a housing authority is concerned about the quality of the resultant product—the redeveloped housing. Designers (and those who work in design, development, and planning sections of housing authorities) tend to measure this quality by the number and kind of awards that professional societies confer on these ventures. Commonwealth and West Broadway each won multiple regional and national design and planning awards, while Franklin Field won none.[16]

More immediately, design quality is measured every day by residents. In our interviews, 81 long-term residents of West Broadway, Commonwealth, and Franklin Field (i.e., those who had lived in one of these places both before and after its redevelopment) were asked to discuss the "most important" physical changes that resulted from the redevelopment. In each case, more tenants stressed changes that had taken place *within their apartments* than any other kind of change. Overall, 44 percent of the most important changes were thought to be apartment centered, 38 percent were building centered, and only 18 percent were site related or programming related.[17]

Most of the changes noted as most important by residents at each development involved such details as larger rooms, more convenient layouts, better kitchen facilities, second bathrooms in larger apartments, and the addition of laundry hookups. Only slightly less central were changes at the scale of individual buildings, such as private entrances, reduction or elimination of common hallways, private yards, elimination of flat roofs (at West Broadway), and better overall appearance. While many residents—especially at Commonwealth—also mentioned site-level improvements such as landscaping, improved parking areas, children's play areas, and new community buildings, these matters were less frequently commented on than changes closer to individual apartments. Resident priorities suggest a considerable desire for expensive changes—involving gutting buildings and reconfiguring them to resemble town houses, maximizing private entrances, and minimizing common hallways.

Design quality may be measured in other ways beyond overtly voiced resident priorities. Perhaps the most significant are the ways that design interventions improve the image of public housing in the eyes of residents, neighbors, and the general public whose political representatives ultimately decide its future funding. Design awards, usually conferred not long after occupancy (if not before it), rarely take into account the social effects of public housing design that ultimately form its most enduring legacy.

Interview respondents from the three developments were asked whether they believed that the development where they lived looked like public housing. Nearly three-quarters of respondents from Commonwealth indicated that they did not think so, markedly higher than the comparable figures for West Broadway and Franklin Field. This is true even though Commonwealth has many midrise elevator buildings—usually the most stigmatized form of public housing—whereas the other two developments are all three-story walk-ups.[18] In other words, the fact that only one-quarter of respondents believed that Commonwealth still looked like public housing is especially impressive, since its redesigners arguably had more stigma to overcome.[19]

At West Broadway, despite some elaborate attempts to deinstitutionalize its appearance, involving the replacement of flat roofs with pitched ones, this image transformation ranked less well than Commonwealth's—40 percent of respondents still said the redeveloped parts looked like public housing. And at Franklin Field, although its buildings were reconfigured in ways similar to the approach at Commonwealth and West Broadway, fully two-thirds of respondents reported that it still looked like public housing. The extreme variation of responses, in itself, does not prove that design changes affect resident attitudes toward their environments, yet residents' explanations of *why* the public housing look persists or has dissipated do suggest powerful ways that design issues are interwoven with other social matters where architects and urban designers exert far less control.

At West Broadway, for example, most respondents chose to make a clear differentiation between those parts of the development that had been redesigned and those parts that remained physically unaltered. The new buildings were described as looking like "town houses" or "condos" or "individual homes," "a nice complex," "more like a development," and "less like projects and more like private homes" (see Vale 1995). Still, as elsewhere, a substantial minority of respondents from West Broadway were not convinced that the redevelopment had done much to change the character of the development: "[You] still can tell it's public housing"; "it's still a project"; "it all look[s] alike." Another respondent, acknowledging that the renovated sections look "less" like public housing, noted that "people still know it's public housing. They know we're here" (cited in Vale 1995). Much of the dissociation from public housing seems to stem from the acts of designers who reconfigured the buildings and relandscaped the site, but a lot of the look of the place seems to be its social appearance. One person explained why she thought Commonwealth did not look like public housing by noting that "people are calm and you don't see them disturbing others on the sidewalks." In the end, there is a merging of these social and physical explanations, since the redevelopment efforts are social processes as well as physical ones, and they yield social as well as physical results (see Vale 1996b).

The success of the design aspect of a redevelopment process has many other social features. Elaborate rehabilitation of buildings necessitates resident relocation, which in turn provides an opportunity for restructuring occupancy before the redeveloped apartments are rerented.[20] More directly, the success of design processes may be measured by their ability to incorporate resident input in significant ways. Rather than simply choosing the colors of kitchen counters and the like, in some cases resident influence over design decisions carried considerably broader import. At West Broadway, for instance, residents succeeded in reversing the BHA plan to begin the phased redevelopment in the most publicly visible place. Instead, they convincingly argued, the redevelopment should begin at the rear, so that the eyesore of the front would remain as a testament to the continuing need for new funds to complete subsequent phases. Design, in this sense, is tenant organizing carried out by other means.

IMPROVED TENANT ORGANIZATION CAPACITY

For community organizers and for many tenants, a key dimension of success in public housing redevelopment is just this—helping the residents become active and influential decision makers in their developments and build their skills to attract additional resources. In each of the three Boston redevelopment cases, housing officials recognized from the outset that such transformations could not simply be imposed on residents but must emerge through negotiation. In two of the three cases, those at West Broadway and Commonwealth, the redesign efforts were preceded by years of resident organizing. Only at Franklin Field, where the redevelopment ultimately proved far less successful in most other dimensions as well, was resident involvement more limited and more belated.

At both West Broadway and Commonwealth, however, the role of the tenants was central. In the interviews conducted in 1993, residents who lived through the redevelopment processes were asked to name those they believed were most important to the process. The results are quite revealing. At both Commonwealth and West Broadway, more than 80 percent of respondents stated that the tenants themselves played the leading role. At Franklin Field, however, only 39 percent gave credit to the tenants, and the majority credited (or blamed) either the on-site management or the BHA for the redevelopment. Moreover, all those at Franklin Field who did credit the tenants credited only "tenant leaders," rather than a broader spectrum of tenant involvement as the Commonwealth and West Broadway respondents often did. Clearly, something went right at Commonwealth and West Broadway that did not happen at Franklin Field. As one of the BHA staff members responsible for coordinating the Franklin Field redevelopment recalled, the tenant organization [at Franklin Field] wasn't terribly strong. There wasn't a long-standing tenant advocacy group the way there was at Commonwealth and D Street. It was one that we at the BHA had to foster and develop the leadership. Because we wanted tenant involvement, we had to have someone to talk to. And so it was more of a top-down situation, as opposed to the other two which were much more bottom-up, people saying "we want to be redeveloped," and pushing themselves to the forefront. (Gilmore 1994)

While there were almost certainly some tenants at Franklin Field who saw themselves as key players in the redevelopment, it seems significant that at least some in the housing authority saw the task of building links to the tenants as a process of inventing someone to talk to.

While it cannot be denied that it was Spence, as receiver, who masterminded the innovative redevelopment schemes discussed here, the degree of tenant involvement at all levels of decision making remains striking. It is not so much that there were so many tenants involved—like most tenant organizations, the efforts at Commonwealth and West Broadway were led by a few committed individuals, though many meetings did attract dozens, if not hundreds, of participants. More than mere numbers, what seems key is the degree to which the redevelopment efforts at these two places were carried out as true partnerships between tenant associations and the housing authority. Rather than simply receive the wisdom of professionals, for instance, the residents hired their own architectural consultants to clarify, defend, and advance tenant interests.

This kind of initiative went beyond design issues as well. At Commonwealth, the tenants association actually entered into a binding agreement with the housing authority and a private management company. This agreement continues to govern the post-redevelopment management of the development and allows the tenants to fire the management with 30 days' notice (Commonwealth Tenants Association, BHA, and Corcoran Management Company 1983). In short, though the vast majority of the money in these redevelopment efforts was spent on physical improvements, a great deal of the time was spent on improving the climate of negotiation in ways that made clear the value of resident input. Just as the physical design alteration was intended to normalize the appearance of the housing, so too the redevelopment process was intended to lessen the social costs of distant and top-down management.

ENHANCED MAINTENANCE AND MANAGEMENT PERFORMANCE

For many in housing authorities and other housing development organizations, the key measure of success in public housing is always management. Measuring the success of management is, in part, a matter of tracking the performance of "official" maintenance and management entities, such things as work order turnaround times. But it is also a matter of assessing the relationship that is built (or rebuilt) between the representatives of management and the tenants themselves. Here, taking account of both quantifiable assessments and the more intangible accounts of tenant-management relationships, the interviews with residents clearly suggest that the privately managed Commonwealth has fared best.[21]

When respondents were asked whether they had experienced problems with the response time of maintenance since the redevelopment, only 10 percent of those at Commonwealth reported problems with Corcoran Management Company, compared with more than one-third at West Broadway and nearly two-thirds at Franklin Field, both of which were still managed by the BHA. The post-redevelopment maintenance problems at Franklin Field were reported to be even greater than those prevailing at the two non-redeveloped sites where interviews were also conducted. BHA-supplied statistics regarding outstanding work orders suggest that these perceptions are not without substance. At the end of 1992, shortly before the interviews were conducted, the quarterly total of outstanding work orders revealed a service backlog of 182 orders at Franklin Field, 319 at West Broadway (including the non-redeveloped part), and only 2 at Commonwealth (BHA 1993b).

When residents were asked about the maintenance of the development as a whole, a similar pattern prevailed. Respondents were asked to rank maintenance in terms of several components: grass, trees, and flowers; dumpster areas; parking areas; and overall cleanliness. When the responses to these are combined to yield an aggregate measure, only at Commonwealth and at West Broadway (despite the fact that the redevelopment there remains incomplete) did a majority of respondents report that development maintenance was either good or very good. Here, too, Franklin Field lagged behind. Like respondents from the two non-redeveloped sites, most Franklin Field respondents rated project maintenance as fair or poor.

The superior performance of Commonwealth's management on maintenance issues is all the more remarkable when compared with pre-redevelopment conditions. Surveys of Commonwealth residents carried out in 1979 (near the nadir of the pre-redevelopment conditions) and again in 1993 (after nearly a decade of reoccupancy) suggest the magnitude of change that has occurred.[22] In 1979, three-quarters of the respondents complained about the inability of maintenance staff to address problems in their apartments; in 1993, only 10 percent indicated that they had experienced any problems with maintenance. Since this measure is taken nearly a full decade after the completion of the redevelopment, and since the 1993 survey was conducted during a time when the Corcoran Management Company was arguing that the BHA provided Commonwealth with a disproportionately low subsidy, the relatively low level of complaint combined with a superb record in the turnaround of work orders surely provides compelling testimony that Commonwealth's management has been in good hands.[23]

What such numbers do not do is offer an *explanation* for this "good" management; most of those at the BHA are personally and institutionally reluctant to say that the Corcoran Management Company succeeds at Commonwealth because it is a private and for-profit organization. All parties do concur that much of the management success at Commonwealth comes from setting and enforcing high standards and from having maintenance carried out by on-site staff trained in multiple trades, rather than—as with the BHA—by centrally administered specialists who work according to union regulations (see Vale 1996a).

At base, Corcoran Management Company succeeds because Commonwealth's residents helped negotiate the terms of the 223-page management plan that remains a reference point for an enormous range of matters (Commonwealth Tenants Association, BHA, and Corcoran Management Company 1983). Tenants at Commonwealth get not just a lease but a set of community rules formulated by their fellow tenants and a commitment by the management to undertake a detailed preventive maintenance program, with written standards for corrective maintenance procedures, janitorial service, and grounds maintenance. At the same time, the management plan describes eviction procedures and spells out charges for damage to apartments. Interviews suggest that Corcoran Management Company and most Commonwealth residents have accepted a sense of coresponsibility for upkeep and behavior in the development; after more than a decade of partnership between residents and management, both groups seem committed to maintaining and enforcing high standards.

IMPROVED SECURITY

Some who participated in the redevelopment efforts argue that, beyond issues of management and maintenance, any determination of redevelopment success must be measured against the security problems that have plagued much of the nation's inner-city public housing stock in recent years. In this sense, success has to do with the ability of residents and management to cope not only with problems internal to a development but also with external forces (such as gangs) whose incursions thwart its manageability. More broadly, this view of success asks that one take into account the socioeconomic context of each redevelopment when attempting comparisons. Socioeconomic trends in surrounding neighborhoods may either help residents of a public housing development change in positive ways or hinder such growth. In this regard, many involved with the redevelopment efforts in Boston emphasize that Commonwealth is located in a stable, economically diverse neighborhood with excellent public transportation access, whereas the pre-redevelopment Franklin Field was one "distressed" piece of a broader distressed neighborhood and remains part of an area that has experienced still further impoverishment and disinvestment since the completion of the redevelopment effort.

When respondents were asked in 1993 whether they believed that most people in the surrounding neighborhoods were "better off than, worse off than, or about the same" as they were 10 years ago, all 23 of the long-term Commonwealth residents who responded to the question indicated that neighborhood residents were better off or about the same; only 46 percent of Franklin Field residents were so sanguine. Respondents were also asked to rank their sense of security as "very safe, somewhat safe, somewhat unsafe, or very unsafe" in a wide variety of settings in and around the development, ranging outward from the interior of their apartments.[24] Two-thirds of respondents from Franklin Field said that they felt somewhat unsafe or very unsafe going into the surrounding neighborhoods at night, whereas only 10 percent of Commonwealth respondents and about one-third of West Broadway respondents felt that way. Even during the daytime, only 14 percent of Franklin Field respondents said that they felt very safe traveling to neighborhoods immediately outside of the development. By contrast, the majority of respondents from both Commonwealth and West Broadway did report feeling very safe in their neighborhoods during the daytime.

Boston Police Department data on reported crimes in Boston housing developments confirm that residents' perceptions are rooted in reality (Boston Police Department 1994). The number of crimes per occupied unit was far lower at Commonwealth, where, taking an annual average for the years 1991 to 1993, there was about one reported crime for every five apartments. At West Broadway there was approximately one reported crime for every two apartments and at Franklin Field approximately two crimes for every three apartments, somewhat higher than the authoritywide mean. Even Franklin Field, however, had fewer reported crimes than some other BHA developments, where, over the 1991–93 period, the annual average of reported crimes exceeded one per apartment.

Such statistics do not distinguish between crimes committed by outsiders and those committed by development residents and therefore do not provide direct evidence of neighborhood problems, yet it seems likely that much of the crime in public housing is related to troubled surrounding areas. This "neighborhood effects" explanation, in turn, makes clear that some measures of redevelopment success have little to do with the bricks-and-mortar investment that required the vast majority of the money.

When residents were asked to name whom they feared most while living in their developments, the most common answer given by respondents from Commonwealth and West Broadway was "nobody"; but for Franklin Field respondents, the most common response was "gangs." On average, respondents from each development said that they felt safer inside their development than they did in the neighborhoods surrounding it, both during the day and at night. Yet, in some places, this reveals little more than the fact that, for many, security was a problem everywhere around them. Even during daylight hours, at Franklin Field only 20 percent of respondents reported feeling very safe in their development, compared with 61 percent of those at West Broadway and 80 percent of those at Commonwealth. At night, only 3 percent of respondents from Franklin Field reported feeling very safe in the development as a whole, and fully 41 percent said they felt very unsafe. At West Broadway, too, perceptions of nighttime safety dipped—only 28 percent reported feeling very safe. Only at Commonwealth did a majority of respondents (66 percent) indicate that they felt very safe in their development after dark, though at least a narrow majority at each place did say they felt very safe within their own apartments at night.

Resident insecurity, both inside and outside their developments, was almost invariably attributed to the presence of drug trafficking, often closely associated in respondents' minds with gangs and violence. Even at Commonwealth, despite its many successes, nearly two-thirds of respondents described drugs as a "major problem" in the development; at the other developments, distress about drugs was even more prevalent.

Moreover, in each place, when respondents were asked to rank the development's greatest problems, most described drugs as the worst and indicated that the drug problem had worsened, rather than improved, during the preceding two years (1991 to 1993). Many Franklin Field residents and others suggest that the epidemic of crack cocaine, and the violence associated with drug dealing, hit this development especially hard in the years immediately following the completion of the redevelopment in 1987, thwarting attempts to sustain what had been achieved both physically and socially. Some desirable design changes, however highly touted as providing "defensible space," have little value for residents in a broader climate of extreme insecurity. There is little purpose in having a private yard if, as at Franklin Field, 80 percent of respondents who have such yards say they are afraid things will be stolen from them, if only 42 percent of respondents report feeling very safe in the yard during the day, and if more than a third feel very unsafe using the yard at night.

One might conclude from all this that violent neighborhoods are a fact of life around most public housing, that matters of insecurity and drug traffic tend to overwhelm efforts at redevelopment, and that some redevelopment efforts—such as the one at Commonwealth—are fortunate that their problems are not quite so severe as those elsewhere. All of that may be true, but there also seems to be some evidence that redevelopment efforts *can* enhance security.

At the heart of any notion of defensible space is the contention that design changes can both enhance the perception of security and reduce the reality of crime. A comparison of resident perceptions of safety in the West Broadway development between those who live in its carefully programmed and zoned redeveloped parts and those who live in the vast undefined expanse of the old part suggests that redevelopment may lead to important gains in security (for greater detail, see Vale 1995). Whether they were talking about their apartments, the area outside their front doors, or the shared courtyards, respondents from the redeveloped part consistently reported feeling safer than did respondents who still lived in the old parts. Conversely, those in the non-redeveloped part were much more concerned about gangs and people from outside the development, while the largest number of respondents from the new part of the development reported that they feared "nobody." While it certainly remains possible that other forces besides the redevelopment led to these differences, it is not at all clear what these would be.[25] Residents frequently voiced pleasure at the control over outdoor space that was possible in the new parts of the development—

especially apparent in the heavily used shared courtyards and the many well-tended private gardens. Many praised the subdivided outdoor space, the elimination of the ability to cut through buildings, and the shared commitment to keeping doors locked, noting that "undesirables" now tended to enter the development through the old part (where resident surveillance had little architectural reinforcement).

However promising, defensible space measures are only a part of a broader effort that is needed to improve security in public housing and in the depressed neighborhoods that so often surround it. When residents were asked about measures that could be taken to improve security, most stressed the need for enhanced community policing, private security firms, and stricter management practices.[26] The central importance of security to residents of public housing cannot be overemphasized, and the ability of development-based or neighborhood-based violence and illegal activities to disrupt a redevelopment effort and limit its sustainability remains a key factor in any assessment of success.

PROGRESS ON SOCIOECONOMIC DEVELOPMENT

Success in public housing redevelopment may also be measured in broader public policy terms in which redevelopment is seen not only as a matter of fixing a housing project but also as an opportunity for addressing the root causes of the poverty that led residents to need public housing in the first place. In some cases, this goal entails policy initiatives directed at economic development of large areas surrounding and including public housing developments. Sometimes initiatives are targeted only to residents within a particular public housing development; sometimes the goal entails sharing facilities with residents of surrounding neighborhoods. In the 1990s, under the Urban Revitalization Demonstration program, many housing authorities have centered redevelopment initiatives on such public policy goals, most frequently on efforts to achieve an economic mix and to develop consolidated and coordinated social service facilities in the name of improving family self-sufficiency.

The three Boston public housing redevelopment efforts of the 1980s also stressed the provision of new community facilities and the need to increase employment among residents but did not make education and job training a central piece of the redevelopment agenda and did little to link these redevelopment efforts to other initiatives in the surrounding communities.[27] Despite active efforts by tenant organizations to raise outside funds for starting or sustaining programs, service provision has remained wholly inadequate even in the most successful of funding cycles. In short, the innovative approaches to physical redesign have not been matched by systematic commitments to exploring new strategies for socioeconomic redevelopment.

Despite the physical improvements that were implemented at Commonwealth, West Broadway, and Franklin Field, it is hard to sustain any claim that the redevelopment efforts have done much to improve the economic circumstances of residents.

Even at Commonwealth, where income data suggest that residents are better off, on average, than those at Franklin Field or West Broadway, less than a quarter of households reported that employment is their principal source of income. This is almost identical to the situation 15 years earlier, before redevelopment (BHA 1979a, 1993a, 1993b).

It is worth noting, however, that this seemingly dismal statistical fact still means that Commonwealth has one of the highest employment rates at a BHA development, and it is more impressive if the 132 households headed by persons over age 62 are not factored in. Nonetheless, Commonwealth still serves a population that is extremely disadvantaged economically, and many of the state-sponsored programs that helped tenants during the 1980s with education and economic development were curtailed or eliminated after 1989 (Braverman 1989; NCSDPH 1992b). At the time of this writing, substantial and sustained investment in education and job training is still absent and, as one newspaper reporter put it, "Commonwealth's social service safety net is hanging by a thread" (Kahn 1993).

If one is looking for signs of modest improvement, however, Commonwealth's marginally better economic showing seems worth further scrutiny. Though the housing authority abandoned early plans to redevelop Commonwealth as mixed-income housing, enhanced tenant screening does seem to have occurred in the years immediately following the completion of the redevelopment, which may well have increased the number of employed residents. Between 1984 and 1988, Commonwealth (like other BHA developments) had its own waiting list and drew new tenants from that list rather than from a citywide list.

Above and beyond the usual BHA screening processes, Corcoran Management Company and the Commonwealth Tenants Association chose to exercise additional control over who was admitted by implementing extensive background checks and home visits. Since 1988, when the BHA entered into a voluntary compliance agreement with HUD that prohibited development-based waiting lists on the grounds that they could be used to foster racial segregation, Commonwealth (despite its being perhaps the most racially and ethnically diverse development in the city) has had to accept tenants from the citywide waiting list and has had no more than an advisory role in keeping out those deemed undesirable.

As of 1995—despite ongoing discussions about the desirability of achieving a greater mix of incomes in public housing—there was no mechanism in place to enable some developments to favor employed applicants, and infrastructure was inadequate for enhancing the employment prospects of those who moved to public housing without a job. While there is presumably much to be learned from other cities where self-sufficiency programs have been attempted in public housing, the consensus seems to be growing that economic development within public housing—given the dire socioeconomic circumstances of the average family—cannot occur only through ambitious programs of on-site services. Given the paucity of employed persons on the citywide waiting lists for public housing, the prospects for sustaining or enhancing the percentages of employed residents depend not only on the expansion of education and job training programs for those already in public housing but also on changes in admissions policies that would import more employed families and on a version of welfare reform that makes employment an economically advantageous and socially possible option for more single-parent families.

Even in advance of all this, however, it seems likely that the restoration of a calm, clean, and secure environment at Commonwealth will contribute to sustained efforts at economic betterment. Moreover, the ongoing presence of a well-managed and well-maintained environment at Commonwealth may even have far-reaching effects on the lives of its residents, effects that are not easily measured in the customary economic terms of jobs and current annual income.

If redevelopment, tenant activism, and private management have increased domestic tranquility, it may be hoped that this, in turn, will enhance the prospects of socioeconomic mobility for the next generation. Though such questions have not yet been addressed as part of the present study, further investigation of the effects of the redevelopment on youth seems warranted. The widely discussed efforts in Chicago to relocate some public housing families to the suburbs have been praised for enhancing the school performance and job prospects of the relocated youth (Rosenbaum 1991); is it possible that well-managed public housing in the city can foster the same kinds of improvements?

The restoration of a peaceful domestic environment is certainly an important starting point, but it is surely not a substitute for enacting the promised improvements in the quality of the city's public schools. At the same time, the social and economic value of learning and earning—and the means for moving in these directions—could be demonstrated more tangibly to jobless residents by enhanced efforts to attract employed residents to public housing. For the time being, however, it seems fair to say that while the BHA likes to regard Commonwealth as its showpiece, the redevelopment effort has attained that status mostly for reasons other than its success at reducing rates of economic dependence among residents.

RESIDENT SATISFACTION

If one potential public policy goal of public housing redevelopment is to foster an economic environment that enables families to afford to leave that housing, then even Commonwealth's success is more limited. If, on the other hand, success in public housing redevelopment is measured by the enhancement of an attractive, safe, and stable community where even many of those who can afford to leave will choose to stay, then the effort at Commonwealth—and, to a great extent, the effort at West Broadway—warrants the highest praise (see Vale 1995, 1996a). Despite the lack of evidence of economic improvement, the long-term residents of Commonwealth and West Broadway who were interviewed for this study overwhelmingly agreed that they were better off than they were 10 years previously, before redevelopment had commenced.

No such positive direction of change was evinced at Franklin Field. There, re-sponses resembled those from other interviews conducted at housing developments that have not undergone a major redevelopment effort, where a majority reported that their circumstances are, at best, unchanged. In the interviews with Franklin Field residents, many actually said that they believed their apartments were better before redevelopment than they were today, chiefly because of more solid original construc-tion, though it seems that they could not fully separate such design issues from the broader feeling of insecurity that continued to pervade the development.

Similarly, when asked to rate how satisfied they were with their public housing development, 90 percent of Commonwealth respondents and 82 percent of West Broadway respondents reported feeling very satisfied or satisfied with the develop-ment, whereas at Franklin Field only 42 percent said they felt that way, and nearly a quarter reported feeling very dissatisfied.[28]

Despite their overall praise, residents of West Broadway and Commonwealth were far more divided over whether, if they were to move elsewhere, they would want to move to a similar place: At each place, about half said yes and half no. As for re-spondents from Franklin Field, 87 percent indicated they had no desire to move to a similar place. The message seems to be that redeveloped public housing can be a more acceptable and desirable form of public housing but that it still falls short of other kinds of living environments.

When asked "How long do you want to live in this development?" two-thirds of respondents from Commonwealth and West Broadway indicated they wished to stay "as long as possible" or "for a while," whereas two-thirds of the Franklin Field re-spondents made it clear they wished to remain "no longer than necessary." Only one-third of Franklin Field respondents said they "definitely would" recommend the development to friends looking for a place to live. By contrast, two-thirds of West Broadway respondents and three-quarters of those from Commonwealth indicated they definitely would do so. Similarly, only 42 percent of Franklin Field respondents agreed that the development was "a good place for raising kids," whereas 69 percent of respondents from West Broadway and fully 82 percent of respondents from Com-monwealth found favor with the child-rearing environment in those places. This last issue underscores the dramatic transformation at Commonwealth quite nicely. When this same question was raised in the 1979 Commonwealth survey, only 19 percent of respondents then felt it to be a good place for raising kids (Community Planning and Research 1979).

In the end, the notion of "resident satisfaction" is a kind of metacriterion for suc-cess. It is, at least in part, an indirect measure of the successes achieved in the other six dimensions. Yet it also may prove to be a deceptive barometer; even high scores may mean little more than temporary stability in high-pressure lives. Alternatively, for some who care about public housing but who do not live in it, high rates of resident satisfaction may even be seen as a liability, if they mean that tenants will make less effort to leave public housing. Ultimately, the questions may be more about which kinds of people are most satisfied and whether these are the kinds of people who are contributing to community stability. Arguably, the most successful public housing communities will be those where many of those most able to leave will choose not to. Yet this community-centered definition of success is in conflict with a more individual-centered and family-centered model of success that is predicated on the development of education, skills, and sustainable employment as a means to exit from public housing and from other sources of government subsidy. Moreover, a community-centered success criterion directly contradicts any lingering belief that public housing developments should be reserved for exclusive use by the most disadvantaged members of society.

Conclusions: Expanding and Applying the Measures of Success

All of the above suggest that public housing redevelopments can, in the best cases, improve residents' satisfaction with their living environments but that some redevelopment efforts will improve resident satisfaction much more than others. Moreover, even where high levels of satisfaction are achieved, redevelopment may do little to ensure that this satisfaction translates to increased residential or economic mobility.

In the end, the complexity of redevelopment processes and the multiplicity of potential redevelopment goals make these processes all too easy to derail. They can be stymied by cost overruns and implementation impasses, by design miscalculations, by the absence of tenant support, by the inability to manage and maintain the changes, by unchecked crime and violence from surrounding impoverished neighborhoods, and by the inability to propose, implement, and sustain commitments to programs that can improve the socioeconomic prospects of residents. Redevelopment efforts can fall short because of a failure in any one of these seven areas, and a failure in one area exacerbates the problems in all others.

Taken together, the three redevelopment efforts discussed here confirm the promise of well-conceived attempts by well-organized communities to implement well-designed redevelopment plans, but they also highlight the ways that equally well-intentioned plans—especially if they lack a solid base of community support, fall victim to implementation snafus, and take place in extremely disadvantaged neighborhoods—may do little to improve the lives of public housing residents. While there is considerable evidence that the physical redevelopment of Franklin Field itself was problematic, it is clear that many of the major problems at that development are driven by the inability to stem the crime that continues to plague the community and by the inability of the management to cooperate with residents. At the other extreme, when comprehensive physical redevelopment is accompanied by adequate security provisions, careful maintenance, and strict rule enforcement, even the enormously high cost (which in Boston has averaged about $100,000 per unit in today's dollars) seems possible to justify.

A full decade after its redevelopment was completed, Commonwealth seems to have sustained its successes in nearly all dimensions. So too, West Broadway—in spite of the failure to complete the redevelopment, and in spite of the added challenges of the racial integration—receives high marks in many dimensions. Even though these redevelopment efforts were centered chiefly on bricks-and-mortar initiatives and have made only minimal progress as economic development ventures, these design changes seem to have generated a more cooperative climate for future initiatives. Creating safe and attractive apartments, buildings, and community facilities may be seen as a crucial first step in rebuilding communities and may serve as a vital haven for individuals struggling to cope with the debilitating psychological and social effects of persistent poverty. The most disheartening aspect of this study's findings, however, is that there are not *three* redevelopment success stories to report. While it is readily apparent that success does not come cheaply, it is also once again all too clear that money, in itself, does not guarantee success. Just as the BHA planning department had hypothesized in 1979, Commonwealth's redevelopment proved most successful, West Broadway achieved many partial successes, and Franklin Field lagged behind.

At a time when federal funding for public housing is once again under attack, what does it mean that the place that had the most perceived advantages when the redevelopment process began also turned out to be the most successful? If it is indeed possible to predict success, what does this suggest for cases where success in any of the seven measures outlined here seems highly unlikely right from the start? Was it a mistake to make such a large public investment at Franklin Field? Is it good public policy to focus only on the projects seen as having the greatest chance of success?

Clearly, every housing authority contemplating large-scale redevelopment would like to replicate the successes achieved at Commonwealth while avoiding the failures of Franklin Field. The core problem here is that all housing developments are not equally promising sites for redevelopment, and a good redevelopment process can go only so far to guarantee success in the most troublesome cases. For housing authorities with several properties that would qualify as severely distressed by almost anyone's measure, the solution would seem to entail choosing for redevelopment only the most salvageable among the most distressed places, even though that choice means failing to help those residents who need assistance most.

Yet if one does wish to focus scarce dollars on the "least disadvantaged" of highly disadvantaged places, what does that choice imply for the places that are most in decline? The key to an equitable and morally acceptable strategy may be for housing authorities to acknowledge frankly that there are some places where—because of the density of impoverished families housed together in a devastated neighborhood—the problems are beyond repair through any existing redevelopment program. In those places, untransformable even through the unprecedented generosity of the Boston experiments or the federal Urban Revitalization Demonstration program, and unlikely to be able to attract a wider mix of incomes, the best solution may be to re-house residents elsewhere through voucher programs and, as that is accomplished, to demolish the projects.

The cases presented here, when taken together, suggest that this kind of triage should, however, be seen as a last resort. To withhold public housing redevelopment dollars from the most distressed neighborhoods will represent yet another blow to the prospects for reinvestment in such places. The story of Franklin Field, for all its problems—before, during, and after its redevelopment—is not necessarily a tale of woe that was either inevitable or irreversible. Before giving up on places like Franklin Field that seem to be at the margins of salvageability, whether in Boston or else-where, it would seem worth trying more of the techniques that seemed to work so well at Commonwealth.

The redevelopment effort at Franklin Field suffered for reasons that went well beyond the problems of its neighborhood and the poverty of its residents. At the heart of the failure was, and is, a level of animosity between tenants and manage-ment that works against the formation of the kind of partnerships that were the hall-mark of the Commonwealth redevelopment effort. One can only speculate whether use of a first-rate private developer and private management team could bring about Commonwealth-type results at Franklin Field–type places, but such measures seem well worth trying, especially in combination with enhanced efforts to recruit and retain a greater economic mix of residents. If privatization is to proliferate, however, it is important to scrutinize the spirit and structure of the Commonwealth redevel-opment process. The public sector has no monopoly on lousy landlords. Com-monwealth's success entailed a carefully considered and scrupulously monitored process of finding not only an available private-sector alternative but the best pos-sible one from among many to meet a variety of goals and to work in partnership with a variety of constituencies. It is not merely that a public agency devolved its responsibilities onto the private sector; it is that a highly intelligent group of thought-ful and motivated housing authority officials, working with a core group of com-mitted and well-advised tenants, jointly developed a vision for a tenant-monitored system of private development and private management. It is not the act of priv-atization itself but the hundreds of hours that went into reaching consensus on the thousands of details that went into both the *Commonwealth Developer's Kit* and the *Commonwealth Management Plan* that laid the groundwork for Commonwealth's sus-tained successes.

Even in these highly touted national success stories there are, unfortunately, clear limits to the range of issues by which such success is being measured. Part of what is needed—at Commonwealth and West Broadway as well as elsewhere—is a broader based definition of success in public housing redevelopment. Achieving success in each of the seven dimensions set out here is certainly daunting, but progress is necessary on all fronts if redevelopment efforts are ever to have a major impact on the quality of life of most residents. To make progress on all seven fronts—design, implementation, tenant organizing, management, security, socioeconomic development, and resident satisfaction—requires a careful articulation of goals right from the beginning and a system of transoccupancy evaluation for monitoring progress toward those goals.

Notes

1. In 1993 and 1994, more than two dozen public housing authorities, located mostly in the nation's largest cities, were awarded federal grants of up to $50 million through HOPE VI. This money is intended to subsidize up to 500 units of redevelopment in a housing project judged to be "severely distressed," according to criteria established by HUD stemming from the report of the National Commission on Severely Distressed Public Housing (NCSDPH 1992a; see also Vale 1993). Unlike past redevelopment initiatives, in which nearly all funds were committed to the costs of physical redevelopment, HOPE VI urged public housing authorities to use 20 percent of the funds for socioeconomic development initiatives.

2. The others are Steamboat Square Development in Albany, Robert B. Pitts Plaza in San Francisco, and Lake Parc Place in Chicago.

3. Other notable examples of similar redevelopment during the 1980s, not discussed in the commission's book, may be found in Cambridge, MA.

4. The 265 interviews include those conducted with residents at two other BHA developments, Bromley Heath and Orchard Park, which had undergone no such large-scale architectural and urban design intervention. Those places are not discussed here, but they provided the author with a broader context in which to assess the three redevelopment efforts. Bromley Heath is run by the nation's oldest tenant management corporation, and Orchard Park has recently been selected for a HOPE VI grant.

5. The residents interviewed constitute a stratified sample that includes approximately 10 percent of households living at the developments as of 1993. The sample includes 59 household heads from West Broadway, 35 from Franklin Field, and 41 from Commonwealth. While not sampled randomly, those interviewed are likely representative of the developments' adult populations, in terms of race, ethnicity, age, sex of household head, length of residence, location of residence within the development, and degree of participation in tenant association activities. Overall (including the respondents from Orchard Park [n = 54] and Bromley Heath [n = 73]), approximately 18 percent of those interviewed were self-identified as non-Hispanic white, 22 percent as Hispanic, 54 percent as black, and 2 percent as Asian. Twenty-seven percent reported that their major source of income came from salary, while the rest reported a variety of other sources (chiefly, Aid to Families with Dependent Children) or refused to answer. The ages of respondents ranged from 18 to 87, and 85 percent were female. Interviews were conducted in English, Spanish, Vietnamese, and Chinese by a multiracial and multiethnic group of residents trained for this purpose by the author and his assistants. All were semistructured interviews conducted on audiotape, each lasting about an hour. They involved a combination of closed- and open-ended questions. The interviewer was asked to record responses directly on the survey instrument, and the responses were verified and amplified by transcription of the tapes by the author and his assistants. The tenants' organization in each development cooperated in the interview process. The whole process was conducted almost completely independently of the BHA and its on-site management and was supported by grant money from the Massachusetts Institute of Technology. In addition to interviews with residents in 1992–93 and site visits beginning in 1986, interviews were conducted with the key

players in each of the three redevelopment efforts, including managers, community organizers, and staff from the BHA. A full discussion of the methodology employed in this study (especially the use of residents as interviewers) is being prepared for separate publication.

6. The BHA's own point system for assessing these data weighted the categories unevenly, allocating 25 percent of available points to site accessibility, 38 percent to physical design, 25 percent to neighborhood characteristics, and 12 percent to tenant characteristics. Even though this weighting favored Franklin Field (given its relatively high physical design scores and its relatively low tenant characteristics score), Franklin Field ranked last, and Commonwealth ranked at the top.

7. It is worth remembering, however, that all these poverty characteristics are defined within the range of the very poor; Franklin Field garnered a "minus" for its 3 percent rate of working adults, but the comparable figures—considered "average" by BHA standards—were only 14 percent for Commonwealth and 12 percent for West Broadway. Similarly, Commonwealth warranted a minus for its 94 percent rate of female-headed households, as did Franklin Field for its 92 percent rate, whereas West Broadway's 78 percent rate ranked as average— earning it the neutral (0) assessment (BHA 1979b).

8. Commonwealth received $31.6 million for 392 units, Franklin Field received approximately $26 million for 346 units, and West Broadway received about $26.5 million, which was expected to cover only the first phases of the redevelopment, with the full costs estimated to exceed $60 million (Massachusetts Executive Office of Communities and Development 1990). Per-unit total redevelopment costs were in the range of $75,000 to $80,000 (all figures here are in 1983 dollars).

9. In 1979, in an internal document, the BHA assigned all of its developments to four categories: sound, slipping, in danger, or seriously distressed. Commonwealth, Franklin Field, and West Broadway were all included in the last category, along with 10 other family developments (BHA 1979c). For detailed accounts of the devastated conditions at West Broadway and Commonwealth at the end of the 1970s, see Vale (1995, 1996a). These two other articles, as well as Vale 1996b, provide much more comprehensive discussion of the redevelopment efforts at those two places than is possible here.

10. A fourth initiative that gained momentum during the receivership was the largest turnaround effort of all—the $250 million transformation of Boston's notorious Columbia Point project into Harbor Point, a mixed-income, privately developed community. Harbor Point no longer formally serves as public housing, although 400 of its 1,283 units are reserved for low-income families; the rest rent at market rate. Since it involved such irreproducibly complex financing and was located on a uniquely attractive waterfront site, this project was not included in the present study, although it certainly represents a plausible alternative approach to public housing redevelopment.

11. As built, the apartments in these developments fell well below the current HUD minimum square footages for the various bedroom-unit sizes. During redevelopment, BHA planners elected to approximate the more generous "contemporary design standards" used by the Massachusetts Housing Finance Agency for its subsidized mixed-income units. This decision resulted in apartments that may well be larger than the average for market-rate units in the city. In contrast to the strict limitations placed on public housing when it was built, the goal here seems to have been to avoid anything that signaled "minimum standards," in terms of either appearance or amenities. These design specifications, of course, did not necessarily entail the management and community improvements crucial to desirable living environments.

12. Since these efforts, defensible space theory seems to have become even more widely implemented. It is fundamental to city and state guidelines such as those contained in the *Redevelopment Handbook* produced by the Massachusetts Executive Office of Communities and Development (1990). The handbook has been touted by the NCSDPH (1992a, 1992b), is heavily funded through HUD's HOPE VI grants, and was championed by HUD Secretary Henry Cisneros (1995) in a widely distributed booklet. The 1980s Boston redevelopment schemes, then, portended something of a national trend.

13. Most of the ideas used in the BHA redevelopment efforts (and in their counterparts in Cambridge) had been discussed or implemented elsewhere, though chiefly with new construction. Most earlier public housing *redevelopment* stressed the site design aspects of defensible space but fell short of the more radical (and expensive) gutting of buildings that allowed for the substantial elimination of common hallways and the creation of private entrances. For discussion of the benefits and limitations of such design interventions, see Vale (1995, 1996a, 1996b). See also Franck and Mostoller (1995).

14. Part of the problem is also lack of accurate or comprehensive data. In 1992, the NCSDPH noted that HUD provided data for only 3 of the 13 measures of "severe distress" that the commission believed should be quantified and tracked (NCSDPH 1992a; see also Vale 1992, 1993).

15. Under the turnkey process, Commonwealth's emptied buildings were turned over to a private developer, who executed the rehabilitation according to a detailed agreement and then sold the revitalized development back to the BHA. By temporarily removing the development from the public sector, the turnkey process allowed the housing authority to use advantageous construction financing terms available from the Massachusetts Housing Finance Authority and to bypass the expense of the public bidding process and union regulations. Although the BHA had developed more than 2,500 units of housing under the turnkey process between 1970 and 1981, most of this was for scattered-site housing and elderly housing, and Commonwealth was to become the single largest such effort (BHA 1981).

16. The West Broadway Comprehensive Renewal Program, a joint venture of Lane, Frenchman, & Associates, Inc., and Goody, Clancy, & Associates, Inc., won the American Planning Association's citation as "most outstanding project in the nation," a *Progressive Architecture* citation for urban design excellence, and an American Institute of Architects national award for excellence in urban design. Commonwealth—a collaboration of developer John M. Corcoran & Company and architects Tise, Wilhelm, & Associates—was featured in the NCSDPH (1992b) case studies book and received an Urban Design Award from the Boston Society of Architects in 1985, a Governor's Design Award in 1986, a Merit Award for landscaping for multifamily housing from the Boston Society of Landscape Architects in 1987, and the Urban Land Institute's 1989 Award for Excellence in the category of Rehabilitation Development. The Franklin Field redevelopment was a joint venture between Carr, Lynch Associates Inc. and Wallace, Floyd Associates Inc.

17. Tables of development-specific responses to the various issues raised in the interviews are available from the author, and some appear in an earlier version of this chapter (Vale 1994).

18. If one compares the results of the interviews at the three redeveloped sites with the responses from residents at a conspicuously non-redeveloped site—Orchard Park—the contrast is even more striking: Fully 92 percent of Orchard Park respondents said that their project looked like public housing.

19. Of course, since there was no comparable survey that asked this question prior to

redevelopment, it is conceivable that Commonwealth residents felt less stigmatized by their surroundings even before redevelopment, perhaps for reasons of neighborhood rather than architecture. Yet, given that the physical conditions at Commonwealth at its nadir were arguably even worse than those at the other places, it seems logical to credit the redevelopment effort with fostering improvement in residents' perceptions about their environment, especially given the amplifications and explanations offered by residents during the interviews. See Vale (forthcoming) for a longer discussion of whether it is possible to destigmatize public housing.

20. In each redevelopment case, the process for rehousing current residents was a major point of contention. Temporary relocation was necessary, whether on site or off site, but the vast majority of residents were able to return after redevelopment—in many cases to locations close to their original apartments and neighbors. At Commonwealth, for instance, some problem families were weeded out through a one-time offer of a housing voucher, and all families who wished to return had to agree to abide by an expanded set of development rules and to commit to a rent arrears repayment plan. In no case was the restructuring of occupancy as extreme as that practiced in places where a major goal of redevelopment is income mixing.

21. Though it was the BHA's decision to go with private management, it was a decision that tenants wholeheartedly endorsed. Beyond the shift to private management, the tenants also wanted to play a substantial role in management themselves—though they evinced little interest in taking on responsibility for day-to-day operations (Commonwealth Tenants Association Management Committee 1981). Commonwealth's tenants have therefore been able to exert a high degree of control over management without attempting to form a tenant management corporation themselves. As of 1995, though some tenant leaders do discuss the possibility of resident management for Commonwealth in the future as a way of removing the influence of the BHA, even this "tenant management" might well involve continuing to contract for management services from a private company such as Corcoran.

22. The two surveys, conducted in 1979 by Community Planning and Research, Inc., and in 1993 by a team under the author's supervision, asked several questions that were phrased and coded identically and reflect remarkably comparable samples. Both were stratified by race, ethnicity, and sex and accurately reflected the breakdown of those living at the development at the time; both used adult respondents with a broad range of ages and length of residency in the development. The 1979 sample contained 80 respondents, representing about 30 percent of the households then living on-site, whereas the 1993 sample contained 41 respondents, comprising about 11 percent of households.

23. As further testimony to the quality of Corcoran's maintenance record at Commonwealth, it is worth noting that Commonwealth is three years older than Franklin Field and, since its redevelopment effort was completed first, might be expected to be the most likely to show signs of decline, rather than the least. Also, unlike those of West Broadway and Franklin Field, many of Commonwealth's buildings have elevators, often a major maintenance problem in public housing.

24. Residents' interpretations of the terms "safe" and "unsafe" may well vary considerably, of course, with residents having different expectations for their own security.

25. The demographic breakdown of respondents from the old and new parts is similar in terms of race, ethnicity, age, and length of residence at the development, and sections of both the new part and the old part face a busy street with a number of bars, reported as a source of much of the trouble.

26. At Commonwealth, where management practices are already strict, many respondents wished that the management company could have more leeway in screening out undesirable new tenants.

27. The principal socioeconomic policy initiative of the Boston redevelopment efforts is of a different nature and involves the desegregation of public housing in South Boston. At West Broadway, one of the three South Boston public housing developments, the population had become nearly all white by the late 1970s, and the redevelopment effort of the 1980s was quickly followed by a far-reaching effort at racial and ethnic integration. In the first five years after the redeveloped site was opened to new residents, the occupancy pattern shifted to 40 percent nonwhite. Despite periodic press reports attesting to numerous acts of racially and ethnically motivated violence, two-thirds of respondents from West Broadway said that they had not experienced such problems while living in the development. While this may still imply a high degree of racial friction, it pales beside the wholesale intolerance that shattered the first attempts to integrate the development, between 1965 and 1975.

28. This level of dissatisfaction is far higher than that reported even at the two nonredeveloped places where interviews were also conducted.

References

Bauman, John F. 1994. Public Housing: The Dreadful Saga of a Durable Policy. *Journal of Planning Literature* 8(4):347–61.

Boston Housing Authority. 1979a. *State of the Development Report.* October. Boston.

Boston Housing Authority. 1979b. *Site Selection Criteria for Substantial Rehabilitation.* December. Boston: Planning Department.

Boston Housing Authority. 1979c. *Occupancy Analysis by Development Classification.* Boston.

Boston Housing Authority. 1981. *Commonwealth Developer's Kit.* Boston.

Boston Housing Authority. 1993a. *State of the Development Report.* Boston.

Boston Housing Authority. 1993b. *Tenant Demographics Report.* April. Boston.

Boston Police Department. 1994. *Reported Crimes in Boston Housing Authority Developments.* Boston.

Braverman, Jane. 1989. Tenant Group Losing Funds. *Allston Brighton Citizen Item,* June 15.

Carr, Lynch Associates Inc. and Wallace, Floyd Associates Inc. 1982. *Franklin Field Redevelopment: Design Report.* February 22. Cambridge, MA.

Chandler, Mittie. 1991. What Have We Learned from Public Housing Resident Management? *Journal of Planning Literature* 6:136–43.

Chermayeff, Serge, and Christopher Alexander. 1965. *Community and Privacy.* Garden City, NY: Anchor Books.

Cisneros, Henry. 1995. Defensible Space: Deterring Crime and Building Community. Washington, DC: U.S. Department of Housing and Urban Development.

Cohen, Bernard. 1981. Is Harry Spence God? Or Is He Just Damn Good? *Boston Magazine,* December.

Coleman, Alice. 1985. *Utopia on Trial: Vision and Reality in Planned Housing.* London: Hilary Shipman.

Commonwealth Tenants Association, Boston Housing Authority, and Corcoran Management Company. 1983. *Commonwealth Management Plan: Memorandum of Understanding.* Boston.

Commonwealth Tenants Association Management Committee. 1981. Memo to Robert Pickette et al., John M. Corcoran Company, and Sandy Henriquez et al., BHA, on "Preliminary Management Recommendations for Fidelis Way." October 7.

Community Planning and Research, Inc. 1979. *The Commonwealth Report: Proposals for Capital Improvements, Management Reorganization and Expansion of Resident Services and Opportunities.* Boston.

Cooper, Clare. 1975. *Easter Hill Village: Some Social Implications of Design.* New York: Free Press.

Epp, Gayle. 1994. Interview by author. April. Boston.

Francescato, Guido, Sue Weidemann, James R. Anderson, and Richard Chenoweth. 1979. *Residents' Satisfaction in HUD-Assisted Housing: Design and Management Factors.* Washington, DC: U.S. Government Printing Office.

Franck, Karen A., and Michael Mostoller. 1995. From Courts to Open Space to Streets: Changes in the Site Design of U.S. Public Housing. *Journal of Architectural and Planning Research* 12(3):186–220.

Garrity, Paul. 1979. Findings of the Massachusetts Superior Court, with Memorandum of Recorded Observations at the Commonwealth Development during the View on April 11, 1979, and Memorandum of Recorded Observations at the Orient Heights, D Street, and Mission Hill Main Developments during the View on April 19, 1979, Perez Case. July 25. *Armando Perez v. Boston Housing Authority.* Boston Housing Authority Archives, Massachusetts State Archives, Boston.

Gilmore, David C. (planner and project manager of Franklin Field Redevelopment, 1982–1984, Boston Housing Authority). 1994. Interview by author. February. Boston.

Jacobs, Jane. 1961. *The Death and Life of Great American Cities.* New York: Vintage.

Jones, Ronald, David Kaminsky, and Michael Roanhouse. 1979. *Problems Affecting Low Rent Public Housing Projects: A Field Study.* Washington, DC: U.S. Department of Housing and Urban Development.

Kahn, Ric. 1993. Brighton Tenants Fear the Bad Old Days. *Boston Globe,* October 10.

Kell, Amy. 1978. *General Management Innovations Developed under the Target Projects Program.* Washington, DC: National Association of Housing and Redevelopment Officials.

Kell, Amy. 1979. *Maintenance, Management, and Administrative Systems under the Target Projects Program.* Washington, DC: National Association of Housing and Redevelopment Officials.

Keyes, Langley C. 1992. *Strategies and Saints: Fighting Drugs in Subsidized Housing.* Washington, DC: The Urban Institute Press.

Kolodny, Robert. 1979. *Exploring New Strategies for Improving Public Housing Management.* Washington, DC: U.S. Department of Housing and Urban Development.

Lane, Frenchman, & Associates, Inc., and Goody, Clancy, & Associates, Inc. 1981. *West Broadway Comprehensive Renewal Program: Master Plan.* October 30. Boston.

Lovinger, Robert. 1981. Can Harry Spence Fix Public Housing? *Boston Globe Magazine,* August 23.

Massachusetts Executive Office of Communities and Development. 1990. *Redevelopment Handbook: Procedures and Guidelines for Redeveloping Public Housing.* Boston.

National Commission on Severely Distressed Public Housing. 1992a. *Final Report.* Washington, DC: U.S. Government Printing Office.

National Commission on Severely Distressed Public Housing. 1992b. *Case Studies and Site Examination Reports.* Washington, DC: U.S. Government Printing Office.

Newman, Oscar. 1972. *Defensible Space*. New York: Macmillan.

Newman, Oscar. 1980. *Community of Interest*. Garden City, NY: Anchor Press.

Peterman, William. 1993. Resident Management and Other Approaches to Tenant Control of Public Housing. In *Ownership, Control, and the Future of Housing Policy*, ed. R. Allen Hays. Westport, CT: Greenwood.

Pynoos, Jon. 1986. *Breaking the Rules: Bureaucracy and Reform in Public Housing*. New York: Plenum.

Rohe, William M., and Michael A. Stegman. 1992. Public Housing Homeownership: Will It Work and for Whom? *Journal of the American Planning Association* 58(2):144–57.

Rosenbaum, James E. 1991. Black Pioneers: Do Their Moves to the Suburbs Increase Economic Opportunity for Mothers and Children? *Housing Policy Debate* 2(4):1179–213.

Sadacca, Robert, et al. 1974. *Management Performance in Public Housing*. Washington, DC: The Urban Institute.

Schill, Michael H. 1993. Distressed Public Housing: Where Do We Go from Here? *University of Chicago Law Review* 60:497–554.

Schneiderman, Eric T. 1982. *Armando Perez v. Boston Housing Authority: A Case Study in Institutional Reform Legislation*. Cambridge, MA: Harvard Law School.

Shlay, Anne B. 1993. Family Self-Sufficiency and Housing. *Housing Policy Debate* 4(3):457–95.

Spence, Lewis H. 1993. Rethinking the Social Role of Public Housing. *Housing Policy Debate* 4(3):355–68.

Vale, Lawrence J. 1992. *Occupancy Issues in Distressed Public Housing: An Outline of Impacts on Design, Management, and Service Delivery*. Washington, DC: National Commission on Severely Distressed Public Housing.

Vale, Lawrence J. 1993. Beyond the Problem Projects Paradigm: Defining and Revitalizing "Severely Distressed" Public Housing. *Housing Policy Debate* 4(2):147–74.

Vale, Lawrence J. 1994. Seven Kinds of Success: Assessing Public Housing Comprehensive Redevelopment Efforts in Boston. In *Future Visions of Urban Public Housing: Proceedings of an International Forum*, ed. Wolfgang F. E. Preiser, David P. Varady, and Francis P. Russell, 327–40. Cincinnati.

Vale, Lawrence J. 1995. Transforming Public Housing: The Social and Physical Redevelopment of Boston's West Broadway Development. *Journal of Architectural and Planning Research* 12(3):278–318.

Vale, Lawrence J. 1996a. The Revitalization of Boston's Commonwealth Public Housing Development. In *Affordable Housing and Urban Development in the United States*, ed. Willem vanVliet, 100–34. Newbury Park, CA: Sage.

Vale, Lawrence J. 1996b. Destigmatizing Public Housing. In *Geography and Identity: Living and Exploring the Geopolitics of Identity*, ed. Dennis Crow. Washington, DC: Institute for Advanced Cultural Studies/Maisonneuve Press.

Walsh & Associates. 1979. *Refinancing and Marketing the Fidelis Way Housing Project*. Boston.

Whittlesey, Robert B. 1976. *Report of the Master in the Case of Perez v. Boston Housing Authority*. CA 03096. Boston.

PART V

Future Directions

RICHARD BEST

9 Successes, Failures, and Prospects for Public Housing Policy in the United Kingdom

Introduction

This chapter gives an overview of some of the main housing policy developments in the United Kingdom since the advent of the first Thatcher government in 1979. It does not present a detailed and comprehensive picture, but rather draws out some of the main themes, looks at their successes and failures, comments on the evolution of policies during the intervening years, and examines the common elements in the prospects for policy development that are likely to find expression regardless of the outcome of the next U.K. general election.

While the main focus is on policies related to public housing, the development of those policies in the United Kingdom can best be understood in the context of policies relating to both homeownership and private rented housing. The single most important feature of U.K. housing policy over the past 15 years has without doubt been the overwhelming priority given to the promotion of homeownership throughout the 1980s, and the subsequent retreat from that policy in favor of policies seeking to reverse the century-long decline of the private rented sector in the United Kingdom.

Public housing was viewed by government in the 1980s as a residual sector for households unable to enter homeownership despite a panoply of schemes designed to aid that process. In contrast, current housing policy debate is more concerned about the balance of the roles between a diversified public sector charging submarket rents and a private sector charging market rents.

Reprinted from *Housing Policy Debate* 7, 3 (Washington, D.C.: Fannie Mae Foundation, 1996). This copyrighted material is used with the permission of the Fannie Mae Foundation.

Definitions and Numbers

The terminology and institutions that predominate in the U.K. housing market are markedly different from those in the United States, and this section gives a short introductory guide to U.K. definitions for readers unfamiliar with the basic structure of the U.K. housing market.

Although this chapter discusses developments in the United Kingdom as a whole, in some cases it focuses on the particular developments in England (which accounts for five-sixths of U.K. households). The legal framework and housing policies are generally similar in England and Wales, but there are some significant differences in housing law and policy in Northern Ireland and Scotland. This chapter indicates only the main differences in housing law and policy between the main "territories" of the United Kingdom.[1]

In the United Kingdom, "public housing" is usually defined as accommodations owned and managed by public—that is, governmental—bodies. Until the 1980s, the principal providers during this century had been the municipalities—the 400 or so democratically elected local authorities. The other substantial suppliers of public housing were the New Town Corporations, although those bodies have now passed the ownership of their properties to local authorities (or, in a few cases, to other non-profit organizations).

In contrast to most developed countries (outside of Eastern Europe), public housing in the United Kingdom has dominated the rented sector since World War II. Public housing reached a peak at 32 percent of the nation's homes during the late 1970s.

"Social housing" is a term used throughout the member countries of the European Union to refer not just to public housing but to other accommodation subsidized by public sources. In the United Kingdom, social housing can embrace public housing (often called "council housing") and also the homes of housing associations. Housing associations are not-for-profit private corporations, many of which are also registered charities, and are similar to community development corporations in the United States.

Housing owned by housing associations, however, was relatively insignificant in comparison with public housing until recent years. Housing associations have been increasing their share of the national stock, but in 1994 local authorities still held almost five times as many properties as housing associations (see figure 9.1).

In the United States, "public housing" is distinguished from "publicly subsidized housing," properties owned by private landlords but subject to a subsidy (a rent certificate or voucher or below-market-rate loan) for a number of years. The U.K. private rented sector—in which about a third of the stock is still subject to rent control—contains many households that receive rent allowances to help them pay their rents, but these homes are not typically described as "publicly subsidized" in the United Kingdom or in other European countries.

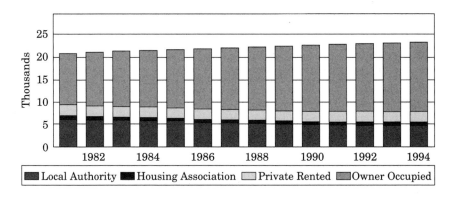

FIGURE 9.1
Dwellings by tenure in Great Britain

Note: Figures refer to December of each year. Local authority includes New Towns.
Source: Housing and Construction Statistics, Department of the Environment.

The private rented sector in the United Kingdom is about the smallest in any developed country, at around 10 percent of the stock. It declined rapidly throughout the century, having comprised some 90 percent of the stock in 1914, under the combined impact of slum clearance programs, rent controls, and unfavorable tax regimes for renting relative to house purchase (Greve 1965).

A recent attempt to attract individuals to invest in renting through private companies, by giving them tax breaks coupled with wider measures to remove rent controls and restrict security of tenure, proved quite successful over the six years ending in 1993–94. But this experiment—although it provided 80,000 extra homes for rent—was not targeted at those with low incomes. The tax concessions covered nearly 40 percent of the cost to the landlord company (averaging more than £18,000 per letting), but rents were at market levels and the renting arrangements were required to remain in place for only five years (Crook, Hughes, and Kemp 1995).

Nor did the scheme prove to be targeted effectively to "entrepreneurial" private landlords; almost half of the lettings under the scheme were made either by housing associations or by university companies set up to provide student accommodation. The scheme has now been discontinued. Over the past two years, the tax advantages of homeownership have been reduced, and it is currently proposed to establish "housing investment trusts," with rather more modest tax breaks, in an attempt to maintain the limited resurgence of private renting that has occurred since 1989.

Policy Change for Public Housing

During the Thatcher years of the 1980s, public housing declined dramatically in importance for British housing. Today it accounts for almost 30 percent fewer homes than at the beginning of the 1980s. This phenomenon followed from central government decisions based on an inherent dislike of public-sector provision and a desire to "roll back the frontiers of the state." There has been an era of conflict between local authorities—where councils have frequently been controlled by the Labour Party or the Liberal Democrat Party—and central government. This conflict has inclined the central government to use its statutory and financial powers to limit the role of the local authority (Bloch and John 1991; Young and Davies 1993).

On the housing side, local authorities were deemed to have failed to supply high-quality homes, a view endorsed by the public at large with respect to the substantial estates of high-rise blocks and unpopular system-built estates constructed in concrete in most major cities in the 1960s and 1970s, some of which were demolished within twenty years of building. Those estates were not, however, typical. At the end of 1977, only 30 percent of council housing comprised flats rather than houses, and less than one-fifth of those were high-rise flats (Department of the Environment 1979).

If that stereotypical image of council housing was far from accurate, it was also the case that existing and emerging problems of social polarization and physical deterioration affected a wider range of council estates, including peripheral estates of terraced and semidetached houses. While estate design and restructuring can reduce crime and improve security, the relationship between social and housing management problems and the built form is far more complex than some architecturally led theorists have wished to believe (Coleman 1985).

The Conservative governments since 1979 have favored the expansion of owner occupation on social and political grounds, believing, as American politicians have also, in a "property-owning democracy." Insofar as subsidized rented housing was a necessity, these administrations favored providing it through the more pluralist housing association sector rather than through the local councils, which were seen as monopoly suppliers in most localities (Rao 1990).

Right-to-buy Sales

The sudden decline of public housing was achieved principally by giving the council tenants the opportunity to acquire their homes, as a statutory right after two years of occupation, at substantial discounts (up to 60 percent off the market value for houses and up to 70 percent for apartments). This has led to the loss from the public sector of 1.5 million homes in Great Britain (table 9.1), out of a total of 6.4 million in 1981.

TABLE 9.1

Right-to-Buy Sales in Great Britain

	1980	1981	1982	1983	1984	1985	1986	1987	1988	1989	1990	1991	1992	1993	1994	Cumu-lative Total
Local authorities	568	79,430	196,430	138,511	100,149	92,230	89,251	103,309	160,569	181,370	126,214	73,365	63,986	60,274	64,332	1,529,988
New towns	227	2,427	3,963	3,638	2,655	2,113	1,656	2,277	3,275	4,608	2,522	1,501	1,182	1,192	1,417	34,653
Housing associations	1,417	2,476	3,936	5,059	4,409	3,985	4,949	5,462	10,221	10,242	6,757	4,259	3,199	2,921	3,201	72,493
Total	2,212	84,333	204,329	147,208	107,213	98,328	95,856	111,048	174,065	196,220	135,493	79,125	68,367	64,387	68,950	1,637,134

Source: Housing and Construction Statistics, Department of the Environment.

The effects of this substantial shift in tenure have been mixed. First, it has given many households the opportunity for a successful transfer into owner occupation on extremely favorable terms. Some of the new owners have taken a special pride in their homes, often borrowing additional money to make improvements.

Second, it has led to a mix of tenure on most council estates, thus retaining people within these communities who might otherwise have moved out to gain the advantages of owner occupation elsewhere. In terms of creating mix and balance within such estates and helping develop leadership skills in people who have a direct interest in the quality of the estate, the outcome appears to be generally positive. However, the level of sales has inevitably been much higher on the most popular estates, where these skills are more plentiful; few sales have taken place in the least desirable estates, particularly those that comprise only apartments, not houses. As a result, the social impact of sales has been mixed (Kerr 1988).

Third, some of the people who purchased, even on these favorable terms, have experienced problems of arrears, possession by the lenders, and homelessness. Economic recession, coupled with a severe slump in the property market at the end of the 1980s, left some purchasers who could not keep up their repayments also unable to find buyers for their properties. During the recessionary years, which followed a house price boom in the late 1980s, the incidence of mortgage arrears rose dramatically, and repossessions increased threefold between 1986 and 1991.

The position has now eased, but some thousand households are still losing their homes each week as a result of lenders' taking possession of properties. Right-to-buy purchasers represented 10 percent of homeowner households in 1991, and survey evidence suggests that, despite their substantially discounted purchase prices, they have been slightly more than proportionately represented among those with arrears. Some 30,000 right-to-buy purchasers had their properties repossessed during the 1989–94 period (Ford, Kempson, and Wilson 1995; Ford and Wilcox 1992) (see figure 9.2).

Fourth, for some, purchase has brought unexpected financial commitments. Individual apartments within larger blocks of rented housing are sold on 125-year leases, with councils retaining the overall ownership of the block (the "freehold"), and consequently control over the upkeep of the structure of the building. Where blocks were found to be in need of substantial repairs, the new apartment owners have faced huge bills for their share of the building works. More generally, some new homeowners have found themselves unable to cope with the cost of maintaining their properties.

Fifth, and probably most important, right-to-buy sales have diminished the pool of homes for rent. In particular, family-sized houses have been removed from the rented sector and are not available to those on the waiting lists of local authorities. The properties still exist, of course, so the shift does not contribute to overall shortage, but it means that opportunities are narrowed for those seeking rented homes. Also, house builders know that first-time buyers can now look to a new market of

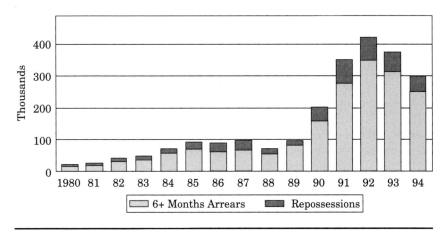

FIGURE 9.2
Mortgage arrears and repossessions

Source: Adapted from Council of Mortgage Lenders.

secondhand ex-council houses, rather than buying new homes. If the homes had been replaced by the provision of a balancing supply of additional rented housing, the whole exercise would have had far fewer critics.

Sixth, a spinoff from right-to-buy sales has been the repayment of debt by local authorities; the central government requires that three-quarters of the receipts that councils obtain from selling the property be used to repay outstanding loans on the council housing stock, thereby reducing the national debt. Altogether, receipts from council house sales have provided windfall gains to the Exchequer exceeding £30 billion. However, the downside has been the disposal of these publicly owned assets at only around half their open-market value, implying a transfer of value to the rather better-off council tenants and, thereby, a reduction in the resources (stock or capital) available for less affluent tenants in the future.

Transfers of Ownership of Public Housing

The Housing Act of 1988 gave all the tenants of local authorities the power, collectively, to exercise "Tenants' Choice" to select a new landlord who would be entitled to take over the ownership of their estate. The government expected housing associations to be the main contenders for the job of managing the stock of public housing. However, almost no tenants have taken up this opportunity. Even where the local authority was apparently acting as an incompetent landlord, and local housing associations appeared to offer a reputable alternative, tenants decided against exercising their new rights. Local surveys of tenants found that they had a firm attachment to the security and traditions of council housing, even when they were critical of the council's insensitivity and inefficiency as a landlord. In only two minor—and somewhat unusual—cases have any estates changed hands through this measure. The government now proposes to abolish the Tenants' Choice arrangements (through the Housing Bill 1996) (Institute of Housing 1990).

Instead, local authorities in some areas—mostly where local politics have coincided with the ideas of the Conservative central government—have decided voluntarily to pass over the ownership of their housing stock to a new enterprise created for the purpose. With only a few exceptions to date, the new enterprise has been in the form of a housing association.

This method—the large-scale voluntary transfer (LSVT)—has been subject to the agreement of tenants; in many cases, tenants have voted for the new arrangement. In contrast to the position of the Tenants' Choice scheme—where tenants might be fighting against their council for control of their homes—the LSVT model has been initiated by the local authority itself and has been carried out with its full backing. The government has learned that the way to secure a change of ownership is not by trying to pit the tenants against their landlords, but by encouraging the landlords to take the step themselves.

Local authorities have strong financial incentives to make this change. Once their properties have shifted into the hands of such an arm's-length separate organization—on which elected councillors can continue to exert some influence (but not control)—it becomes possible for the new body to raise funds in the private market and spend more on improving the condition of the housing stock. In accounting terms, the new landlords are private not-for-profit corporations with a minority public-sector influence, and conventional loan finance is raised on the strength of future rent streams and the underlying security of the housing stock.

Many estates are in serious disrepair through a lack of investment (often attributed to government spending restrictions). For England as a whole, it has been estimated that roughly £20 billion would be required to undertake a comprehensive program of repairs and improvements to bring all council housing estates to current standards. That such public funds will become available is highly unlikely (Hawksworth and Wilcox 1995).

However, if the housing is transferred into the hands of the newly created organization—usually constituted as a housing association—it breaks free of the constraints on public borrowing. Government also gains, since henceforth the new organization's investment in old or new housing stock does not count toward the public-sector borrowing requirement (the key U.K. government budget deficit measure), which government is constantly striving to reduce. Moreover, if a surplus is created from the sale proceeds, both the authority and—through repayment of debt—the central government can gain.

Until April 1995, fewer than 180,000 homes in England had been transferred out of the public sector and into new ownership in this way (Wilcox 1995, table 60). Tightening constraints on public spending will coerce more local authorities to consider this option. The arrangements for such a transfer can have beneficial side effects: The transfer can be to two or more organizations, thereby creating competition within the same area between new managers striving to provide the best service.

Diversification in the ownership of rented housing in big cities has brought with it the opportunity for tenants to become more involved in the management of their housing. Indeed, the statutory requirement that tenants must be consulted and balloted prior to a transfer of stock has typically resulted in the presence of a number of tenant representatives on the managing bodies of the newly created housing associations (Mullins, Niner, and Riseborough 1995).

Between 1988 and March 1995, forty local authorities in England undertook LSVT. However, councils there have made no large-scale stock transfers in Wales and only one in Scotland, where the financial arrangements for council housing are markedly different. An alternative approach in Scotland has been the transfer of a number of individual council estates into the ownership of tenant cooperatives.

The government has now accepted that local authority councillors can play a more significant (but still not controlling) role than has been so far permitted within the newly created landlord bodies, and it can be expected that transfers to newly formed housing associations, or local housing companies, will accelerate in the years ahead (Wilcox et al. 1993).

More Emphasis on Resident Involvement in Management Decisions

Tenant participation has been a muted theme in public housing for more than two decades. The late 1960s slogan "Power to the People" did not mean much in the housing world, but advocates of community development stressed the need for bottom-up decision making. Over the past decade, however, even as public funding has declined, government policies have favored greater resident involvement in management. For example, Department of the Environment funding for estate improvements, under the Estate Action program, has been conditional on greater tenant involvement.

During John Major's premiership, policies have been linked to the Citizen's Charter, the quasi-contractual relationship between the individual and the providers of public (and private) services. The charter is sometimes seen as an antidote to the overweening power of local or central government bureaucracies. Such measures raise consumers' expectation that the service providers have clear responsibilities toward them.

A variety of approaches to encouraging tenant involvement have been tested in the public housing sector, and a number of models are outlined below. While some of the models are well established, others are more recent innovations, at least in the United Kingdom.

The different approaches range from a higher level of informal tenant consultation—usually following devolution of management to local offices—to the creation of various forms of Tenant Management Organizations (TMOs) that enable tenants—while not becoming actual owners—to run their own affairs collectively, to a greater or lesser extent.

Community development trusts are bodies that are set up outside the structures of housing management but that seek to influence it regularly. They are managed by elected members from the community, and their activities are likely to stretch beyond participation in the consultative processes of estate management to campaigning for amenities and organizing community activities (Gibson and Todd 1993).

Participation of residents' associations has greatly increased in recent years, to the point that the whole estate decision-making process is directly affected. Access to good-quality, independent advice has often been crucial in unlocking the residents' initiative. A Technical Aid Network supplied consultants whose job was to empower residents. It is becoming more common for residents to be closely involved in the design of estate improvements—preparing design briefs independently of the landlord, meeting directly with the project architect, and monitoring outcomes. Design can capture the imagination of a group and prove a good route to wider involvement in local management (Watson 1994).

Some housing authorities use estate agreements as contracts without legal sanctions, to formalize the arrangements for delivering services. These agreements can cover repair times, appeal mechanisms, consolidation duties, and so forth. Sometimes, more ambitiously, an agreement can embrace other agencies handling social services such as education or policing. Interagency collaboration, with a need for coordination across a range of governmental activities, can be hard to formalize. Nonetheless, it represents an important next stage and a successful involvement of residents in managing their estates (Zipfel 1994).

Estate Management Boards involve both the tenants' representatives (usually drawn from elected residents' associations) and the municipal authorities' officials. The housing authorities' delegates to these boards make decisions on management and maintenance matters, sometimes with substantial budgets.

Residents' Democracy is a fairly recent model imported from Denmark. Key to this model is formation of a residents' board that meets regularly with a local manager and has formal input from residents. The estate budget is developed by agreement between the board and the manager, but the landlord retains full responsibility for service delivery (Aldbourne Associates 1994).

This landlord responsibility distinguishes the Residents' Democracy model from tenant management cooperatives, in which tenants collectively take over direct control and responsibility for day-to-day management and repairs on their estates. However, the landlord generally retains responsibility for the upkeep of the basic structure of the buildings and for major repairs (Power 1988).

Weaving all these strands together, it can be seen that public housing in the United

Kingdom is gradually evolving toward a model in which tenants are at the center. In some localities, the process is far more advanced than in others. But everywhere the tenor of management is changing from treating tenants as passive recipients of the housing authority's munificence to considering them as customers or as partners in the enterprise.

These attitudinal changes have been reinforced by the 1993 introduction of a legal "right to manage" for those council estates with properly constituted TMOs. These can take the form of either Estate Management Boards or tenant management cooperatives in their constitutional makeup, but they are more like the cooperatives in that they assume the direct responsibility for day-to-day management and repairs (Newell 1994).

In the long run, these changes, which involve a shift in the balance of power toward tenants, may prove to be as important as any other alteration in public housing in the late twentieth century.

A Switch from "Bricks-and-Mortar Subsidies" to "Personal Subsidies"

In the past, general subsidies to public housing producers have ensured relatively low rents (probably half the market levels). This situation has led to accusations that many of those housed have been subsidized unnecessarily—they could afford to pay more.[2]

Over recent years, the subsidy arrangements have been transformed. Local authorities have been pressured to increase rents well in excess of inflation on the basis that the U.K. Housing Benefit scheme would enable lower-income tenants to meet the cost of higher rents. For tenants with very low incomes, at or below the level of the basic state assistance provided by the Income Support scheme, Housing Benefit generally meets the full rent. For tenants with slightly higher incomes, the level of Housing Benefit is progressively reduced.

Now instead of central government providing general subsidies, the policy shift toward higher rents has led many local authorities in England and Wales (with the benefit of low historical capital costs) to move from deficit to surplus. These surpluses are artificially generated, however, in the sense that constraints on local authority borrowing have made it impossible for councils to spend more on rectifying deficiencies in the current stock; they have been compelled to generate surplus income from rents, which they are then obliged to use to reduce the cost to the central government of providing Housing Benefit to poorer tenants. In 1995–96, for example, council rent surpluses will meet almost a quarter of the total costs of Housing Benefit for council tenants in England and Wales. Between 1980–81 and 1995–96, general subsidies to council housing in Great Britain fell from £4.8 billion to a net figure of £–0.3 billion (at 1995 prices).

In Britain, no allowance is made for housing costs in basic social security payments. This policy means that persons who depend on the government for their weekly income—pensioners who receive only the state pension, single mothers with no other income, unemployed households, people with disabilities who are unable to work—can all receive Housing Benefit to cover their rent in full, in addition to their basic social security payments (whether in the form of Income Support, Unemployment, or Incapacity Benefit).

As rents rise in real terms, the burden of these "targeted" Housing Benefit payments—coinciding with a rise in the number of unemployed—generates public expenditure almost equivalent to the savings from cutbacks in the general subsidies to producers. Between 1980–81 and 1995–96, for example, the gross cost of Housing Benefit to council tenants rose from £1.9 billion to £5.5 billion (at 1995 prices). It has been a matter, therefore, of passing the parcel between government departments and programs, but without significant savings (Wilcox 1995).[3]

Meanwhile, the other housing subsidy not targeted—the tax relief on mortgage repayments for homeowners—is also being cut back. This subsidy proved costly and inefficient. With the departure of Margaret Thatcher, the great champion of subsidy for homeownership, mortgage interest tax relief (MITR) has been eroded by lowering the rate of relief for eligible mortgage interest costs against tax, from a maximum of 40 percent in 1990–91 to just 15 percent in 1995–96.

In part, these reductions were made possible by the fall in average mortgage interest rates from 15.0 percent in 1990 to just 7.7 percent in 1994, so that average net mortgage payments fell substantially despite the cutbacks in MITR. The government's resolve to press ahead with the MITR cuts has been reinforced by its commitment to low inflation as a cornerstone of economic strategy and by a recognition of the dangers to that strategy posed by the instability of house price cycles.

In real terms, the cost of MITR has fallen rapidly, and dramatically, from its peak of £9.2 billion in 1990–91 to just £2.7 billion in 1995–96 (all figures at 1995 prices) (see figure 9.3). But that fall resulted as much from the reductions in prevailing interest rates as from the policy cutbacks in MITR rates.

Housing associations have faced a similar transition in financial support. Since they are not public bodies, the government cannot control them directly. Nevertheless, when the government cuts housing association grants, these organizations are obliged to raise rents (from levels that were already higher than council rents). The high-rent, high-benefit-dependence regime affected the housing associations much as it affected local authorities, even though these not-for-profit organizations are generally loath to impose financial burdens on their tenants.

Some shift in subsidies from providers to users had been advocated by the Inquiry into British Housing chaired by the Duke of Edinburgh, which reported in the mid-1980s (National Federation of Housing Associations 1985). However, when this same Inquiry produced a second report in the early 1990s, it raised anxieties about the extent to which this policy had been pursued and pointed out the disadvantages of taking this switch too far (Joseph Rowntree Foundation 1991).

It has now become apparent that this policy can have adverse effects. First, to

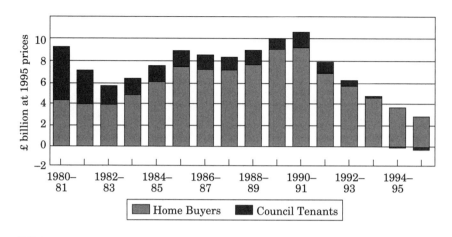

FIGURE 9.3
Phasing out general subsidies

Note: All figures refer to Great Britain.
Source: Wilcox (1995). Courtesy Joseph Rowntree Foundation.

operate a system of means-tested subsidies for millions of individuals, rather than a formula-based subsidy system for hundreds of landlords, is administratively more expensive and more bureaucratic—as well as more likely to cause delays and mistakes.

Second, subjecting those in low-paid employment to a means-tested benefit—which is withdrawn as income rises—is the equivalent of taxing earnings at a prohibitive level (see figure 9.4). The bus driver, post office worker, or bricklayer may now require Housing Benefit to afford a rented home, but once the benefit is accepted, the individual will lose up to 97 pence from every £1 earned when the benefit is withdrawn after payment of income tax and national insurance contributions.

Higher rents have extended the income range over which such work disincentives operate, although there have also been some limited measures to ameliorate those problems, particularly with respect to child care costs, introduced in the last few years. More fundamental benefit reforms to ease work disincentives are held back by the lack of hard evidence on their behavioral impact and by concerns about public expenditure (Wilcox 1994).

Third, higher rents make public housing a less attractive option for households who can afford equivalent accommodation outside the sector. This situation leads to a flight of those who are employed, intensifying the poverty on council estates and accelerating the marginalization or "residualization" of council housing, particularly on estates that have not attracted significant levels of right-to-buy sales.[4]

Fourth, there are wider implications for public spending. Because the rents are

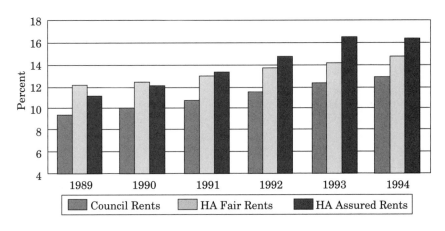

FIGURE 9.4
Rents rise as a percentage of average manual male earnings

Note: HA = housing association.
Source: Wilcox (1995). Courtesy Joseph Rowntree Foundation.

met for so many households through Housing Benefit, the cost of switching subsidies does not present much of a saving to the government. But because rents are part of the calculation for the Retail Price Index, upon which various wage claims, social security payments, and index-linked pensions are based, higher rents increase costs to employers and to the government well beyond any savings (Meen 1994).

There is now a general view that the policy of targeting subsidies to individuals, rather than paying similar amounts to housing providers, has run its course in the United Kingdom. The policy is now having negative effects on individual households and the national economy. Indeed, in the 1995 budget, government ended the upward movement in council rents and took measures to restrain housing association rents (Best 1994a).

Increased Support for Housing Associations

For the decades up to the middle of the 1970s, public housing through local authorities was the dominant method of providing affordable homes. At its peak, in 1964, council house building reached 200,000 homes in a single year. Housing associations had built only 50,000 homes over the previous twenty years.[5]

Following the Housing Act of 1974, the then Labour government greatly increased the role of housing associations. Associations were to be found, operating on a small scale, in many areas, and the oldest of these organizations were charitable trusts that dated back several hundred years. They saw their work program magnified by substantial injections of public money in the 1970s, to the point that they were obtaining approvals for up to 50,000 homes in a single year by the end of the decade.

With the Conservative administration's arrival in 1979, the production line of local authorities was fairly swiftly phased out: Their program of house building fell from 65,000 homes in 1979 to just a handful by 1994. Meanwhile, the housing associations, while not experiencing a corresponding growth, nevertheless saw their work program broadly maintained and then increased in the early 1990s (see figure 9.5).

With funding through the Housing Corporation (and equivalent bodies in Scotland and Wales), associations were encouraged to meet the needs of homeless families, elderly people, and people with a range of special needs. They also undertook a low-cost homeownership program based on the "shared ownership" model, in which occupiers purchase a share in the ownership of their home and pay rent for the remaining share.

This growth, however, was obtained at a price. First, to get more homes for the available public money, levels of grants to housing associations for each new scheme were cut back. This meant associations had to borrow more money to undertake each development, which led to the higher rents shown in figure 9.4. More than 80 percent of new housing association tenants now rely on Housing Benefit to pay their rent (Housing Corporation 1994).

Second, the pressure for growth led to intense competition between housing associations and some undercutting of costs. Each association can bid for the available

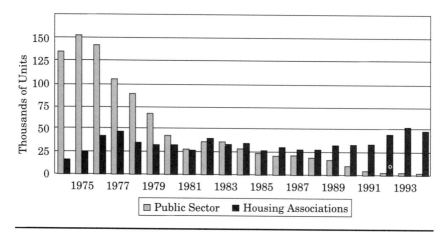

FIGURE 9.5
New Social Housing provision for Great Britain

Note: Housing association figures include both new build and rehabilitation schemes.
Source: Housing and Construction Statistics, Department of the Environment.

resources, and those who can produce the most homes for the lowest cost can be rewarded with housing association grants. As a result, some associations charge rents approaching market level but also cut quality standards, particularly space standards (Karn and Sheridan 1994).

Third, to secure the private loans they need, housing associations pledge the equity from their older property as security for their borrowing. Eventually the associations run out of equity and can pledge no more; as this moment approaches, they become anxious that their capacity to fund further new developments will be exhausted.

Fourth, to gain economies of scale, housing associations, in many cases, developed larger estates than in the past, thereby leading to concentrations of low-income households, with the inevitable problems of overload for the statutory services and the communities themselves. While the problems are not on the scale of those on the residualized—and least popular—council estates, it is a remarkable achievement of current policies that associations have found themselves dealing with similar social and community issues on new estates from the first days of their occupation (Page 1993).

Unmet Housing Needs

Despite the growth in housing association new building, the far greater decline in new council house building and the impact of right-to-buy sales in diminishing the existing council sector stock contributed to a significant rise in the incidence of recorded homelessness during the 1980s. Other key factors were the continuing decline in the private rented sector and a rise in mortgage-to-income ratios for house purchases. Even so, the recorded homelessness does not generally reflect trends in single-person homelessness or the limitations of programs to provide "care in the community" for people previously housed in large mental institutions (Evans, Dix, and Allen 1994).

More recently, the incidence of "statutory" homelessness, a situation in which local authorities have accepted that they have a legal duty to secure accommodation for "priority need" households, has fallen slightly since peaking at just under 180,000 in 1991 (see figure 9.6). This easing of a still-severe shortage corresponded with a modest reversal in the century-long decline in the private rented sector, a fall in house-purchase entry costs, and the boost in lettings to new tenants in 1992–93 and 1993–94, primarily as a result of a one-time increase in housing association investment. As a result, social sector lettings to new tenants were 20 percent higher in 1993–94 than in 1989–90.

The one-time increase in housing association investment was, however, part of a budgetary package designed primarily to ameliorate the economic and political impacts of the then-prevailing private housing market recession and was introduced following the expulsion of sterling from the European Exchange Rate Mechanism

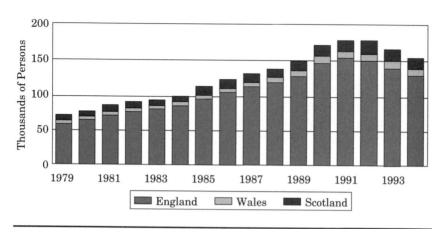

FIGURE 9.6
Rise and fall in level of statutory homelessness

Source: Wilcox (1995). Courtesy Joseph Rowntree Foundation.

in 1992. It did not signify a renewed political commitment to the provision of social rented housing, and subsequent budgets have seen successive cutbacks in the provision for new housing association investment.

Consequently, the shortfall in the availability of social sector rented housing is now set to grow again, as the numbers of lettings fall, because of those cutbacks and the increasing impact of right-to-buy sales on the vacancies available to new tenants from the remaining council sector stock.

Holmans' authoritative study of demographic and housing market trends in England concluded that close to 100,000 new social sector rented dwellings must be built each year over the next decade to deal with the shortfall in dwellings likely to be provided by the homeowner and private rented sectors under current policies.

That analysis assumes some growth in the private rented sector in response to the effective demand arising from the trend for younger households in the United Kingdom to be more likely to rent than to buy. Otherwise, however, under the current tax and subsidy arrangements, there is no other expectation that the sector is likely to grow.

Compared with that analysis, under current expenditure plans new housing association investment (in all its forms) will produce only about 40,000 additional lettings each year. Unless there are further policy initiatives, whether they are to boost the provision of public or of private housing for lower-income households, levels of homelessness and density of occupation will increase, as will the pressures on access to social sector housing (Holmans 1995).

Urban Renewal: Resources and Competition

Housing has, until recently, been at the heart of government investment strategies in urban areas. But urban renewal strategies have gone beyond demolition and replacement and are quite distinct from the slum clearance programs popular in the United States during the 1960s and 1970s.

In targeting public investment on urban regeneration, government has sought to secure both the maximum impact for every public pound spent and the involvement of private-sector interests. Turning away from local authorities as the main instruments for delivering urban renewal, government established new Urban Development Corporations in the 1980s, with board members drawn from the business communities. The emphasis has been primarily on physical regeneration, with efforts to leverage private-sector investment.

One of several recent initiatives in England has been the City Challenge scheme. This scheme required those bidding for public resources to form coalitions, with involvement of the public, private, and voluntary sectors.[6] In response to competitive bidding, the government allocated more than £1 billion, spread over five years, to thirty-one City Challenge schemes. Although those whose bids failed have expressed considerable disappointment, some have argued that the exercise in partnership has been beneficial to their city. The same pattern reportedly has occurred in the United States with failed bids for empowerment zones. The schemes' targets relate to generating employment and reclaiming land as well as to building or improving housing. While focusing primarily on housing to rent, some 10 percent of the new or improved housing has been for homeownership (Department of the Environment 1995).

Recent research commissioned by the Department of the Environment to consider the impact of investment in the 57 designated "urban priority areas" indicates that the City Challenge approach worked well where there was local consensus but was undermined where there were conflicts between local interests. Local authorities were placed at the center of these initiatives and, after many years of feeling undermined by financial restrictions and poor relationships with the central government, expressed some enthusiasm for these arrangements.

This important new research, released in July 1994 (by the University of Manchester; John Moores University, Liverpool; and the University of Durham), indicates that sustained government investment does both increase employment opportunities and improve residential attractiveness. However, the research also indicates that in the most deprived areas, this input was not able to make significant inroads into socioeconomic problems. Indeed, the worst areas declined still further despite investment targeted at them, and "there is consistent evidence of increasing degrees of polarization between the worst and the best areas" (Robson et al. 1994).[7]

A More Holistic Approach to Urban Regeneration

Robson's study criticized urban policy both for its emphasis on the physical refurbishment of buildings and for the lack of coordination and coherence between the approaches of different central and local government departments to the problems of each area. The study also contributed to a growing awareness in policy debates that public housing investment is not just about keeping the homeless off the streets or keeping property in reasonable repair (though these remain important), but that it is also about the basis for "community," for civilized society.

As a result of these debates, programs for investment in housing have become increasingly linked with investment in the economic and social development of areas where employment and other opportunities have been in decline. In 1994, the U.K. government integrated the regional offices of four government departments (Environment, Transport, Employment, and Trade and Industry) to provide a clearer focus for public funding to these areas.

The twenty individual regeneration programs from those four departments (plus one program from the Department of Education) were at the same time brought together into an agency referred to as the Single Regeneration Budget (SRB), which operates under the Local Development Group of the Department of Environment. The idea is to form the connections between education, training, and job creation, or between improvements to the environment, job creation, and the strengthening of the capacity of local communities.

This approach agrees with the thinking in the European Community about organizing the distribution of resources on a regional basis (e.g., metropolitan Birmingham). Integrated programs, with interagency collaboration between the different parties, are to be delivered at a local level but within the broader context of the region. The SRB is now attempting to channel resources in a coordinated fashion to achieve greater efficiency. While this effort has been broadly welcomed, officials operating in urban areas—now that they see the individual programs subsumed within this new budget—remain concerned that the total level of resources has been diminished in the process (from £1.6 billion in 1993–94 to £1.3 billion in 1995–96).

One of the main programs that the SRB inherited from the Department of the Environment was the Estate Action program. Estate Action schemes had a firm base of housing investment for major refurbishment works, and in many cases elements of demolition and rebuilding. The schemes, however, have also typically addressed housing management and community involvement, as well as wider issues such as crime, security, and traffic management.

The Estate Action program, which accounted for a fifth of all investment on renovation of council estates in England in 1994–95, is now being phased out by the SRB, while the new integrated SRB schemes are directed primarily toward economic and employment issues and generally have only a limited housing investment content (Dunmore, Ayriss, and Hughes 1996).

Looking to the future, in the steps that follow from the repackaging of available resources in these ways, a greater emphasis must be placed on the role of the local residents in tackling the problems of multideprived communities; this seems particularly important for the areas experiencing economic restructuring on an unprecedented scale following the collapse of major industries.

A comprehensive approach has been suggested that would blend support for economic and social recovery and would stress the ways the local communities could themselves be centrally involved. Current ideas include creating new community enterprise agencies owned and governed by the community, bidding for funds from a community enterprise corporation, and using local authorities as the sponsors and facilitators (Taylor 1995; Thake and Staubach 1993).

Conclusion

During the 1980s and early 1990s, the primary emphasis of government housing policy was on the extension of homeownership. Now at about 68 percent, homeownership exceeds that in the United States, but there are signs that its growth may have repercussions for the wider economy. Most homeowners have mortgages, and in the United Kingdom these are normally on a variable interest rate. Rises or falls in interest rates translate quickly to increased or reduced expenditure. When monetary policy is used to regulate the economy—raising or lowering interest rates—its impact is swift and unsettling.

Most people in the United Kingdom have the greatest part of their wealth tied up in their houses. If values are rising, the feel-good factor means that they save less and spend more. Correspondingly, if prices are falling, sometimes to the point where the mortgage debt is greater than the value of the property, the opposite holds true and the economy can be plunged into deeper recession.

Government now recognizes the economic instability and volatility created by the rapid growth in owner occupation. It has cut the level of support for homeownership paid through MITR. The value of these subsidies has fallen from nearly £8 billion in 1990–91 to less than £3 billion in 1995–96. This perception of the economic instability linked to homeownership has also resulted in calls for more emphasis on the rented sectors—private renting for those with better incomes but for whom the commitment of homeownership is not appropriate now, and social renting for those on lower incomes (whether from benefits or low-paid work) (Maclennan 1994).

However, this chapter paints a picture of the decline of the public housing sector in the United Kingdom. The Conservative governments since 1979 sought to diminish the role of local authorities as providers of housing, compensating slightly by boosting the work of the not-for-profit housing associations.

Although steps have been taken to expand the role of the private rented sector, the role of a revived private landlord has been seen principally as providing for middle-income, young, and mobile people. Private landlords are interested in relatively short-term lettings to secure the opportunity for sales with vacant possession, and in market rents that are outside the reach of people with low incomes. Efforts to use such short-term lettings to supply accommodation to families who need permanent homes and are in relatively low-paid work seem unlikely to succeed on any significant scale (Best 1994b).

Meanwhile, the local authorities that continue to provide public housing and the housing associations that have taken over development of new social housing are looking increasingly beyond the provision of rented homes. The interest is in area regeneration, with local authorities wishing to be at the heart of initiatives—like the City Challenge scheme—that produce partnerships for economic and social change, and the housing associations seeking to develop and strengthen communities, not simply to build houses (Page 1994).

It can be predicted that the trend for local authorities to transfer their stock voluntarily to newly formed housing associations or local housing companies—and thereby free themselves from restrictions on the amounts they can borrow and spend—will accelerate. And, with more similarities than divergences between the new thinking of the Labour Party and the post-Thatcher thinking of the Conservative Party, the striving toward an unfettered market-oriented approach of high rents and low subsidies would appear to have come to its natural end, both for local authorities and for housing associations. A growing consensus is possible based on the recognition that—in a more pluralist form—subsidized housing is necessary for perhaps 25 percent of the population, and that this is best delivered in a wider context of economic renewal, in cooperation with local communities.

Acknowledgments

This chapter was revised and updated by Steve Wilcox, Senior Research Fellow, University of York.

Notes

1. For a more complete summary of the distinctive characteristics of housing policy in Scotland and Wales, see Smith and Williams (1995) and Maclennan and More (1995).

2. This criticism of "bricks-and-mortar" subsidies has lost some of its sting as so many of the better-off council tenants have purchased their own homes, but there remain some tenants for whom higher rents would not present an intolerable burden.

3. The Department of the Environment is responsible for both producer and benefit subsidy for council tenants, while the Department of Social Security is responsible for benefit subsidy for housing association and private tenants.

4. In terms more familiar in the United States, these higher rents are among the factors leading to segregated ghettos of benefit-dependent households.

5. Housing associations are the not-for-profit agencies with unpaid committees that were set up by churches, community groups, or citizens keen to see improvements in local conditions.

6. Some emphasis was placed on participation by local communities themselves, although this has been a somewhat muted theme.

7. See Vale (1996) for parallel findings related to distressed American public housing developments.

References

Aldbourne Associates. 1994. *Can Housing Managers Learn to Dance?* Aldbourne, England.

Best, Richard. 1994a. The Duke of Edinburgh's Inquiry: Three Years On. In *Housing Finance Review 1994/95*, ed. Steve Wilcox, 7–17. York, England: Joseph Rowntree Foundation.

Best, Richard. 1994b. Backdoor. *Roof,* November, p. 44.

Bloch, Alice, and Peter John. 1991. *Attitudes to Local Government.* York, England: Joseph Rowntree Foundation.

Coleman, Alice. 1985. *Utopia on Trial: Vision and Reality in Planned Housing.* London: Hilary Shipman.

Crook, Anthony, John Hughes, and Peter Kemp. 1995. *The Supply of Privately Rented Homes.* York, England: Joseph Rowntree Foundation.

Department of the Environment. Various years. *Housing and Construction Statistics.* London: HMSO.

Department of the Environment. 1979. *National Dwelling and Housing Survey.* London: HMSO.

Department of the Environment. 1995. *Annual Report 1995.* London: HMSO.

Dunmore, Kathleen, Louise Ayriss, and Margaret Hughes. 1996. *Housing and the SRB Challenge Fund.* Coventry, England: Chartered Institute of Housing.

Evans, Angela, Jackie Dix, and Chris Allen. 1994. Homelessness: The Problem That Won't Go Away. In *Housing Finance Review 1994/95*, ed. Steve Wilcox, 40–45. York, England: Joseph Rowntree Foundation.

Ford, Janet, Elaine Kempson, and Marilyn Wilson. 1995. *Mortgage Arrears and Possessions: Perspectives from Borrowers, Lenders, and the Courts.* Department of the Environment. London: HMSO.

Ford, Janet, and Steve Wilcox. 1992. *Reducing Mortgage Arrears and Possessions.* York, England: Joseph Rowntree Foundation.

Gibson, Tony, and Linda Todd. 1993. *Danger Opportunity.* Neighbourhood Initiatives Foundation. Pamphlet.

Greve, John. 1965. *Private Landlords in England.* Occasional Papers in Social Administration, no. 16. London: Bell.

Hawksworth, John, and Steve Wilcox. 1995. *Challenging the Conventions: Public Borrowing Rules and Housing Investment.* Coventry, England: Chartered Institute of Housing.

Holmans, Alan. 1995. *Housing Demand and Need in England, 1991–2011.* York, England: Joseph Rowntree Foundation.

Housing Corporation. 1994. *Grant Rates for 1995/96.* London: Housing Corporation.

Institute of Housing. 1990. *Social Housing in the 1990's: Challenges, Choices, and Change.* Coventry, England.

Joseph Rowntree Foundation. 1991. *Second Report, Inquiry into British Housing.* York, England: Joseph Rowntree Foundation.

Karn, Valerie, and Linda Sheridan. 1994. *Standards in Housing Association Homes.* Manchester, England: University of Manchester.

Kerr, Marion. 1988. *The Right to Buy.* London: HMSO.

Maclennan, Duncan. 1994. *A Competitive UK Economy: The Challenge for Housing Policy.* York, England: Joseph Rowntree Foundation.

Maclennan, Duncan, and Alison More. 1995. Scottish Housing and Policy Since 1989: Contrasts with England. In *Housing Today and Tomorrow,* ed. Mary Smith, 134–61. London: Housing Center Trust.

Meen, Geoff. 1994. *The Impact of Higher Rents.* Housing Research Findings, no. 109. York, England: Joseph Rowntree Foundation.

Mullins, David, Pat Niner, and Moyra Riseborough. 1995. *Evaluating Large Scale Transfers of Local Authority Housing.* Department of the Environment. London: HMSO.

National Federation of Housing Associations. 1985. *Inquiry into British Housing.* London.

Newell, Wendy. 1994. The Right to Manage. Module 12 of *Competition and Local Authority Housing Services: A Guidance Manual.* London: Association of District Councils and Chartered Institute of Housing.

Page, David. 1993. *Building for Communities: A Study of New Housing Association Estates.* York, England: Joseph Rowntree Foundation.

Page, David. 1994. *Developing Communities.* Teddington, England: Sutton (Hastoe) Housing Association.

Power, Anne. 1988. *Under New Management: The Experience of Thirteen Islington Tenant Management Co-operatives.* London: Priority Estates Project.

Rao, Nirmala. 1990. *The Changing Role of the Local Housing Authority.* Prepared by the Policy Studies Institute for the Joseph Rowntree Foundation. York, England.

Robson, Brian, et al. 1994. *Assessing the Impact of Urban Policy.* London: HMSO.

Smith, Robert, and Peter Williams. 1995. The Changing Nature of Housing Policy and Practice in Wales. In *Housing Today and Tomorrow,* ed. Mary Smith, 120–33. London: Housing Center Trust.

Taylor, Marilyn. 1995. *Unleashing the Potential: Bringing Residents to the Center of Regeneration.* York, England: Joseph Rowntree Foundation.

Thake, Stephen, and Reiner Staubach. 1993. *Investing in People: Rescuing Communities from the Margin.* York, England: Anglo-German Foundation and Joseph Rowntree Foundation.

Vale, Lawrence J. 1996. Public Housing Redevelopment: Seven Kinds of Success. *Housing Policy Debate* 7(3):491–534.

Watson, Dick. 1994. *Putting Back the Pride: A Case Study of a Power Sharing Approach to Tenant Participation.* Liverpool, England: ATAC.

Wilcox, Steve. 1994. The Costs of Higher Rents. In *Housing Finance Review 1994/95,* ed. Steve Wilcox, 46–60. York, England: Joseph Rowntree Foundation.

Wilcox, Steve, ed. 1995. *Housing Finance Review 1995/96.* York, England: Joseph Rowntree Foundation.

Wilcox, Steve, Glen Bramley, Alan Ferguson, John Perry, and Colin Woods. 1993. *Local Housing Companies: New Opportunities for Council Housing.* York, England: Joseph Rowntree Foundation, in association with the Chartered Institute of Housing.

Young, Ken, and Mary Davies. 1993. *The Politics of Local Government.* York, England: Joseph Rowntree Foundation.

Zipfel, Tricia. 1994. *Multi Agency Working on Difficult to Manage Estates.* London: Priority Estates Project.

MARY K. NENNO

10 *New Directions for Federally Assisted Housing*

An Agenda for the Department of Housing and Urban Development

A Clear Focus on Housing Supply and Condition in Local Markets

Over the last two decades, there has been an increasing trend to focus HUD resources on rent allowances (certificates/vouchers) for families living in private rental housing, most of which is in standard condition; this constitutes a form of "income support" for families with high rent burdens. At the same time, new authorizations for the construction or substantial rehabilitation of low-income housing have declined. In fiscal year 1976, certificates comprised 52 percent of newly authorized assisted housing units; by the end of the 1980s, this proportion had risen to more than 80 percent. Appropriations for FY 1995 provided that 74 percent of newly authorized assisted lower-income housing units be allocated to certificates/vouchers.

Since 1995, there has been a limited swing back to housing construction assistance, reflecting the adoption of the new HOME program in the National Affordable Housing Act of 1990; a 1995 HUD report covering 45,000 completed units for fiscal year 1992 and most of fiscal year 1993 documented that 15 percent involved new rental housing construction or rehabilitation, with the balance in owner-occupied rehabilitation (36 percent), rent allowances (29 percent, to be converted later to Section 8 certificates), and assistance for first-time home buyers (20 percent) (U.S. Department of Housing and Urban Development 1995a). In late 1994, the Clinton administration proposed eliminating all low-income project-based housing

The findings of this chapter are in large part excerpted from the author's recent book, *Ending the Stalemate: Moving Housing and Urban Development into the Mainstream of America's Future* (Lanham, MD: University Press of America, 1996).

205

assistance (except for a block grant program built on the HOME program) in favor of tenant-based rent certificates; this included the 57-year-old public housing program and the 35-year-old Section 202 housing program for the elderly/handicapped. This proposal was revised in 1995 and 1996 (discussed below). Documentation included in the FY 1996 HUD budget indicated that by the year 2000 about two-thirds of *all* new HUD budget authority would be used for certificates/vouchers. Following the 1994 HUD proposal, the issue of rent allowances versus project-based assistance took on new momentum as a subject for debate in the 1995 and 1996 sessions of Congress, controlled by the Republican party.

The forces that support the use of family rent allowances as the primary method of housing assistance are strong, based on the finding that a large proportion of housing need is related to family income inadequate to pay housing costs. This finding has been well-documented in "Whose Shortage of Affordable Housing?" (Nelson 1994) and "To Whom Should Limited Housing Resources Be Directed?" (Nelson and Khadduri 1992). The Joint Center for Housing Studies at Harvard University estimates that there are some 4.5 million households with incomes of 50 percent or less of their area's median income who do not receive housing or income subsidy; they live in "adequate" housing but have a severe rent burden—that is, they pay 50 percent or more of their incomes for gross rent. "Adequate" housing is defined in terms of presence or absence of plumbing fixtures, heating equipment, and other mechanical sub-systems, and in terms of repair and upkeep of the properties (Joint Center for Housing Studies 1993).

The move to family rent allowances has also been stimulated by the assumption that the costs of rent allowances are less than those of new project-based housing. Findings by Mark Matulef are ambiguous; his analysis shows a cost advantage for project-based new public housing construction over rent allowances beginning in the sixteenth year (Matulef 1988, 1989). Clearly, additional analysis is required with special attention to relative costs over the long term.

One factor that has not been emphasized in past studies is that construction programs produce a publicly owned capital asset, which if properly maintained, has a useful life of forty to fifty years for occupancy by succeeding numbers of low-income families. HUD's FY 1996 budget proposed to convert all existing public housing support to vouchers for residents. Although this proposal was not ultimately adopted, it resulted in a further debate over the comparative cost figures in early 1995. The results of these analyses depended on the cost factors that were included, particularly the percentile break point used in establishing fair market rents (FMRs) for certificates/vouchers based on the cost of available housing in the local community, the base of public housing units used in the calculations, and the public housing modernization cost figures. Of the five analyses developed, two were calculated on nationally based factors—the analyses by HUD and by Peter Henderson of the National Association of Housing and Redevelopment Officials (NAHRO) (U.S. Department of Housing and Urban Development 1995b; Henderson 1995).

The HUD analysis used a proposed 40th percentile of the cost of available housing as the basis for setting the fair market rent ceiling, whereas NAHRO used the 45th percentile (authorized in early 1995). This shift by HUD had the effect of lowering the cost to the federal government and also reducing the availability of rent certificates for lower-income worker families. (Congress approved HUD's request to lower the basis to the 40th percentile later in 1995.) Another difference in the analyses was HUD's inclusion of only those occupied units receiving operating assistance; NAHRO used the larger inventory of "units less units expected to be demolished in the near future." HUD included the costs of all physical improvement programs available to local housing authorities; NAHRO utilized only the major modernization programs available to all authorities. Based on these differences, the HUD analysis showed a $41 per month cost advantage of certificates/vouchers over public housing units, whereas NAHRO showed a $46 advantage for public housing.

Another issue raised in regard to the support of family rent allowances is the charge that low-income housing construction programs have been plagued by scandals. There is no evidence that all project-based housing development has a record of scandal, however. In fact, there is a long record of largely scandal-free, project-based assisted housing administered by local housing authorities and Section 202 elderly/handicapped nonprofit housing sponsors. In 1994, HUD indicated in its evaluation of local housing authorities that 3,300 of the 3,400 authorities (97 percent) were "well performing" (U.S. Department of Housing and Urban Development 1994).

In February 1996, then HUD Secretary Henry Cisneros released a revised version of the agency's "Reinvention Blueprint," which left any conversions of public housing and Section 202 assistance to certificates/vouchers to "local discretion." This proposal became a part of the deliberations on the 1996 proposed reform legislation before Congress, which was not adopted.

In any event, the need for rent allowances for families living in standard housing who have high rent burdens is not the whole story. There is evidence of a substantial housing need related both to an inadequate supply of low-rent housing and to deficiencies in the structural condition of the housing. In terms of supply, there is serious concern about the massive losses of low-cost housing. The Joint Center for Housing Studies at Harvard University documents that the low-cost housing stock (gross monthly rents of $300 per month or less) declined by an average of 130,000 housing units annually between 1985 and 1991, whereas new multifamily housing construction, especially for low-cost units, dramatically slowed. The limited numbers of new multifamily units being put in place were primarily in suburban areas in higher cost units. In 1993, new permits for the construction of multifamily housing were off 70 percent or more in most states from their 1980 peaks (Joint Center for Housing Studies 1993, 1994). A basic question is whether there is a sufficient supply of standard vacant housing units to re-house families living in deficient housing. Recent analysis has shown agreement that there are serious shortages of rental housing units for the lowest-income families (Joint Center for Housing Studies 1993;

Nelson 1994), but this market cannot be reached under the HOME program or through housing supported by Low-Income Housing Tax Credits without further rent support. This is a market that is reached by public housing and the Section 202 elderly/handicapped assistance programs through operating subsidies attached to the housing developments. The question, then, is how the additional rent assistance should be provided—through rent supplements given directly to families or through operating assistance attached to housing developments.

The issue of the structural condition of housing remains critical. The Harvard studies report structural problems in both the lowest- and lower-income ranges. In 1991, a total of 1.7 million unsubsidized households with incomes 50 percent of the area median or below lived in inadequate housing. This included 22 percent of the lowest-income renters, with incomes less than 25 percent of the area's median income; among households in the 25 to 50 percent of median income range, 16 percent lived in inadequate housing. Even among households with incomes in the 50 to 80 percent of median income category, 12 percent lived in inadequate units.

Two additional studies bring evidence to this question, one by the Congressional Research Service of the Library of Congress (Milgram, Foote and Bury 1994) and the other an analysis published by the Urban Institute (Newman and Schnare 1992). The Milgram report reviews surveys in twenty-two metropolitan areas to determine if there is a sufficient number of standard quality vacant units of the proper size to re-house all households living in unsatisfactory housing. The size of the available standard units was a critical factor in this analysis. A gross comparison of inadequately housed families against the number of vacant standard units showed that in all but four areas there appeared to be a sufficient number of vacant units to re-house all needy families; however, when size of the vacant units is considered, only in one area (Pittsburgh) are all families able to move to satisfactory housing. In all other areas, there is a shortfall in the number of larger vacant units. This study concludes that its simulation "gives a ballpark estimate of a real inadequacy of supply in the existing stock regardless of any income supplement the households may receive." The Newman–Schnare analysis estimates the potential impact on housing quality if welfare shelter allowances were raised to the level of HUD-determined FMRs. Based on an analysis in fifty-one local market areas, the predicted percent improvement in the average welfare recipient's housing quality would be only 20 to 30 percent in the majority of areas.

An additional factor to be considered is the extent to which rent allowances or low-income housing developments contribute to neighborhood improvement. A study examining the relative impacts of federal assistance programs (Varady 1982) concluded that neither form of assistance, standing alone, resulted in a measurable impact on neighborhood upgrading. However, this study cited general agreement that programs that are concentrated on particular blocks and in particular neighborhoods are more likely to have an impact on increased property values in the surrounding area. It also cited general agreement that success in upgrading neighborhoods involved combining housing improvements with strategies to upgrade community services and facilities. This latter finding is confirmed in the recent study of experience in the Community Development Block Grant (CDBG) program conducted over a three-year period, which included extensive field examinations (Urban Institute 1995). This analysis found that neighborhood improvement was a complex process involving existing conditions and dynamics of change: almost all neighborhoods credited with stability or improvement contained a mix of income groups and land uses; some neighborhoods measured improvement unrelated to CDBG investment. At the same time, the study concluded that the most success in neighborhood stabilization and revitalization occurred in cities which concentrated investments and linked housing, economic development, social service spending, and citizen participation in neighborhood planning. This finding is relevant to the question of whether HUD should emphasize rent allowances or housing development. Which approach can best concentrate assistance in specific locations related to strategies for neighborhood and community revitalization?

My conclusion is that low-income housing development (including acquisition and rehabilitation of distressed properties) in specific locations in support of community improvement strategies has a clear advantage over the scattered pattern of individual family-based rent support. This is not to negate the value of rent allowances to assist families to meet their housing costs; but allowances can be linked only in a general way with community revitalization efforts. The Joint Center study (1993) cited above concludes:

> To be sure, insufficient income is the primary problem of most extremely low-income families. Housing assistance could help more poor families, however, if these programs were better linked with other income support efforts. Added income cannot eliminate the widespread problem of structurally inadequate housing or stem the ongoing loss of low-cost units. Added income also cannot erase the blight that undermines the quality of life in many low-income communities or confront the persistent discrimination that limits the housing market opportunities of many minorities. Efforts to expand economic opportunity and eradicate poverty should therefore be accompanied by equally strong efforts to promote the revitalization of distressed communities, to eliminate housing market discrimination, and to preserve and expand the stock of affordable and adequate housing. (Joint Center for Housing Studies 1993)

The above quotation supports the thesis of this chapter that rent allowances (income support) for families with high rent burdens living in standard housing should be a responsibility of mainstream income support programs, not a responsibility of HUD. There are political implications in removing rent allowances (income support) from HUD, including the question of whether HUD could retain the funding currently allocated for this purpose. However, the diversion of HUD's traditional funding to rent allowances could support restoration of HUD funding to its original statutory purposes. HUD has a prime statutory mission to improve the supply and condition of housing, particularly lower-income housing, in conjunction with its programs to revitalize neighborhoods and communities. The mission of HUD, dating back to its creation in 1965 and still extant in the enabling statute, is to remove slums and expand the supply of low-income housing in conjunction with revitalizing neighborhoods and communities in both central cities and metropolitan areas (Section 2, U.S. Department of Housing and Urban Development Act, Public Law 89–174).

REFINED ANALYSIS OF LOCAL HOUSING MARKETS

Current HUD assisted housing policy sets family eligibility solely on the basis of income—i.e., family income related to median income in the local area. Whereas FMRs are used to determine the ceiling on rent assistance to be provided, they are not used to determine family eligibility for assistance. In the original 1937 Housing Act, eligibility was determined by a family's inability to afford private-market housing within a given percentage of family income, originally 20 percent. This formula provided a range of eligibility that directly related family income to housing costs in the local housing market. This approach should be reconsidered under a more refined housing market study that includes a "rent gap" analysis—i.e., the gap between a family's ability to pay for housing (based on the average housing expenditure of the income group) and the supply of standard housing available at that rent (Alexander and Nenno 1974).

The Comprehensive Housing Affordability Strategy (CHAS), established by the 1990 National Housing Affordability Act, is the basis for allocating HUD housing assistance and requires a five-year projection focused on the housing needs of individual households, current housing market conditions, and the impact of local land-use and tax policies. The Consolidated Community Development Plan, adopted in 1994, is designed to meet the minimum statutory requirements for Community Development Block Grants, the HOME program, Emergency Shelter Grants, and Housing Opportunities for People with AIDS under a consolidated application document. Its five elements include developing partnerships, improving citizen participation, identifying housing and community development needs, putting together a housing and community development strategic plan, and developing an action plan for one year's use of funds. The annual plan must describe the eligible programs, projects, and activities and their relationship to priority housing and community development needs. It must specify numerical affordable-housing goals; this is a linkage with the CHAS. These instruments are important elements in a revived strategy for community improvement; but do they meet the full tests of housing market analysis linked to community revitalization in changing urban areas?

In terms of local housing market analysis, we have yet to address adequately the dynamics of change in local housing markets. As Michael Stegman, former HUD

Assistant Secretary for Policy Development and Research points out, we need to en-large data collection to include the design and implementation of empirical studies to help us understand the economics of privately owned, low-rent and inner-city hous-ing markets and how they have changed over the past fifteen years. We need to know who now owns and manages this stock; how changes in marketing, financing, taxes, and social conditions have contributed to the inventory decline. We need, in par-ticular, more information on issues related to the decline in the affordable housing supply (Stegman 1992). A study by the Urban Institute called for local housing strat-egies based on more accurate projections of area shifts in household growth, and in-come and age distribution; it advocated a ten-year assessment of the changes in housing quality and housing locations in metropolitan areas to determine a range of possible government housing policies as well as to capture the impact of the hous-ing situation on a range of people who are differentiated by race, income, and fam-ily type (Struyk, Marshall and Ozanne 1978). Such an assessment would move beyond identifying housing needs at one point in time and relate them to the dynamics of community and metropolitan change and revitalization plans. The Urban Institute report includes a housing market simulation model incorporating the ten-year as-sessment calibrated to different types of metropolitan areas. In terms of the poten-tial for implementing such a model, the report concludes that:

> [I]t may be unrealistic now to believe that local planning officials have the resources
> to evaluate the long-term effect of strategies they put forward, or to make reason-
> ably accurate projections of area shifts in household growth, income and age distri-
> butions. These limitations, however, argue persuasively for local housing strategies
> that are within general guidelines set by (1) area trends in basic economic and de-
> mographic forces and (2) the potential long-term effects—both direct and indirect—
> of alternative strategies in similar metropolitan areas. (Struyk, Marshall, and Ozanne
> 1978, 9)

As a beginning initiative, there is a need to incorporate some of the provisions and factors contained in the Housing Assistance Plan (HAP) of the 1974 Housing Act (now replaced) into current housing and community development strategies. The HAP was designed to provide a direct linkage between housing assistance and com-munity development programs by making it a requirement for receiving CDBG fund-ing, and by requiring the coordination of the locations of assisted housing with existing or planned public facilities, with services such as schools, transportation, police and fire protection, and recreational facilities, as well as with job opportunities. It in-cluded a component to measure the housing needs of those "expected to reside" in the community in the future (Alexander and Nenno 1974). A direct linkage between HUD's housing assistance programs and its community development functions is required. Today, the emerging importance of the "urban region" that ties together the interests of the central city and the outlying area makes it critical to incorporate a metropolitan dimension in housing and community development strategies.

Sound and Livable Housing Developments

A number of past and current HUD assisted housing policies run counter to the goal of achieving sound and livable housing developments. These include, first, a well-intentioned but failed policy to concentrate assistance on the poorest households, which makes it difficult to locate assisted housing developments with this concentrated occupancy in many communities. Management of housing developments with concentrations of very-low-income residents is particularly difficult in large cities with an inventory of large public housing developments located in areas that are severely distressed. A second HUD housing policy that needs new attention is an explicit effort to encourage housing settings and structural designs that respond to diverse household needs. This kind of approach has not been encouraged by federal policy, except in the case of developments for the elderly, and to a lesser extent, for disabled or homeless persons. A third HUD policy that needs new attention is an expanded effort to make housing developments places of opportunity for residents to achieve maximum independence. This includes supportive services for the large numbers of frail elderly persons living in federally assisted housing to enable them to continue to live in their assisted housing units without premature placement in nursing homes. It also includes expanded resources to assist non-elderly households to increase their incomes and self-sufficiency with the goal of moving into the private housing market. The provision of family support services is not a priority HUD function, but the Department can take actions to stimulate the provision of such services in its assisted housing developments by social service agencies, as described below.

"MIXED-INCOME" HOUSING DEVELOPMENTS

Initially, federally assisted housing occupancy policy under the U.S. Housing Act of 1937 was based on serving a range of families in the local housing market who could not afford to pay for standard, available housing. This produced housing developments occupied by a variety of people within income eligibility limits—working families as well as those receiving public assistance. It also produced both social and fiscal stability for the housing development with working families serving as models for those striving for more self-sufficiency and paying higher rents, which helped support those families at the lowest-income range. This occupancy policy was gradually changed as the housing needs of very-low-income families escalated, until in 1981 (under the Omnibus Budget and Reconciliation Act of that year), occupancy was basically restricted to those households with incomes of 50 percent or less of the median income in the local area, largely a dependent population. While this occupancy policy has a philosophical and political attractiveness in concentrating limited housing resources on those with the most severe problems, it creates housing developments that are not socially or fiscally sound—and that do not provide models for an expanded program. This occupancy policy also denies housing assistance to many moderate-income working families who cannot afford local housing costs. In 1992, a survey of public housing occupancy showed that the median income for households in family developments (excluding elderly developments) was 43 percent below the poverty level for a family of four; large proportions of households in these developments (as high as 59 percent in developments with more than 4,000 units) had public assistance (Aid for Families with Dependent Children) as their main source of income; and only 26 percent of families in these developments had earned income as a primary source (Djoko and Sherwood 1992). This occupancy pattern creates major obstacles for the families involved, for housing management, and for the local community. Yet, in 1996, HUD still supported heavy concentrations of very-low-income families in public housing, advocating at least 40 percent of newly admitted households in individual developments below 30 percent of area median income, with the remainder below 60 percent of the median (Stegman 1996). This issue was still being debated in 1997.

As early as 1974, there were efforts to move toward "mixed-income" housing developments. Under the Housing and Community Development Act of that year, Congress directed HUD to move the public housing program to occupancy by a range of incomes as soon as possible; but this statutory directive was never implemented. Many state-financed housing assistance programs, however, have reported successful mixed-income experience, including the Massachusetts State Housing Finance Agency, which in 1993 reported an inventory of 572 rental housing developments representing 69,638 mixed-income units, many in suburban locations (Massachusetts Housing Finance Agency 1994). The Housing Opportunities Commission (HOC) of Montgomery County, Maryland, has also followed a number of different mixed-income housing approaches, including a zoning law which supports low-income family occupancy in privately developed middle-income subdivisions. In 1994, the Commission owned about 1,400 homes in more than 125 different subdivisions. In addition, HOC developed its own mixed-income communities through different funding packages, including the issuance of tax-exempt mortgage revenue bonds, loans from the state and county governments, and resources generated from market rents. Three mixed-income rental housing developments totaling 588 units were constructed during 1992 and 1993, and another three developments with 709 units were under construction in 1994, one of which utilizes assistance under the federal HOME program. All of these developments include a broad range of family incomes (Siegel 1994).

It is important to note that none of the "mixed-income" programs in Montgomery County are under the federally assisted public housing program but were developed under additional financing powers available to the Housing Opportunities Commission under Maryland state law, an option not available to most local housing authorities. Although the income level in Montgomery County is comparatively high relative to other jurisdictions, resulting in higher income limits for admission into assisted housing, it is the policy of the Housing Opportunities Commission to reach as many very-low-income families as financially feasible. Many of the county's mixed-income developments include occupancy by families from the public housing waiting list. Significantly, the new HOME program of the 1990 National Affordable Housing Act provides at least some additional flexibility in occupancy requirements by allowing 90 percent of admissions to be at 60 percent (instead of 50 percent of median income) and by not requiring other admission priorities that are required by some federally assisted programs.

A recent analysis of the record of "mixed-income" housing development is contained in an August 1995 article by Morton Hoffman documenting not only the Montgomery County (Maryland) and the State of Massachusetts experience, but also that of the Illinois Housing Development Authority and the states of Maryland and New Jersey. The ingredients for success include land planning, unit mix, architectural considerations, and site location. The last condition is particularly important if an area has already absorbed a significant number of "mixed-use" developments and is concerned about "over concentration" (Melton 1995). Hoffman concludes:

> For a long period, conventional real estate analysis held that most families seek identified one-class developments. Many state housing finance agencies . . . have successfully fostered housing for low-, moderate-, and middle-income families and encouraged mixed-income or income integrated developments. (Hoffman 1995, 45)

A very important step in moving toward a more balanced occupancy in federally assisted housing was taken by HUD in January 1995 when it announced that local housing authorities and housing sponsors could establish a local admission preference for working families (*Federal Register*, January 18, 1995). This was consistent with the final HUD preference rule, issued on July 18, 1994 but which, under the terms of HUD's Fiscal Year 1995 Appropriations Act, applies to fiscal 1995 only. This rule makes it possible to increase the average income of families in assisted housing, reducing the federal subsidy as well as providing for a stable social environment. The New York City Housing Authority was the first to implement the new policy, citing it as an effort to achieve an occupancy pattern of one-third welfare families, one-third elderly households, and one-third working families. In making the change, a New York City Housing Authority official stated: "Projects that are economically integrated just work better. . . . [T]hat has been demonstrated in city after city across the country." HUD's Assistant Secretary for Public and Indian Housing stated that "the goal of the new policy is to do away with the concentration of poverty that public housing has become. . . . [F]ostering an economic mix is the most direct way of achieving this, along with a combination of modernization and changing rent rules (*The New York Times*, February 4, 1995). This policy was extended on a year-to-year basis in the FY 1996 and 1997 appropriation acts.

ASSISTED HOUSING AND SOUND NEIGHBORHOODS

The relationship of low-income housing to neighborhoods has been a critical one from the beginning of federally assisted housing programs. Housing developments should be integral parts of the neighborhood and the local community; this relationship is critical to the welfare of both. Incorporating factors to identify general housing locations that support sound relationships to the neighborhood and community (as called for in the 1974 Housing Assistance Plan requirement described above) is important as a component of the 1995 Consolidated Community Development Plan.

Newly constructed public housing developments over the last decade, although limited in number, are represented in all sizes of communities and are neighborhood assets. The high quality of these developments in a variety of structure types is recognized and accepted. The public housing design award winners illustrated in the *Journal of Housing* (Henry 1994 and 1995) are representative of quality development. Although type of structure and quality of housing design are very important in facilitating locations in good neighborhoods, the occupancy pattern of the development also carries important influence in gaining neighborhood support. In the past, assisted housing locations have been constrained by federal policy that has restricted occupancy to very-low-income families, including large numbers of welfare-assisted families. The FY 1996 and FY 1997 legislation authorizing occupancy by "worker families" (as described above) could be an important factor in opening more housing locations.

The relationship of housing sites to the surrounding neighborhood is a particularly difficult one in many large cities because of past history. Initially, under the U.S. Housing Act of 1937, federally assisted public housing had to be developed on slum-clearance sites, leading to locations that were surrounded by neighborhood areas with serious physical, economic, and social problems. The accompanying policy was that the housing developments should be of sufficient size to influence the sound direction of the adjacent area. With the passage of the Urban Redevelopment Program in 1949, slum clearance became a responsibility of the new program, and this requirement was removed from the public housing program. However, an inventory of large-city public housing surrounded by troubled areas remained. The hope that large-scale housing developments would influence the restoration of these areas was unrealized; instead, in many instances, the housing developments became islands in a sea of blight. With the growing demand for housing for very-low-income families in the 1950s, occupancy in these original developments, as well as in the new large-scale public housing developments of that period, resulted in a continually increasing pattern of concentration of low-income families. This was accompanied by the escalation of occupancy by poverty-level families in the rapidly deteriorating areas surrounding the housing developments.

The 1992 report of the National Commission on Severely Distressed Public Housing pointed out that conditions in the surrounding areas had critical impacts on the environment of housing developments, and that solutions to a housing development's problems must involve multifaceted approaches to deal with conditions in the surrounding area (National Commission on Severely Distressed Public Housing 1992). Certainly, improvements in surrounding areas would include rehabilitation or removal of substandard housing or other detrimental conditions; the establishment of adequate schools; programs of street repairs and street lighting; expansion of police activity to reduce crime, drugs, and violence; and new resources for family support and job opportunities. Improvements to reverse conditions in severely distressed public housing in large cities should be undertaken jointly with improvements in surrounding areas. Adding this as a specific factor in documenting local public housing needs under the Consolidated Community Development Plan (described above) would be valuable. The lesson for future policy is that assisted housing developments must recognize that sound neighborhood conditions and environment are critical factors in housing locations; sound and livable housing developments cannot be created in isolation from the surrounding neighborhood. Comprehensive efforts should be undertaken to improve neighborhood conditions, along with the revitalization of existing housing developments—or replacement housing on more appropriate sites. Most importantly, future assisted housing should be located in sound neighborhoods with linkages to all community resources.

QUALITY AND DIVERSITY IN HOUSING DESIGN

Other elements in the effort to create sound and livable housing developments are the housing setting and the design of housing structures, particularly in response to the varying needs of different types of households. In a seminal article in 1962, the houser-planner-architect Albert Mayer reviewed the atmosphere in which public housing architecture had developed. He cited the fact that public housing was forced to operate in a way that would offer no possible alternative to private enterprise and had to be built to standards of the direst minimality, placing it into a position apart from the mainstream. This had a traumatizing influence on the livability and architecture of public housing development. Housing officials, both federal and local, were placed on the defensive, seeking to escape criticism, practicing stark economics, squeezing down space, and minimizing community facilities. The results were developments of the bare essentials of safety, decency and economy. There were some individual breakthroughs when local authorities insisted on better quality, but it was a hard fight (Mayer 1962). Further perspectives on the experience in public housing architecture are presented by Alexander von Hoffman in chapter 1 of this volume and by Karen Franck in chapter 5.

Another influential factor cited by one of the founders of public housing,

Catherine Bauer, was that after World War II as many Americans were moving to single-family homes in the suburbs, public housing was constrained to follow the directions in the urban design profession to use the new technological advances in building construction to build high-rise, high-density housing in the inner city for the low-income families left behind by the suburban exodus. Many public housing developments literally turned their backs to the surrounding neighborhoods (Bauer 1957). Many small- and medium-sized cities succeeded in developing small-scale row houses and apartment structures, but they were still faced with restrictive federal cost regulations that made imaginative design or housing quality almost impossible. Further roadblocks to the development of quality design and livability in public housing came in the decade of the 1950s, when new construction technology made possible the development of high-rise buildings in central cities, and the values of designers favored these new approaches. In addition, high densities allowed more families to be served by the government dollar. Increasing occupancy of these high-rise structures by very-low-income, deprived families also brought with it management problems.

The decade of the 1960s saw the first major breakthrough in public housing architecture with the opening of public housing for elderly occupancy. Led by Public Housing Commissioner Marie C. McGuire and Albert Mayer (Mayer 1962), a new drive for excellence in design was launched, along with special design features and facilities to respond to the special needs of elderly households. The result was an explosion of well-designed, low-income elderly housing in virtually every section of the country (*Journal of Housing* 1963).

In addition to the elderly and the handicapped, federally assisted housing programs have been slow to respond to the special housing needs of other types of households. Standardized apartment-type development has continued to be the model. The design of "shelters" for the homeless and "group homes" for the mentally disabled has drawn some attention (Greer 1985), but there has been no widespread movement to rethink the housing settings and design requirements in permanent housing for "special needs" households as part of the total community.

In 1974, the need to reconsider housing design for changing household types was recognized in national legislation. In that year, Congress authorized $10 million in additional research authority for HUD to undertake special demonstrations to determine "the housing design, the housing structure and the housing-related facilities and amenities most effective or appropriate to meet the needs of those with special housing needs including the elderly, the handicapped, the displaced, single individuals, broken families and large households." The HUD Secretary was authorized to utilize this additional research funding in conjunction with funding authority under assisted housing programs to construct demonstration housing. This demonstration authority is still in the statute but has never been implemented.

One of the special household groups needing particular attention in terms of housing settings and design is that of single mothers with children. A supportive housing

setting can be an important factor in stabilizing family life for single parents in prepa-
ration for moving to increased independence in private housing and in providing
housing models for single parents in the general population. There has been a rapid
growth in this type of household in the population as a whole, in public housing,
and among the homeless. In the nation as a whole, the number of single mothers
with children doubled between 1980 and 1988, to a total of 8.2 million single women
raising 13.5 million children, more than half living in poverty. Fortunately, there are
signs that the special needs of these families are beginning to be recognized. In 1991,
a Boston architect, Joan Forrester Sprague, applied new understanding to the physical surroundings of these households by focusing on a pattern of social interaction
that relates their needs as individuals to those of their households, the immediate
community of households, and the neighborhood. She advocated new design of residential spaces that would nurture and support their particular needs, such as having
opportunities to socialize, obtain peer support, have informal access to information,
observe role models, and have opportunities to share household responsibilities such
as cooking or child care. Ms. Sprague documented examples of such new approaches
across the country—fifty different models from eighteen states (Sprague 1991). Her
contribution builds on pioneering work by others. One option she puts forward is
the use of "cluster" housing, which involves the construction or rehabilitation of small
developments with units built around a central core of community space that can
be utilized for common household activities (Nenno 1991).

This new flexibility in design related specifically to the needs of elderly or physically handicapped persons and was not geared to meet the needs of developmentally
disabled persons (e.g., mentally disturbed). The recognition of the special design needs
of the elderly, however, did bring attention to the special housing requirements of
other households, including the physically handicapped, single parents with children,
single persons, and homeless persons.

An increasing number of households in need of housing assistance are households
with these special design needs. HUD could accelerate the effort to provide sound
and livable housing developments for their occupancy by implementing the 1974
research authority and by reviewing its construction guidelines to provide more flexibility for new design models.

OPPORTUNITIES FOR HOUSEHOLD INDEPENDENCE

Another critical element in achieving sound and livable assisted housing developments involves facilities and support to help resident families achieve their maximum level of independence; this applies to family groups, the elderly, and
handicapped persons. For families with an adult member capable of working, particularly families headed by single mothers, there is a need for appropriate settings
and a structured program to assist the potential worker, in a given time period, to

achieve a level of employment sufficient to provide basic family needs including standard private housing. This move toward independence has been accelerated by the provisions of the 1996 welfare reform act (the Personal Responsibility and Work Opportunity Reconciliation Act of 1996). In the case of an elderly or handicapped person, the need is for supportive assistance to enable that person to maintain independent living as long as possible, without premature placement in a nursing home.

Initially, the occupancy in public housing, representing a significant number of upwardly mobile families, did not require structured efforts to assist families in moving toward independent living; but with increased occupancy by very-low-income disadvantaged families whose income derives primarily from public assistance, the situation changed. Over the past decade, there have been an increasing number of efforts designed to aid families living in assisted housing to move toward a more independent status. A major impetus was given to this movement by Project Self-Sufficiency (PSS) begun by HUD in 1984, involving 155 communities in thirty-seven states, Guam, Puerto Rico, and the District of Columbia. PSS was designed to help single parents in poverty situations obtain decent, affordable private housing and economic self-sufficiency through a broad range of locally sponsored education, counseling, training, and employment programs, as well as other supportive services. An incentive for participants was the provision of Section 8 certificates or vouchers. The initial results were promising: a 1988 HUD progress report indicated that 42 percent of nearly 10,000 individuals who had participated in 134 local programs had either obtained full-time jobs with growth potential or were enrolled in two- or four-year college programs (U.S. Department of Housing and Urban Development 1988). A more recent perspective on family self-sufficiency in Seattle is presented by Rick Kustina (1994).

Although no follow-up analysis was conducted to determine how many participants actually attained a new stage of self-sufficiency, the preliminary results were encouraging enough to extend the PSS effort in 1989, under the title of Operation Bootstrap. This program involved sixty-one communities and covered all types of low-income households, not just single-parent families, and placed more emphasis on employment (McGovern 1991). The 1990 National Affordable Housing Act made a family self-sufficiency program a requirement for local housing authorities (with limited exceptions) in both the public housing and the Section 8 programs. In addition to the federal programs, many states and localities have undertaken a variety of family self-sufficiency efforts (National Association of Housing and Redevelopment Officials and the American Public Welfare Association 1989). State programs have focused largely on families receiving assistance under the Aid to Families with Dependent Children (AFDC) public assistance program, building on the Family Support Act of 1988 which provided federal funding for a program of assistance to enable families to move to independence. Public welfare program regulations have prevented using support services available under the 1988 act from being targeted to AFDC families living in public housing, however. In addition, Congress has not appropriated monies to the level authorized in that act. HUD makes available only public housing or Section 8 certificate/voucher assistance; support services must be funded at the local level, and this has caused serious constraints for local housing authorities since there are many other demands on local social support resources. However, Congress has authorized the funding of "social service coordinators" for housing authorities undertaking self-sufficiency programs.

One of the most promising approaches for meeting the need for self-sufficiency efforts was the creation by Congress in the 1990 National Affordable Housing Act of the Family Investment Center (FIC), based on a number of models initiated by local housing authorities and in particular, the Lafayette Courts public housing development in Baltimore. Under this approach, family services to support family self-sufficiency are brought directly into community space in the housing development, avoiding the need for families to search out services from different agencies throughout the community. Federal funding can be used to construct or rehabilitate space for the centers; 15 percent of the funding can be allocated to the cost of services, providing an incentive for service matching at the local level. In 1996, although the Lafayette Courts public housing development was demolished in favor of a smaller-scale housing development, the FIC was retained in an alternate location within the neighborhood.

Despite promising initial results, there is no adequate long-term evaluation of the success of self-sufficiency programs, or tested experience as to how long it takes for a family to move to independence, or when assistance should be terminated. These were all issues under discussion in 1996 in relation to the welfare reform legislation. However, there is encouraging evidence of family movement under a variety of self-sufficiency efforts (National Association of Housing and Redevelopment Officials and American Public Welfare Association 1991a.) If future efforts are to be successful in federally assisted low-income housing, they must incorporate ways to link the family support assistance of federal and state social welfare programs to subsidized housing developments. HUD should not be the primary source for support services.

A possible model for HUD is the FIC program noted above, under which HUD provides 15 percent of service costs as an incentive for other matching funds. This program could operate in conjunction with the provisions of Community Development Block Grants, which stipulate that up to 15 percent of block grant funds can be used for "public services," including family support services.

The second area of need relative to achieving independence for residents of federally assisted housing concerns frail elderly persons. In 1989, it was estimated that there were between 75,000 and 135,000 households residing in federally assisted housing with at least one frail member (Struyk et al. 1989). Thirty-three percent of residents in elderly public housing developments are between 66 and 75 years of age; 45 percent are more than 75 years of age. These statistics document the aging in place of many people who became public housing residents in the mid- to late 1960s, when a number of elderly developments opened. The emerging need to address the situation of the elderly was recognized in the Housing and Community Development Act of 1978, which created the Congregate Housing Services Program (CHSP) demonstration. Between 1980 and 1990, thirty-three public housing agencies and thirty nonprofit sponsors of Section 202 elderly housing provided support services to some 2,000 frail elderly and handicapped persons. The demonstration funded a package of services tailored to the needs of each individual to enable the person to maintain independent living.

An evaluation by Congress released in 1987 found positive results both in terms of resident satisfaction and cost savings over nursing home care (U.S. House of Representatives, Select Committee on Aging 1987). The 1990 National Affordable Housing Act made CHSP a permanent program, and funding was expanded under the 1992 Housing and Community Development Act. Funding is authorized for retrofitting space to accommodate the CHSP program and for providing services under a matching formula, requiring a 40 percent federal contribution, a 50 percent local contribution, and a 10 percent contribution by the service recipient. The fiscal year 1993 federal appropriation was $21 million to cover existing contracts and a possible extension of service to 2,000 additional persons, bringing the total to 4,000 elderly persons. Administrative regulations limit this funding to services only, not physical retrofitting, which is far short of the estimated need in federally assisted housing, as indicated above. Unfortunately, new authorizations in support of the CHSP have not been requested by the administration or approved by Congress in the fiscal years since 1994, despite its successful record. The future of this effort could well depend on how services are provided. A 40 percent share from HUD may be too high; a greater federal share perhaps should come from other federal resources. The solution could well involve the merging of services for frail elderly persons in assisted housing with the federally supported long-term care programs, now restricted to elderly persons in nursing homes. A solution should also involve the expansion of integrated housing/nursing home delivery systems at federal, state, and local levels from social service agencies (National Association of Housing and Redevelopment Officials and American Public Welfare Association 1991b).

In particular, states have a critical role since they receive federal funding for elderly services from the Administration on Aging (AOA) and also administer Supplemental Security Income (SSI) and Medicaid, which can be linked with assisted housing developments. There are encouraging signs that states are beginning to take a leadership role in this area (National Academy for State Health Policy 1992). The cost to states of providing services for aging persons in congregate housing developments, preventing premature institutionalization, is far less than in nursing homes.

New Directions in Federally Assisted Housing: 1997

Legislative action affecting HUD's housing assistance programs in the last three fiscal years has tended to maintain the status quo, despite numerous reform efforts. The predicted elimination of the Department or drastic reductions in program funds, under serious debate since 1995, have not materialized. Total appropriation levels for the Department remained relatively constant at $18 billion to $19 billion (Table 10.1). Individual program levels also stayed relatively constant. The trend away from funding project-type housing assistance continued, but there has also been increasing restlessness about the level of funding required to renew Section 8 leases.

In the case of public housing, the FY 1997 Appropriations Act continued the incremental reform provisions of the FY 1996 Act. These include flexibility in the use of modernization funds, repeal of federal admission preferences, one-for-one replacement of demolished units, and a new minimum rent requirement at the discre-

TABLE 10.1

Appropriations for Major Programs of the
U.S. Department of Housing and Urban Development:
FY 1995, FY 1996, FY 1997
(in $000,000s)

Program Appropriations	FY 1995	FY 1996	FY 1997
Community Development Block Grant (CDBG)	$4,600	$4,600	$4,600
Home Investment Partnerships	1,400	1,400	1,400
Homeless Assistance	1,120	823	823
Public Housing Modernization	2,500	2,415	2,500
Public Housing Operations	2,900	2,800	2,900
Distressed Public Housing	500	480	550
Section 8 Contract Renewals	1,231	4,007	3,550
Section 8 Amendments	735	610	850
Section 8 Incremental (New)	830	–	290
Section 202 Elderly	1,279	830	645
Section 811 Disabled Housing	387	258	196
Housing, Persons with Aids	171	171	171
Total, Department of Housing and Urban Development	$18,395	$19,176	$19,446

Source: Compiled by the author from the Appropriations Acts for the departments of Veterans Affairs, Housing and Urban Development and for Independent Offices for fiscal years 1995, 1996, and 1997.

tion of local housing authorities of $0 to $50, eliminating the need for hardship waivers. But these changes were based on year-to-year appropriations acts; they fall short of permanent reforms in authorization legislation. The public housing reform bill of 1996 was not enacted.

In a move toward housing program consolidation, the FY 1997 Appropriations Act combined nine assisted housing accounts into three primary accounts: Development of Additional Subsidized Housing, Prevention of Resident Displacement, and Preservation of Existing Housing Investment. The FY 1997 HUD Appropriations Act also contained language to extend the HUD demonstration program to restructure the HUD inventory of FHA-insured project-based Section 8 multifamily housing properties; but this restructuring still fell short of a comprehensive solution.

Among the public reform amendments under consideration in the 1997 Congressional session were the issues of rent charges, the proportion of occupancy to be targeted to low- and moderate-income families and the method of fund delivery (either to local housing authorities or to local governments), the degree of flexibility to be granted local housing authorities in the administration of their programs, and approval for housing authorities to own or operate mixed-income projects. The Section 8 program could also be affected, particularly in regard to the proportion of very-low-income families to be given assistance. Reform legislation was drafted by the Senate, the House of Representatives, and the administration, with different provisions in each bill. Whether a final act would emerge in the 1997 Congressional session was unclear at the time this chapter was written.

Future directions in federally assisted housing are far from solidified. They are strongly influenced by larger issues on the political agenda including the drive to cut government costs and to implement devolution, i.e., to shift responsibility to state and local levels. Hopefully, the recommendations in this chapter will contribute to the long-term debate on housing policy. They clearly favor a return to HUD's primary statutory missions of improving the supply and condition of housing in conjunction with the revitalization of neighborhoods, cities and, increasingly, metropolitan areas.

References

Alexander, Robert C., and Mary K. Nenno. 1974. *Required: A Local Housing Assistance Plan.* Washington, DC: National Association of Housing and Redevelopment Officials.

Bauer, Catherine. 1957. The Dreary Deadlock of Public Housing. *Architectural Forum.* May and June.

Djoko, Yves S., and Wayne Sherwood. 1992. *Public Housing Demographics.* Washington, DC: Council of Large Public Housing Authorities.

Federal Register. 1995. Preference for Working Families in Public Housing. Washington, DC. January 18.

Greer, Nora Richter. 1985. *The Search for Shelter.* Washington, DC: The American Institute of Architects.

Henderson, Peter H. 1995. *Comparing Public Housing and Section 8 Costs.* Washington, DC: National Association of Housing and Redevelopment Officials.

Henry, Marilyn J. 1994. NAHRO's H/CD Awards Winners. *Journal of Housing* 51(1):24–30.

_____. 1995. NAHRO Excellence Award Winners. *Journal of Housing* 52(1):27–30.

Hoffman, Morton 1995. Mixed-Income Housing: A New Direction in State and Federal Programs. *Real Estate Issues* 20(2).

Joint Center for Housing Studies, Harvard University. 1993, 1994. *The State of the Nation's Housing.* Cambridge, MA.

Journal of Housing. 1963. Public Housing for the Elderly Expands in Numbers, Ideas. 20(2):77–78.

Kustina, Rick. 1994. Seattle Housing Authority's Experience with the Family Self-Sufficiency Program. In Wolfgang F. E. Preiser, David P. Varady, and Francis P. Russell, eds., *Future Visions of Urban Public Housing.* Proceedings of "Future Visions of Urban Public Housing: An International Forum," held at the University of Cincinnati, Cincinnati, Ohio, November 17–20.

Massachusetts Housing Finance Agency. 1994. *Annual Report.* Boston, MA. Matulef, Mark. 1988. *More Accurate Estimates of Assisted Housing Costs.* Washington, DC: National Association of Housing and Redevelopment Officials.

Matulef, Mark. 1989. *More Accurate Estimates of Assisted Housing Costs* (Update). Washington, DC: National Association of Housing and Redevelopment Officials.

Mayer, Albert. 1962. Public Housing Architecture Evaluated from PWA Days Up to 1962. *Journal of Housing* 19 (8):446–456.

McGovern, Julia D. 1991. Linking Housing and Human Services: Lessons from Project Self-Sufficiency and Bootstrap. *Family Self Sufficiency: Linking Housing, Welfare and Human Services.* Washington, DC: National Association of Housing and Redevelopment Officials.

Melton, R. H. 1995. New View on Housing in Liberal Montgomery. *The Washington Post.* October 16.

Milgram, Grace; Bruce E. Foote; and Robert Bury. 1994. *Existing Housing Resources vs. Need, Revisited.* Washington, DC: Congressional Research Service, Library of Congress.

National Academy for State Health Policy. 1992. *Building Assisted Living for the Elderly Into Public Long-Term Care Policy: A Technical Guide for States.* Portland, ME: Center for Health Policy Development.

National Association of Housing and Redevelopment Officials and American Public Welfare Association. 1989. *Findings, Initiatives and Recommendations: A Report of the Joint Advisory Panel on the Housing Component in Welfare Reform.* Washington, DC.

National Association of Housing and Redevelopment Officials and American Public Welfare Association. 1991a. *Family Self Sufficiency: Linking Housing, Welfare and Human Services.* Washington, DC.

National Association of Housing and Redevelopment Officials and American Public Welfare Association. 1991b. *Developing an Integrated Family Self-Sufficiency System: Roadblocks, Key Elements and Recommendations for Action.* Washington, DC.

National Commission on Severely Distressed Public Housing. 1992. *Final Report of the National Commission on Severely Distressed Public Housing: A Report to the Congress and the Secretary of Housing and Urban Development.* Washington, DC: U.S. Government Printing Office.

Nelson, Kathryn P. 1994. Whose Shortage of Affordable Housing? *Housing Policy Debate* 5(4):401–442.

Nelson, Kathryn P., and Jill Khadduri. 1992. To Whom Should Limited Housing Resources Be Directed? *Housing Policy Debate* 3(1):1–55.

Nenno, Mary K. 1991. Wanted: New Housing Design. *Journal of Housing* 48(5):219, 221.

New York Times. 1995. Housing Projects to Give Priority to the Employed. February 4.

Newman, Sandra J., and Ann B. Schnare. 1992. *Beyond Bricks and Mortar: Reexamining the Purpose and Effects of Housing Assistance*. Urban Institute Report. Washington, DC: Urban Institute Press.

Siegel, Joyce. 1994. *Mixed Income Housing Experience of the Montgomery County Housing Opportunities Commission*. Kensington, MD.

Sprague, Joan Forrester. 1991. *More Than Shelter: Lifeboats for Women and Children*. Boston, MA: Butterworth Architecture Press.

Stegman, Michael A. 1992. Comment on Kathryn P. Nelson and Jill Khadduri's "To Whom Should Limited Housing Resources Be Directed?" *Housing Policy Debate* 3(1): 57–66.

———. 1996. Stegman Argues Case Against Income Targets in House Bill. *Housing and Development Reporter* 23(44):675–676. March 11.

Struyk, Raymond J.; Sue A. Marshall; and Larry J. Ozanne. 1978. *Housing for the Urban Poor*. Washington, DC: The Urban Institute.

Struyk, Raymond J.; Douglas B. Page; Sandra J. Newman; Makiko Veno; Barbara Cohen; and Paul Wright. 1989. *Providing Supportive Services to the Frail Elderly in Federally Assisted Housing*. Washington, DC: Urban Institute Press. Report 89–2.

U.S. Department of Housing and Urban Development. 1988. *Partners in Self Sufficiency*. Washington, DC.

U.S. Department of Housing and Urban Development. 1994. *Preliminary Results Under the Public Housing Management Assessment Program*. Washington, DC.

U.S. Department of Housing and Urban Development. 1995a. Memorandum of the Office of Policy Development and Research on HOME, Resident Income Data from CMI. Washington, DC. January 30.

U.S. Department of Housing and Urban Development. 1995b. Will It Cost More to Replace Public Housing with Certificates? Washington, DC. March.

U.S. House of Representatives, Select Committee on Aging. 1987. *Dignity, Independence and Cost Effectiveness: The Success of the Congregate Housing Services Program*. Washington, DC.

Urban Institute. 1995. *Federal Funds, Local Choices: An Evaluation of the Community Development Block Grant Program*. Prepared for the U.S. Department of Housing and Urban Development. Washington, DC.

Varady, David P. 1982. Indirect Benefits of Subsidized Housing Programs. *Journal of the American Planning Association* 48(4):432–440.

Von Hoffman, Alexander. 1996. High Ambitions: The Past and Future of America's Low-Income Housing Policy. *Housing Policy Debate* 7(3):423–446.

IRVING WELFELD

11 *Gautreaux: Baby Steps to Opportunity*

In 1966, Dorothy Gautreaux of Chicago and her family of six were living in a one-bedroom apartment. She moved into public housing; however, she was unhappy. She had wanted to live in an integrated building, but no openings were available. Although at the time the Chicago Housing Authority had 30,000 units and sixty-four projects, sixty of the projects were 99.5 percent black and four projects were 95 percent white. Mrs. Gautreaux and a number of similarly minded residents sued. In the ensuing legal controversy the Chicago Housing Authority (CHA) and HUD were found guilty of violating the equal-protection clause of the Constitution and the Civil Rights Act of 1964 in operating a public housing program that segregated black families.

The courts had difficulty fashioning a remedy. After four trips to the Circuit Court of Appeals, the case landed in the lap of the Supreme Court in 1976 (*Hills v. Gautreaux*). The Supreme Court turned its attention to HUD, in part because during the intervening years, the CHA, in response to several court orders directing it to build small projects in primarily white areas, had built sixty-three new units. The Supreme Court determined that the effect of HUD's actions had been to confine families eligible for public housing to one segment of a housing market that was metropolitan in scope. However, the court would not interfere with suburban governments that had not been implicated in HUD's conduct (even though many, in fact, had avoided public housing like the plague). The Supreme Court sidestepped the dilemma by indicating that HUD could bypass local governments and deal directly with private owners of apartments in the suburbs. HUD could provide subsidies under the Section 8 program to enable low-income families to lease units throughout the metropolitan area. The Supreme Court then remanded the case to the district court to work out the details (Welfeld 1976).

226

In June of 1976, following the Supreme Court ruling, HUD agreed with the attorneys for the plaintiffs to undertake a demonstration program to assist Gautreaux-class families in finding housing in suburban and non-minority areas of the Chicago SMSA. Four hundred Section 8 rental assistance certificates were made available for the first year (1977–1978) and 470 for the second year. The program continued informally until it was institutionalized through a consent decree in 1981 by the U.S. District Court (*Gautreaux v. Landrieu*). Under the consent decree, HUD agreed to set aside 7,100 Section 8 slots to be used to assist public housing residents (and those on the waiting lists) to move to areas of the city and suburbs where the population was either less than 30 percent black or to revitalized low-income urban black neighborhoods that provided better housing than the projects.

The program was and continues to be administered by the non-profit Leadership Council for Metropolitan Open Communities in Chicago. The *modus vivendi* until quite recently was that the council would locate landlords willing to participate in the program. The "client"—typically a single black woman in her mid-30s with two or three children, the youngest about eight years old—would visit the unit and the community. Although the "clients," in theory, had the choice to accept or reject the unit, in actual practice they were placed wherever the program happened to have housing openings at the time. The apartments in the suburbs have typically been in areas with an average white concentration of 96 percent. The city apartments have been in areas that are 99 percent black (Rosenbaum et al. 1991).

Gautreaux's "Moving to Opportunity" approach became a model in the 1980s and 1990s for other cities in settling discrimination lawsuits against public housing authorities (Cincinnati, Memphis, Dallas, Las Vegas, Hartford, Boston, and Yonkers). The program has received much favorable publicity. Congress concluded that the Gautreaux approach was sufficiently promising to appropriate $50 million to the program in 1993 and $171 million in 1994. David Broder, the noted *Washington Post* columnist, concluded that the "potential consequences are enormous" (1994).

Unfortunately, Mr. Broder's prediction of the future was no more accurate than predictions by political pundits in 1996 of the winners in the early Republican presidential primaries. At best, we are dealing with minimal consequences.

A Step Forward; A Step Backward

How many families are now *in the suburbs* as a result of the Gautreaux program? The total number of households placed, through 1992, is approximately 4,500 (Rosenbaum et al. 1991; Rubinowitz 1992). However, documentation about the number of families placed specifically in the suburbs, for most of the period, is difficult to come by. The figures are contained in an unpublished report by Paul Fischer of Lake Forest College, using Leadership Council data covering the years 1983 to 1992. Fischer's report shows that of the 3,080 placements (609 of which were in

HUD-assisted projects), 1,300 families were placed in Chicago and 1,748 were placed in the suburbs. Fischer's report also documents that a significant shift in the program occurred in 1992. Between 1983 and 1991, the average number of placements per year was 291, with 50 percent in the suburbs. In 1992, however, the total number of placements was 462, with 99 percent in the suburbs. Is it possible that the Chicago suburbs are going through an age of enlightenment (or more accurately "endarkenment"), or is it that the rules have changed? Apparently neither. The overall pattern through 1993 and 1994 is consistent with the earlier figures. A 1995 HUD report (Goering et al. 1995) notes that between 1976 and 1994, 5,600 families participated in the program, with 3,000 families (53.6 percent) being dispersed among roughly 115 Chicago suburbs.

How many of the families placed still reside in the suburbs? There are only strands of evidence. One report shows that by May of 1979, 18 percent of the initial suburbanites had dropped out of the program (Peroff et al. 1979). In 1982, a random sample of participants who had children of school age was taken; seven years later, more than 40 percent of the sample could not be located (Rosenbaum 1994). An estimate of a 25 percent return-to-the-city rate would give a cumulative 17-year total of 2,225 families remaining in the suburbs (an annual net rate of 132 families). That total is only 5.2 percent of the 43,000 families (Peroff et al. 1979) who were originally eligible for the program. The initial goal of 7,100 units that was seen as a modest first step has become a long march.

In the meantime, the world has not stood still. While Gautreaux has trudged forward, the number of black poor living in census tracts in Chicago designated as "poverty," "extreme poverty," or "underclass" grew by 80,000 between 1970 and 1990, to a total of 354,194 (Kasarda 1993). Between 1980 and 1990, the number of tracts designated as at or below poverty levels increased from 574 to 669. Significantly, a large portion of the increase in the number of poverty areas is due to the departure of 84,000 middle- and upper-income blacks from the city to the suburbs during the 1980s (O'Hare and Frey 1992).

WHY SO FEW?

Most blacks are initially reluctant to pioneer in all-white areas (Farley et al. 1993). At the outset, the Gautreaux program, with its dispersal strategy, probably raised the initial diffidence level. The family would be, for a good number of years, one of very few black families in the area. In 1979, of the 22,655 families notified about a briefing session for the program, only 1,823 attended (Peroff et al. 1979).

But when the choice is between being strangers in a strange land and living in a daily nightmare, the former becomes more attractive. Nowadays, the choice is between the Robert Taylor Homes or Cabrini-Green—centers of drug and gang culture, where a walk to the grocery or to school is fraught with danger—and an apartment in a relatively safe middle-class neighborhood in the suburbs. And, the rent is the same! Even given the diversity of preferences among 43,000 eligible families, by the mid-1990s, the program ought to have been able to draw a more-than-sufficient number of potential movers.

Another possible explanation for the low number of successful placements may lie with the selection process. The Leadership Council is not a "pie in the sky" group that has sought out the worst-need cases and trooped them off to Gallopoli, thereby decimating the program. The Council wanted to reward good tenants and provide private landlords with attractive candidates. The tenants needed persistence and luck just to get through to the switchboard, which closed after 2,000 families were selected for the waiting list. Since little more than 300 were chosen in an average year, a multi-year wait has been the norm.

Waiting has not been the only requirement. Thirty percent of the families selected for the program couldn't pass through the Council filter (Rosenbaum 1994). The applicants chosen had to have a good rental and credit record (rejection rate: 12%), an apartment kept in accord with the expectations of a private landlord (rejection rate: 13%), and fewer than four children (rejection rate: 5%). In the initial years, the selection process excluded families with criminal records, alcoholics, and those without cars.

Although the demand was more than adequate, the supply of units was modest and halting. The easiest areas, the parts of the suburbs in which there were blacks and in which many landlords accepted Section 8 certificates, were mostly off-limits. The possibility of resegregation conflicted with the goals of the Leadership Council and the desires of the black and white residents of the area. Much of the litigation in opposition to subsidized housing and its residents is based on class. The plaintiffs, in many cases, include middle-class blacks living in integrated communities (*Shannon v. HUD; King v. Harris*).

HUD did require assisted housing developers to set aside a portion of their new units for the program. (Although federal appropriations declined dramatically in the early 1980s, the lengthy development "pipeline" meant that new housing was available until the late 1980s.) Elsewhere in the private market, however, the Leadership Council had little leverage. There wasn't much doubt that some housing was withheld for racial and class reasons. Moreover, even when there was evidence from trained testers, the Leadership Council was playing with a weak hand. As one commentator noted:

> The council's dual role was particularly problematic . . . since the program depended so heavily on landlords' voluntary participation. Any Leadership Council investigation or lawsuit related to the Gautreaux program could have endangered carefully cultivated relationships with that landlord, and risked alienating others as well. (Rubinowitz 1992)

Many landlords saw little reason to get involved in the government's social engineering, especially if they didn't have much difficulty obtaining occupants. Less than half of all landlords will accept a tenant bearing a Section 8 certificate in all their units (Goering et al. 1995). In the case of the Gautreaux families steered by the Council, 63 percent of the tenants were placed in the newly developing far northwestern suburbs. The unguided Section 8 program run by Cook County, on the other hand, resulted in the vast majority of the black families being placed in clusters of tracts immediately south of Chicago (e.g., Calumet City) and the relatively few white families placed to the north of Chicago (Burke 1996). There are, thus, vast areas of the suburbs where the landlords are less than eager to engage in a program that attempts to achieve racial and economic integration.

The need to use the Section 8 program as the subsidy delivery mechanism created other problems for the program as well. To qualify for the program the units had to meet HUD's quality standards, procedures, and contract provisions. As a Northwestern law professor, who was closely involved in the evaluation of the program, has written:

> Many landlords viewed [HUD as] intruding inappropriately on their discretion in selecting tenants. Suburban landlords expressed concerns that if they accepted one Section 8 tenant . . . they would not be able to limit access of low-income families. This "floodgate" led some landlords to avoid the program. [This requirement was removed in the 1990s.] Section 8 requirements also included procedures for landlords to follow. Perhaps most significantly, evictions required adherence to HUD-specified procedures. (Rubinowitz 1992)

More Jobs than Jobholders

Employment results have also been less than spectacular. In recent decades, large numbers of low-skill jobs have left the cities and relocated in the suburbs. Chicago had 68 percent of the region's jobs in 1960, for example, but only 41 percent in 1981. Between 1972 and 1989, Chicago lost 133,965 jobs, while the suburban portion of the six-county region gained 427,952 jobs, with the largest growth in suburban Cook and DuPage Counties (Rubinowitz 1992).

The spatial mismatch hypothesis (Kain 1992) posits that geographical distance between home and work has limited employment for low-income blacks who are confined to inner cities. Shouldn't the low-income black women who moved to the suburbs have experienced significant gains in employment by relocating?

In the fall of 1988, a random sample of demographically similar Gautreaux participants—224 in the suburbs and 108 in the city—were surveyed. Of those who were employed before the move, the suburbanites fared 13.9 percent better than the city residents in obtaining employment. Among the previously unemployed, the suburbanites fared 53 percent better than the city residents in finding jobs, leading the principal researchers of the labor market experiences, James Rosenbaum and Susan Popkin, to conclude:

> [L]ow-income urban blacks experience significant gains in employment by moving to middle-class suburbs. Thus, housing assistance may be an effective alternative to traditional welfare-to-work programs. (Popkin et al. 1993)

However, the enthusiasm of the researchers seems to have outrun their findings. The percentages are statistically significant, but statistics is a refined science that can turn a small change into a meaningful event. One would expect that in a city losing jobs, the number of jobs obtained by low-skilled workers would decrease. And so they did. The intra-city movers had ten fewer jobholders. One would further expect that in the suburbs adding low-skilled jobs, the number of jobs obtained by low-skilled workers would increase. Not 50. The number of jobholders before the move was 144. The number after the move was 143. Significantly, their hourly wage and the number of hours worked per week were the same as the city dwellers. In other words, the suburbanites may have fared better than the intra-city movers, but they still didn't fare very well.

The suburban movers are still a long way from self-sufficiency. A market monthly rent of $600 is more than 70 percent of the income of the household that has an average weekly wage of $200. The families in the suburbs still faced hurdles. Besides the internal barriers (many of the movers were second generation AFDC recipients), the lack or absence of a reliable car, inadequate child care, and low skill levels hinder the families' ability to make substantial economic progress. It takes more than a ticket on the suburban job merry-go-round to capture the brass ring of success.

What's more, the spatial mismatch theory has not held up well to subsequent research. Christopher Jencks and Susan Mayer (in Kain 1992), after reviewing twenty-five empirical studies, concluded:

> Taken together, these findings had a very mixed story. They provide no direct support for the hypothesis that racial segregation affects the aggregate level of demand for black workers. They provide some support for the idea that job proximity increased the supply of black workers, but the support is so mixed that *no prudent policy analysis should rely on it.* Those who argue that moving blacks to the suburbs would improve their job prospects, or improving public transportation would reduce unemployment in the central-city ghetto, must recognize that there is as much evidence against such racial claims as for them. [emphasis added] (Kain 1992)

Education—Pain and Gain

The children that moved to the suburbs encountered very different school systems. The suburban educational standards were undeniably higher. The level of curriculum in Chicago was one to three years behind the suburban grade level (Rosenbaum et al. 1991) The adjustment was initially painful. Nineteen percent of the children were placed in special education programs (compared to 7 percent pre-move). An unknown percentage was set back a grade or placed in lower ability groups.

Some of the mothers complained of racial discrimination in the suburbs. However, most of the anger was vented on the Chicago schools. As one mother said, "It was like he hadn't even gone to school in Chicago for three years. And he was going every day and he was getting report cards telling me that he was doing fine" (Rosenbaum et al. 1991).

The suburban teachers provided help to the children and were more responsive to their educational needs than their city counterparts. However, more than a few of the teachers were less than tolerant, and a request for help would sometimes result in the singling out of the child as not as smart as the other children in the class. As the researchers commented, "These incidents not only had negative ramifications for the children involved, and other black children; they are also likely to have fostered racial prejudice in these schools" (Rosenbaum et al. 1991).

The educational gap between the city and suburban schools was also present at the high school level. The suburban schools had significantly higher reading scores than the city schools. On a scale of 1 to 500, Chicago eleventh graders were at 198 and suburban eleventh graders were at 259. Many of the Chicago students never even took the test. The high school dropout rate in Chicago was more than 65 percent; in the suburbs, the rate was less than 15 percent. The norm in the city school was not to graduate; the norm in the suburbs was to graduate (Kaufman and Rosenbaum 1992).

The Gautreaux youth in the suburbs held a clear advantage over their Chicago counterparts. Forty percent of the movers were in college track classes versus 24 percent in Chicago. Of the fifty-five youths who were older than eighteen (41 were in the suburbs and 14 were in the city), 27 percent of the suburban youths were in four-year colleges (11) and 27 percent were in community colleges (11). Of the fourteen city youths in the sample, 21 percent (3) were in four-year colleges. Seventy-five percent of the suburban youths were employed versus 40 percent in the city (Kaufman and Rosenbaum 1992).

Although the percentages amplify the results, they prove that superior schools turn out students who are better prepared for the future than do mediocre schools.

Conclusion

The Gautreaux program produced a cottage industry for researchers but modest results for public housing tenants. The vision of the initial plaintiffs lies in the distant past. The chance of getting a unit in an integrated building in Chicago public housing is still slim. The program's most significant accomplishment has been to enable a relatively few families over many years to escape from the mean streets and mangy apartments of Chicago's inner-city public housing. The economic opportunity of being closer to a richer job pool allowed the suburban group to maintain their tenuous position in the job market but resulted in no real advances. The change in educational systems, after causing some emotional pain, did produce gains, but only when compared to the school conditions in the city.

The good news is that the Gautreaux program is replicable in other suburban areas. The bad news is that the process will be long and laborious and that the results will be so microscopic that it will take sophisticated and talented social scientists to uncover them.

A POSTSCRIPT

In 1994, residents of Baltimore County, Maryland, objected to HUD's decision to move 285 inner-city residents to new neighborhoods in the city and county under the Moving to Opportunity program. In July of 1994, the administration's request for $149.1 million to expand the program came before the Senate Committee (chaired by Barbara A. Mikulski of Maryland). The committee earmarked no funds for the program in 1995 and reached back and reprogrammed the previous year's unspent money ($171 million) to a general Section 8 counseling program.

References

Broder, D. 1994. For the Urban Poor. *Washington Post* (op-ed). June 8.

Burke, P. 1996. *A Picture of Subsidized Housing. Midwest* 5:41–3. Washington, DC: U.S. Department of Housing and Urban Development.

Farley R.; C. Steeh; T. Jackson; M. Krysan; and K. Reeves. 1993. Continued Racial Segregation in Detroit: "Chocolate City, Vanilla Suburbs" Revisited. *Journal of Housing Research* 4(1):1–38.

Gautreaux v. Landrieu. 523 F. Supp. 665, 674 (N.D. Ill 1981).

Goering, J.; A. Haghughi; H. Stebbins; and M. Siewart. 1995. *Report to Congress: Promoting Housing Choice in HUD's Rental Assistance Programs.* Washington, DC: U.S. Department of Housing and Urban Development.

Hills v. Gautreaux. 425 U.S. 284 (1976).

Kain, J. 1992. The Spatial Mismatch Hypothesis: Three Decades Later. *Housing Policy Debate* 3(2):371–460.

234   IRVING WELFELD

Kasarda, J. 1993. Inner-City Poverty and Economic Access. In *Rediscovering Urban America: Perspectives on the 1980's*, eds. J. Sommers and D. Hicks, 1–60. Washington, DC: U.S. Department of Housing and Urban Development.

Kaufman, J., and J. Rosenbaum. 1992. The Education and Employment of Low-Income Black Youth in White Suburbs. *Education Evaluation and Policy Analysis* 14(3):229–40.

King v. Harris. 464 F. Supp. 827 (1979).

O'Hare, W., and W. Frey. 1992. Booming, Suburban, and Black. *American Demographics* (September):30–38.

Peroff, K.; Cloteal Davis; and R. Jones. 1979. *Gautreaux Housing Demonstration: An Evaluation of Its Impact on Participating Households.* Washington, DC: U.S. Department of Housing and Urban Development.

Popkin, S.; J. Rosenbaum; and P. Meaden. 1993. Labor Market Experiences of Low-Income Black Women in Middle-Class Suburbs: Evidence from a Survey of Gautreaux Program Participants. *Journal of Policy Analysis and Management* 12(3):556–73.

Rosenbaum, J. 1994. Changing the Geography of Opportunity by Expanding Residential Choices: Lessons from the Gautreaux Program. FNMA (Annual Housing Conference 1994), *Access to Opportunity: Understanding Its Influence on Urban Lives*, 1–31.

Rosenbaum J.; H. Kulieke; and L. Rubinowitz. 1988. White Suburban Schools' Responses to Low-Income Black Children: Sources of Successes and Problems. *The Urban Review* 20(1):28–41.

Rosenbaum, J.; S. Popkin; J. Kaufman; and J. Rusin. 1991. Social Integration of Low-Income Black Adults in Middle-Class White Suburbs. *Social Problems* 38(4):448–61.

Rubinowitz, L. 1992. Metropolitan Public Housing Remedies: Chicago's Privatization Program. *Northern Illinois Law Review* 12(3):589–669.

Shannon v. HUD. 436 F. 2d 809 (1970).

Welfeld, I. 1976. The Courts and Desegregated Housing: The Meaning (If Any) of the *Gautreaux* Case. *Public Interest* 45 (Fall):123–135.

PART VI

Epilogue

JAMES G. STOCKARD, JR.

12 *Public Housing— The Next Sixty Years?*

Introduction

Overall, public housing in the United States is a success. It has been so, to a great extent, since its formal creation through the Federal Housing Act of 1937. For nearly sixty years, this program has created millions of jobs, helped eliminate devastated portions of our cities, and provided affordable housing for poorer Americans. Although some have criticized the quality of this housing, its residents consistently report that it is significantly better than they could hope for in the private sector. The program has not been flawless, but that is no reason to deny its overall success or to fail to learn from an accurate understanding of its performance.

Many readers, including those who have examined some of the chapters in this volume, may find these assertions surprising. But they are not the emotional cries of an advocate. Rather, they are the reality-based conclusions to which any dispassionate observer must come if he or she examines the public housing program thoroughly and honestly. Of course, public housing has not been a total success:

- It has not entirely eliminated poverty, although it has provided economic breathing space that has allowed many to climb out of that state.
- It has not turned every neighborhood in which it is located into a Norman Rockwell painting, although many neighborhoods without public housing are far worse than areas with public housing. Some developments, especially those that serve the elderly, have anchored successful turnarounds.[1]
- It has not protected every resident from all the dangers of life in America

today, but the private sector in poor neighborhoods has not been significantly more successful at this task.

Public housing has, indeed, not been perfect. But then, no program—public or
private—ever is.

The conference out of which this volume grew ("Future Visions of Urban Public
Housing: An International Forum") was dedicated to assessing the impact of public
housing and the prospects for its future. If we are to seriously pursue this matter,
the reasonable question is not: "Has public housing been perfect?" Rather, we need
to ask whether the effort has accomplished some significant part of its mission, especially in light of the context in which it has operated. The answer to this question
may tell us what elements of the program have led to its successes, what elements
have been a drag on the program, and how the program might be modified to serve
its goals more fully.

This epilogue will assert that, when measured against its goals, its resources, and
its environment, public housing can be called an overall success. Further, it will argue that America's public housing program contains within its history and practice
many elements of a vision for even better ways to provide decent, safe, and sanitary
housing for Americans who cannot afford what the private market provides. This
vision is compelling: strong, independent, local public agencies operating decent housing for a wide range of residents (with a focus on the poor) at affordable rents, using
modest federal subsidies. A number of chapters in this volume (especially those by
Alexander von Hoffman, Gayle Epp, Lawrence Vale, Peter Marcuse, Mary Nenno,
and Richard Best) hint at this vision, and it will be the purpose of this concluding
chapter to pull it into focus.

Every community in our nation benefits when it has three strong actors in the
housing marketplace—private for-profit organizations, private nonprofit entities, and
public agencies. In most cases, each of the entities focuses on serving the needs of a
particular part of the population in the community. At any given point in time, the
effectiveness of each sector is shaped by the financing available to it (both public
and private), the subsidy dollars available to it (direct or through the tax code), and
the leadership of the organizations in that sector. When one of these sectors "fails,"
it is important that there be other alternatives that can take over where there is a
vacuum. If there is no longer a public agency that can own and manage housing
units, then the community has lost one-third of its ability to respond to certain housing needs. And, certainly some PHAs have failed in the past. On the other hand,
strong, creative PHAs, such as the Housing Opportunities Commission in Montgomery County, Maryland, until recently under Bernard Tetreault; the Norfolk
Redevelopment and Housing Authority led by Dave Rice; the Richmond Redevelopment and Housing Authority with Rick Gentry; the Dade County Department
of Housing and Urban Development under Greg Byrne; and the Cambridge, Massachusetts, Housing Authority led by Dan Wuenschel are reshaping their communi-

ties by stepping beyond the traditional roles for PHAs. They are undertaking new and unusual partnerships, contracting with private entities for services long undertaken only by PHAs, providing financing for other housing ventures, creating new forms of affordable housing, participating in mixed-income developments, and generally leading the way in resolving major housing issues in their communities.

This volume asks the question, "What is the role of the public housing program in this nation's future?" From the chapters included here and the examples of good public housing programs before us, we now know there is no single answer to this question. The role of public housing is very different from community to community. In order to create the public housing program of the future we will need to pay attention to what we have learned from the history of this program and to make the changes that will free it to operate effectively in the future. Chapters by Peter Marcuse, Gayle Epp, Mary Nenno, Richard Best, and others in this volume are particularly helpful in pointing us in this direction.

A Brief History of Public Housing

Public housing was created six decades ago as a major part of the response to several problems threatening the nation—unemployment, the decay of rapidly expanding cities, a crippled economy, and . . . oh, yes . . . inadequate housing resources. This New Deal program was designed to serve the temporarily disenfranchised middle class, especially the younger members who had not yet secured their first independent home. They were to wait and rent (at affordable prices) until the economy recovered; then, they would find the jobs for which they were destined, and move to their own homes. At first, these homes were to be in the "better" neighborhoods within the city. Later, after the second wave of major economic dislocation (World War II), their future destinations became the newly emerging suburbs. Since then, we have asked this program to continue housing poor people while responding to new realities every few years, including dramatic changes in the economy, two more international wars, the substantial aging of our population, radical changes in the racial and ethnic makeup of our cities, and fundamental alterations in the shape of the American family and the social mores surrounding it. We have required this to be done by an inadequately funded, heavily regulated, local public agency ostensibly autonomous, but often fully enmeshed in the political life of its city.

Following both the Depression and World War II, the housing industry, including the large public housing sector, led the economic recovery. The program created millions of jobs and stimulated the construction materials industry. Thousands of acres of "slum housing" were cleared and redeveloped with vastly improved housing—much of it public housing. When the property acquired and vacated was not actually used for public housing, it was often public housing that provided relocation resources to make the clearance possible. Millions of Americans, unable to afford

decent housing, have been provided with this critical resource over the past sixty years
through a tenure in public housing.

STATISTICAL FACTS

As noted, there have been some dramatic and very public failures in the public
housing program. But, even today, statistics and serious evaluations of public housing paint a picture of a program with many fewer failures than one would anticipate
from reading the dramatic headlines or the sensational exposés about public housing. President Bush's National Commission on Severely Distressed Public Housing
found, in 1991, that 94 percent of the nation's 13,741 public housing developments
(commonly referred to as "projects") were providing "decent, safe and sanitary housing at an affordable price" (National Commission on Severely Distressed Public Housing 1992). Some have questioned the thoroughness of this assessment. For example,
many of the failed developments are the vast high rise-buildings for families that, in
total, include more than 6 percent of the public housing units (apartments) in the
nation. No one would defend them as a reasonable method for housing large numbers of poor families. In fact, HUD has not allowed such buildings to be constructed
since 1971. Still, such developments are but a very small percentage of all properties, and therefore the total number of "failed" apartments is not significantly larger
than the 6 percent figure given above.

It is also true that definitions of "successful" and "troubled" are debatable, and
the measures implied in these terms are partially subjective. But there is no research
of which this author is aware that details a greater number of unsuccessful properties across the country. It appears that declarations of the failure of public housing
have been based on a very narrow view of the program. Advocates, journalists, academics, politicians and others can target Robert Taylor Homes in Chicago, or Desire in New Orleans, or Richard Allen Homes in Philadelphia, and declare them
failures. They can cite receiverships in Washington, D.C., Kansas City, and Boston
as indications of entire city programs where clearly more than 6 percent of all units
or developments are troubled. Rarely do these same opinion leaders consider life at
Washington Elms in Cambridge, or Commonwealth in Boston, or Diggstown in
Norfolk, or hundreds of other successful family-oriented public housing developments
across the nation. And they seem to ignore the public housing programs in Seattle,
Milwaukee, St. Paul, Miami, Louisville, Richmond, Norfolk, Omaha, and many other
large cities that serve their residents in a highly professional manner. Nor do most
critics think to consider the nearly 40 percent of all public housing developments
that serve senior citizens. Somehow, this housing is considered a different category
and its widely perceived success cannot be called a success for public housing. Even
if the numbers of troubled developments cited in the Commission's study were
doubled, the general level of success would still be very significant.

As another measure of success or failure, we might consider HUD's own system of evaluating housing authorities, the Public Housing Management Assessment Program (PHMAP). Under this system, every PHA in the nation is evaluated each year on twenty-two indicators of performance (e.g., vacancy rate, rent collection rate, work orders completed). As of September 1994, 97 percent of PHAs were evaluated at standard or high performance levels. Only 3 percent of all agencies (91 in number) were designated as "troubled" (Public Housing Management Assessment Program System for Management Information Retrieval—Public Housing 1995).

Some other statistics about this program are surprising as well. The more than 3,400 public housing agencies serve over 1.25 million households (HUD System for Management Information Retrieval—Public Housing 1995), 43 percent of whom have elderly or disabled heads. Only 18 percent of the families have three or more children. The median income of all these households is $6,420 (U.S. Department of Housing and Urban Development 1995), clearly not enough to afford even the meanest housing in virtually any corner of the nation. For two-thirds of these households the main source of income is Social Security, pensions, or wages—not welfare. And the median length of time for which families rely on public housing is four years. Forty percent of all families stay for fewer than three years and 71 percent leave within ten years (U.S. Department of Housing and Urban Development, forthcoming). Many of those who stay longer are elderly or disabled. They truly have no other choices.

It is not only true that public housing has largely served its purpose well in the past, but it is also clear that the program is vitally necessary for the foreseeable future. The essence of public housing consists of homes owned by a local public agency and affordable by people at any income level. One and one-quarter million poor households currently live in such housing, and an equivalent number are on waiting lists for this housing. Surely, these people would make other choices if all public housing were so undesirable. Even if the desirability is relative, only the cruelest of policymakers would advocate eliminating the best alternative for the poorest families. In addition to those on waiting lists, millions of other families who are eligible for public housing currently pay more than 50 percent of their income for their housing, live in substandard dwellings, or are overcrowded in their homes (Joint Center for Housing Studies 1996, Chart 27 and Table A-12). This is more than adequate testimony to the continuing need for the current number of public housing units and more. These homes must be available at deeply subsidized rents or they are of no value to this population. At least some of the housing must be owned by public agencies because there has been no demonstration that the private sector alone, whether for-profit or nonprofit, is capable of housing this population in adequate numbers, or at rents they can afford, and in locations which are reasonable. Should this public resource disappear, or be significantly reduced, hundreds of thousands of American families and individuals will find themselves without decent housing. This is simply unacceptable.

How is it that the public housing program that has met so many needs in the past, and that is so necessary for our future, is in such ill repute? The average person in the street will tell you the program has been a failure, as will almost anyone else, including the typical Congressperson who must vote on the future of public housing. Why is this the case? And what is to be done about it? Is there a better alternative? And if there is not, what should be done about the nature and the image of the public housing program so that it can be even more successful over the next sixty years than it has been over the past sixty? One thing is clear: Change must occur.

PROBLEMS IN PUBLIC HOUSING

A knowledge of the history of public housing, from its emergence as an idea in the early 1930s through the current debates about its future, is very important to an understanding of the program as it exists today. Chapters in this volume by Peter Marcuse, Alexander von Hoffman, and Karen A. Franck are helpful in this regard, particularly Franck's discussion of societal values and their reflection in design. Listed below are the major problems of public housing.

Image. In a few very prominent locations, public housing provides unconscionably bad environments for its residents. Between intolerable physical conditions, woefully inadequate services, and very real dangers to life and limb, these properties can reasonably be considered by all decent people to be disasters. These are the properties that make up most of the failures cited by the National Commission on Severely Distressed Public Housing. Many of them are high-rise properties for families, a housing type that has failed in many locations (with the notable exception of New York City). But this style of housing constitutes only a tiny minority of all public housing units. While these apartments frequently deserve condemnation, they are not representative of the entire public housing program and, therefore, they are not grounds for destroying the program. For more than twenty-five years, HUD has forbidden the construction of any housing for families that exceeds three floors. Still, high-rises are the buildings that appear on the evening TV news, the front page of the local paper, and in the latest speech by an opportunistic politician. In turn, these visual and rhetorical images shape the public's view of this program. The result is an almost total lack of support for the continued funding of public housing.

A marginalized group of beneficiaries. Because of the image issue, the federal mandates regarding who is to be admitted, the local politics which also shape admissions policy, and other factors, the population of public housing has become increasingly poor, increasingly dominated by single-parent–headed households and families of racial and ethnic minorities, and increasingly troubled. Finally, for a wide variety of reasons, this population tends not to vote. In the current political and social climate in this nation, such families have fewer and fewer advocates and allies. Social facts like these do not make public housing worse, but they make it less popular. These factors make it easier for politicians and bureaucrats to ignore this constituency. (For a more detailed explication, see Peter Marcuse's excellent chapter.)

Financial starvation. Federal funding for public housing has always been less than adequate. In a number of cases over the past decade, Congress has not even appropriated the funding levels "guaranteed" by the Performance Funding System, a formula which was created to determine how much money PHAs should receive to conduct their normal property management operations. This constant underfunding has meant that needed repairs have been postponed. Hard choices have been required. Frequently, the care of the grounds has been deferred in order to complete repairs inside apartments and buildings. This has led to more low-maintenance asphalt and less grass with the result of yet more image problems. Beyond normal operations, capital improvements have been, and still are, severely underfunded. They have lagged well behind the levels recommended by the Abt Associates study (1987) of public housing capital improvement needs conducted a decade ago. Similar financial shortfalls have affected other areas of service to residents. Until the early 1990s very little money had been set aside for security or resident services such as training, youth sports, day care, or job placement. These services could be provided only by reducing other line items in PHA budgets.

Housing of last resort. PHAs are unique bodies. They are, typically, independent public agencies rather than city departments. They often do not even appear on a city organization chart. But their commissioners are usually appointed by elected officials who therefore have a great deal of leverage on these key policymakers, without having to be accountable for their performance. When local officials (from the city or the authority itself) substitute their personal or political agendas for the professional standards of providing good housing, authorities become troubled.[2] Personnel decisions, admission choices, maintenance priorities, and other critical elements of the PHA can often be adversely affected by such actions. In addition, local courts typically treat public housing as the housing of last resort, refusing to allow PHAs to evict or otherwise discipline residents, even when no one disputes that lease violations have occurred. Judges frequently wonder: "Where will this family go if they are evicted from public housing?" Absent a convincing answer, they may order the PHA to retain the family,[3] thus sending a clear message to all tenants that paying the rent and obeying the rules are not necessary in order to stay in their housing. In this way, the label "housing of last resort" becomes a self-fulfilling prophecy. Worst of all, decent residents tend to leave public housing (as they do in nearly any multifamily situation) when the management is not able to remove troublesome neighbors from the property.

Negative incentives. As documented in many studies, the package of incentives that emerges from the maze of regulations surrounding programs that serve poor Americans such as welfare, food stamps, Medicaid, and public housing, tends to drive these families away from the economic mainstream rather than toward it. Public housing's contribution to this problem is the rent formula. On the one hand, the idea of basing rent on income is extremely helpful to poor families. On the other hand, the fact that the percentage is taken on adjusted *gross* income, rather than *net*, and the lack of ceilings on rents, discourages people from choosing to work. Basing rent on a percentage of adjusted gross income means essentially that the rent comes out of a person's earnings *before* the taxes come out. Since welfare payments are not taxed, the amount received is a net income. Effectively, the rent for a person on welfare is based on their net income. But even low working wages are taxed. Therefore, every extra dollar residents earn when they move from welfare to work costs them not only 30 cents in rent, but another 17 cents or so in taxes. Furthermore, as families move up the economic ladder, their public housing rent can become substantial if there are no ceiling rents. At $25,000 gross income, monthly rent is $625. At $30,000 (for example, a married couple, each with a $15,000 job), monthly rent is $750. Although there are not a large number of public housing residents with incomes in this category, the changes in the funding levels for PHAs may mean there will be more households in this range in the future. Rents will go up rapidly for these families, and there is often a gap between what feels burdensome in a public housing unit and what it may take to secure a significantly better dwelling in the private sector. In many cases, the wise, *rational* decision—the decision anyone would make for his or her family if presented with the options facing many poor households in our cities—is to stay on welfare. While the wave of welfare "reforms" may move many people off welfare rolls, early indications are that it may not necessarily move many of them to the kind of employment that will enable them to pay their rents and have enough left for the other necessities of life. Public housing legislators and regulation writers have not created this perverse incentive system by themselves, but they have contributed to its powerful negative impact on the lives of poor Americans.

Public housing is unfair—it is not an entitlement program—so some people get a very substantial benefit, while others get nothing, even though they are working hard. There are many, many people working at low-paying jobs in our communities who live in far worse housing (and who pay far more for it) than their public housing neighbors. Some of these families are on public housing waiting lists and would like to live in public housing some day. Others have no desire to live in these properties, but they feel as though they are being treated unfairly, since they may receive no subsidy at all for their housing while public housing residents receive a large benefit. This has not gone unnoticed in some cities and provides the grounds for additional sentiment to cut or eliminate the program since, in this context, it is inherently unfair.

The industry is dramatically overregulated and micro-managed. In spite of the original resolve to make public housing a local program operating simply with federal grants for construction, HUD has grown into a dominating master, instructing local agencies in the most minute details of how to do their job. Thousands and thousands of pages of regulations control every element of housing authority operations. Worst of all, nearly every decision must be submitted to HUD to be matched against libraries full of regulations. In many cases, particularly those where the public housing program has performed poorly, this has slowed the process and reduced many initiatives to the lowest common denominator. Currently, HUD administrators are endeavoring to reduce these regulations and turn many competent authorities loose to pursue housing strategies that are the best for their communities. Although this direction is positive, it is likely to take many years to break the old habit of turning to a regulation handbook to find out how something is done or why it can't be done.

POSITIVE ASPECTS OF PUBLIC HOUSING

The preceding list of public housing problems was easy to create. Even people who are not intimately familiar with public housing can make this list if they have read the appropriate newspaper articles. But the other side of the picture is less well-known. Cited below are some of the positive aspects that public housing is adding to our cities.

The vast majority of public housing is in decent condition. If one takes the word of the National Commission on Severely Distressed Public Housing (1992), then 94 percent of all public housing developments are providing decent shelter for their residents. HUD's PHMAP system, another national evaluation program, indicates that 97 percent of all authorities are doing at least an adequate job of providing housing for those of modest means. These two studies, one a "photograph" taken in 1991, the other an annual assessment, might be biased. But there is no data other than anecdotal to support a significantly contrary opinion. And for every story about a tragic public housing environment, there are hundreds of stories to be told about quiet, modest-sized developments that provide good shelter for families and elderly households.

Thanks to recent major capital improvement funding programs (CIAP, Comprehensive Modernization, MROP, HOPE VI), a number of family public housing developments around the country have become showpieces and are regularly confused with market-rate condominiums. Gayle Epp's chapter describes how these funds are being used and documents some of the outstanding early results that are occurring. Older modernization efforts, such as those at Washington Elms in Cambridge (ten years old) and Commonwealth (15 years old) in Boston, demonstrate that where good management follows good rehabilitation, the improvements can be sustained over a long period of time. Lawrence Vale's chapter in this volume documents the seven ways in which major redevelopment efforts must succeed if they are truly to make a difference in the lives of their residents. He shows how those standards have been met at two Boston developments, though not at a third. The great secret of public housing is that it is quietly performing a very tough assignment quite well in most of the 3,400 communities throughout the nation in which it exists. We seem finally to have learned some very important lessons about how to provide decent homes for poor households, and these lessons are being applied in important revitalization efforts.

One very legitimate issue that cannot be ignored, however, is the impact of the surrounding neighborhood on the conditions at any particular development. It is clearly difficult to maintain a good housing environment when the adjacent blocks are unattractive, dangerous, and lacking reasonable amenities. Certainly, some public housing properties have fallen prey to poor locational choices and to subsequent neglect of their neighborhoods. On the other hand, where site choices have been made wisely, and where the public sector has kept its commitment to serve all neighborhoods with good transportation, reasonable police and fire protection, decent amenities and regular services, public housing developments have remained decent. These observations help to confirm what we all know intuitively—that housing never stands in isolation from its surrounding neighborhood. The particular situations where public housing has failed are often those where both neighborhood and site are troubled.

Compared to the other alternatives, public housing is a very good choice. Children and parents interviewed recently for research on growing up in public housing were crystal clear about their homes. While there were problems and aspects of the housing they would change if they could, the overwhelming sentiment was that the housing was better than they would have been able to afford in the private sector. People said things like: "If we didn't live in public housing our family would be split up by now"; and "The only reason me and my brothers and parents aren't dead by now is that we got into public housing" (New Community Services, Inc., Reese Fayde and Associates, and Stockard & Engler & Brigham [forthcoming]). Unlike their counterparts in the private sector, public housing residents always know where to find their landlord; in fact, the owner is required to have a 24-hour response system for emergencies. Furthermore, the owner is not suddenly going to decide to leave the program; residents cannot be evicted without cause; and rent is tied to income.

A particularly important portion of the public housing story involves the properties serving the elderly. More than 34 percent of all public housing households are headed by elderly residents and 9 percent by people with disabilities (U.S. Department of Housing and Urban Development 1995). These units have provided affordable shelter, often with associated services, for a portion of the population living on low fixed incomes who have no real alternatives for housing. Almost without exception, the same critics who condemn the public housing program in general praise this portion of the program. Clearly, this element of the public housing program works well and may prove useful in constructing public housing programs for the future.

It is all too easy to think that if poor households did not live in public housing, they would live in idyllic urban or suburban townhouses or pleasant garden apartments with helpful managers to assist them in going about their daily business. In fact, given what low-income families and individuals can afford to pay, the alternative may well be a unit in a marginal or troubled neighborhood. And compared to a typical public housing unit, the private apartment is quite possibly in worse condition, has a higher rent, and, in some cases, is owned by a less-than-responsible land-lord. There is no reason to believe, for example, that a low-rent private unit has had lead paint removed, whereas the vast majority of public housing units are now lead-free. Before we lose too many of the 1.4 million units from the public housing stock, we should listen to residents, old and young, about the other alternatives facing them.

Public housing is more efficient than any of the other forms of assisted housing. Public housing construction was financed entirely through tax-exempt bonds. The private stock rented through vouchers under the Section 8 program, on the other hand, was built with more costly private financing. The vast majority of these public housing construction bonds were sold in times when interest rates rarely climbed above 5 percent. What's more, construction costs were lower for many public housing struc-tures because of economies of scale, cost limitations on development, and the small size of apartments. As to operating costs, the Performance Funding System (PFS), mentioned above, has kept costs low for many years. Basically, HUD calculates an Allowable Expense Level (AEL) for each authority using a mathematical formula. It then subtracts the amount of rent the PHA expects to receive and sends the rest to the authority as an operating subsidy.

Over the years, the PFS formula has kept operating costs lower than typical equiva-lent private housing,[4] in part because the PFS mechanism does not have to provide operating subsidies to cover profit margins. Nor are there major tax waivers (such as the Low Income Housing Tax Credit or the income tax deduction for property own-ers) in the public housing program, as there are in virtually all other forms of as-sisted housing. The actual numbers support this circumstantial evidence. In city after city, the sum of rent receipts plus the operating subsidy, modernization grants, and an imputed amortization cost is substantially lower than the Section 8 Fair Market Rent, or the typical rent in the marketplace.

Another indication of the cost-effectiveness of public housing financing can be seen from the treatment of the Section 8 Certificate and Voucher program by Con-gress and HUD in the mid-1990s. HUD issued its first "reinvention" document in 1993, calling for the conversion of the entire public housing program to a voucher program. After several years of reflection, that idea is largely off the table, in part because of the cost issues involved. In a similar vein, Section 8 Certificate contracts between HUD and the PHAs that used to be for twenty years, and were then re-duced to ten and later five years, are now down to one and two years. The primary reason is the great expense involved in subsidizing rents in the private sector. Projec-tions of the costs for simply maintaining the current level of Section 8 housing are prohibitive. (FY 1996 was the first year since the inception of the program that no new certificates were authorized.) Our leaders in Washington continue to return to the traditional public housing formula—a grant for construction and an operating subsidy—as the most effective way to use our public dollars for housing.

There are still some very good professionals working in this field. Distinguished public servants are working hard at every level to make public housing serve its original intent—decent homes for people of modest means. The housing authorities in Cambridge, Louisville, Miami, Milwaukee, New York City, Norfolk, Omaha, Richmond, St. Paul, and Seattle are but a few of the very fine public agencies headed by outstanding professionals. While many other fine individuals have left because of the fear they would not be allowed to undertake the professional work they needed to do, they would be back in a flash if they knew the opportunity existed to do the job right. Witness the excellent people that have been recruited as receivers (court-appointed chief administrators who take over troubled PHAs)—e.g., Harry Spence in Boston, Jeff Lines in Kansas City, and David Gilmore in Washington, D.C.

The Clinton administration and Congress seem determined to change the shape of public housing dramatically. Some of their proposals, such as the elimination or substantial renovation of many of the most troubled developments, the reduction in regulations, and the encouragement of more mixed-income developments, are very positive. On the other hand, the significant cuts in funding, the refusal to fund new development of additional units in the face of long waiting lists, and the move to raise rents for poor families are clearly misguided and shortsighted actions. They fly in the face of important conclusions we can draw from our experience with public housing programs. So, what is to become of the public housing program?

A NOTE ABOUT PERSPECTIVE

As mentioned earlier, it is important to remember the history of this program. This is not the first time that public housing has not been politically popular. In the early 1970s, the infamous Nixon Moratorium halted nearly all housing programs that benefited low- and moderate-income citizens. Shortly after that, however, a determined Congress and different national leadership restored programs in new and improved formats. In its early days, the Reagan administration announced plans to reduce the public housing budget by 25 percent annually—totally terminating it within four years. Once again, a strong Congress and determined citizenry resulted in a stronger public housing program than ever. History tells us this program does not die easily.

Logic also favors the retention of some housing stock for families that cannot pay market rates. Every time public officials edge up to the conclusion that some form of housing voucher is a better system, somebody calculates the cost and has second thoughts. Additionally, many families will never be able to find a unit with a voucher because the private marketplace simply will not respond to them, regardless of whether they can pay the rent or not. Those needing a wheelchair-accessible unit, those with a large number of children, those with a shaky rental history, and, in many places, those who are members of racial and ethnic minority groups, face barriers other than cost. The only way these families will find a decent place is if an organization with a firm and formal commitment to meeting the needs of *all* those who are not served by the marketplace actually controls some housing units. Other alternatives for this population—doubling up with friends, living in shelters, tolerating substandard and hazardous housing units—are far more costly in the long run than simply providing decent housing units.

Finally, the American public is not nearly as mean-spirited as the current political winds seem to indicate. When, a decade ago, the problem of homelessness became so public, the Congress *and* a conservative administration created a generous source of funding (the McKinney legislation) that has provided temporary and transitional housing for many of our most vulnerable citizens. At different times, when veterans, or senior citizens, or battered spouses, or those living with AIDS have needed housing resources, the nation has embraced these populations.

In short, this period in the history of public housing should be viewed as a valley, not the bottom of a cliff. This is not the moment to give up on the program and relegate it to the scrap heap of public policy history. Rather, it is a time to reshape the program in order to strengthen it for the climb out of the valley, up to a place where it is a valued part of the overall housing policies of the nation.

Ten Points on Which to Build Public Housing Over the Next Sixty Years

The ten principles suggested below can help guide policymakers and administrators as this program is reshaped.

1. *Housing is especially important to children in shaping their view of the world and their ability to control their future.* As obvious as this might sound, it is a fact that policymakers sometimes lose track of. What does a child of six expect when he or she opens the front door in the morning? Are there safe but exciting adventures waiting to happen with friends? Are there interesting places and people to encounter? Is there a playground with new challenges? Is it safe and convenient to begin learning to take on the world by going to the store for milk? Will there be flowers, attractive buildings, and some people out and about to greet? Or will there be dangers lurking outside that front door? Will everything encountered be ugly and dirty? Will there be few people on the streets with whom to have a positive interaction? Will there be no stores or playgrounds nearby? Will there be other children their parents want them to play with? When strolling the marble halls of Congress, reading polls about "what the public thinks," it is easy to forget what public housing really means to the people who live in it. It is equally easy to forget that public housing deserves some reasonable place in the public policy priority lists, since few leaders seem to want to talk about the issue. We must reshape the public housing program as if housing really mattered to people—because it does.

2. *Poor people cannot afford to pay the legitimate costs of decent housing.* Many people seem to think the reason housing is unavailable to people of modest means is that private developers and landlords are greedy, or public and nonprofit agencies waste money. Although some examples of each of these conditions undeniably exist, they are by no means the major problem. In most cities of any size and many rural areas, a substantial portion of the population (as much as 20 percent in many locations) (Joint Center for Housing Studies 1996, Tables A-1 and A-12) simply does not earn enough money to pay for the fair costs of housing (land, materials, labor, financing and operations) produced by the marketplace. Once this shortfall in income is acknowledged, it becomes reasonable to have a discussion about how to deal with this gap in housing affordability. The problem impacts middle- and upper-income families as well, but we have a way to deal with it—the income tax deduction for real estate taxes and mortgage interest for residential property. Together these constitute the largest housing subsidy we have, both in overall terms, and, in the case of the wealthy, on an individual household basis. While this policy makes good sense as a stimulant for homeownership (a very sound national policy), it also undeniably brings a higher level of housing into the range of middle- and upper-income families than they could afford without the benefit. It seems reasonable to do the same for poorer families.

3. *The marketplace will not sort out housing needs and provide appropriate housing for everybody.* There are those who argue that if the marketplace were left alone, it would sort out housing needs reasonably on it own, and that we only make the problem worse by interfering with natural forces. This posture simply ignores the reality of private residential real estate. If the marketplace were able to perform this sorting process reasonably and in the public interest, how can we explain these phenomena: racial discrimination; the lack of decent housing for low-income residents; the lack of housing for those who require physical accommodations; the continued existence of poisonous lead paint and asbestos in many housing units; high vacancy rates in some neighborhoods, while others are overcrowded; and all the other gross imperfections in the housing arena? Once again, the excellent chapter by Peter Marcuse is instructive on this point. There clearly must be other actors in the housing arena if all our citizens are to have decent homes.

4. *If people do not have decent housing, other bad things happen in their lives. In coping with these problems, society incurs other costs—mental health, crime, divorce, family abuse, fires, and so on.* Because housing is so important, people almost always find some way to cope with meeting their needs. They double up with some other relative or friend; they live in very inadequate and unsafe housing; they move to a remote location where no jobs are accessible; they "live" in the shelter system; or they commit too much of their money to housing, and are unable to adequately feed and clothe their family and meet other needs such as medical care. All of these alternatives

have consequences, and many of these consequences have costs to the community at large that are greater than the cost of supplying public housing. In this context, decent housing is a real bargain.

5. *It is better for people to live in the midst of economically and demographically diverse communities than to live in isolated developments of only a single category of residents.* This is an issue about which reasonable people can differ. Thousands of public housing developments, as well as many properties owned and managed by good for-profit and nonprofit organizations, have demonstrated for many years that it is possible to operate healthy and stable communities made up exclusively of low-income residents. This does not mean, however, it is the most desirable situation possible. Mixed-income developments are less susceptible to stigma, more difficult to isolate and underserve, and easier to integrate into the normal fabric of the community. In the final analysis, everybody gains from encountering a variety of people in their neighborhoods. It is the most important way of learning that people need to be treated as individuals and not as members of a stereotyped demographic category. It is the most natural way to offer children the widest variety of possible role models from which to choose the path they want to follow in life. And such mixed-income developments require less subsidy than those that serve a 100 percent low-income population. It would not be reasonable, practical, or necessary to argue that all low-income housing properties be broken up. But in those situations where it is possible to create more heterogeneous communities, it makes sense to do so.

6. *None of the three basic forms of organizations (private for-profits, private nonprofits, public agencies) has a record of total success or total failure at developing and managing housing, especially for those who cannot afford to pay the full costs of that housing.* Broadly speaking, we have tried each of these three forms of organizations in our national quest for a solution to the affordable housing issue. Beginning in 1937 and continuing through the 1940s and 1950s, we responded to the failure of the private market to provide housing for these families by creating public agencies to do the job. In the 1960s and 1970s, dissatisfied with the success of these organizations, we offered significant incentives to the private, for-profit sector to do the job, i.e. Section 221(d)(3) and (d)(4), Sections 235 and 236, Section 8 New Construction and Substantial Rehabilitation. When it became clear that too many of these actors were failing to perform adequately, we turned, in the 1980s and 1990s, to the private nonprofit sector. In the past twenty years, nonprofit organizations and neighborhood-based community development corporations have grown into a substantial force in the affordable housing field, developing expertise and knowledge. Many of these properties exist on very fragile financing and subsidy arrangements, however. Although this group of organizations has developed a substantial number of units, it is not clear whether they will fare better (or worse) than the other actors who have tried. Building and managing decent affordable housing is very complex work, and no one

is perfect at it. Organizations of all types change over time; leadership comes and goes; politics change; economics, at both the macro and micro scale, change; and programs are funded more and less generously. This complex picture argues in favor of keeping all three options available to provide housing—the quantity of which will vary with time and from place to place.

7. *Resident-based subsidies are a good idea, but they will not work for everybody, and they are often more costly than site-based subsidies, especially over the long haul.* Rental vouchers should be an important part of any comprehensive affordable housing program: They allow many families to stand on their own in the housing marketplace; households avoid the stigma of being labeled a "project" family; homes remain on the tax rolls of the local community; and people have access to a wider range of locations than they otherwise would. However, as stated above, this form of housing assistance is frequently more expensive than providing actual units for low- and moderate-income families, and a voucher program simply will not serve all the families that need assistance. We need both types of programs, as Mary Nenno argues so persuasively in her chapter in this volume.

8. *Over the long term, decent housing for low- and moderate-income people will thrive only if it develops a broader constituency.* Programs that serve only poor people or other marginalized constituencies will always be fragile in our society. A primary reason for this is that some of the individuals in these categories are not ones who are naturally seen as "deserving" by the public at large. In addition, poor families and individuals are a minority of our population (thankfully), and they typically do not vote in high numbers. For these reasons, it is an easy population to write off, both electorally and financially. A broader advocacy group for affordable housing needs to be developed, including all those who benefit from the range of housing assistance programs. This would mean, as Peter Marcuse suggests, building coalitions across class lines—a difficult, but arguably logical and certainly necessary task.

9. *The biggest single problem in the implementation of affordable housing programs over the past sixty years has been the lack of consequences for failure (to anybody except the residents).* If the public is to support housing for those who cannot afford to pay for it, someone must be accountable to ensure that success in providing this form of housing is rewarded and failure is punished. It is unconscionable that a housing authority such as the Department of Public and Assisted Housing in Washington, D.C., could have remained on the "Troubled Housing Authority" list for more than seventeen years with no significant sanctions. Neither the city nor HUD was willing to take the actions necessary to preserve the rights of the 12,000 households who deserved better. It took strong residents, resourceful lawyers, and a courageous judge to finally wrest this agency from its downward spiral, as it did in Boston, Kansas City, and Chester, Pennsylvania—other sites of receiverships in public housing.

Thankfully, the current HUD administration is beginning to take more definitive action in selected cases (e.g., Chicago, New Orleans, San Francisco) where failure has gone on for too long. Slowly, people are being held more accountable. But similar stories of poor performance can be told of housing complexes under every affordable housing program in the nation's history. Providing housing for families that are outside the economic mainstream of the culture is a difficult task. The rewards for doing this work well are extremely minimal—and mostly internal. When there are no sanctions for failing, it is all too easy to do so. A truly successful system of housing *all* of our people must include meaningful sanctions for failing. And some significant rewards for succeeding wouldn't hurt either.

10. *The important goal is maximum affordable-housing-unit–months over the long term—not the preservation of any particular institution, program, or financial structure.* One of the great threats to the creation of innovative and sustainable solutions to the housing issues that face poorer Americans is the determination of some to defend to the death some part of the status quo. These individuals and organizations want to build a barricade around particular programs (public housing, Section 8 vouchers); entities (housing authorities, CDCs); jobs ("Whatever happens, I need to still be the director of development for something"); financial arrangements (Low Income Housing Tax Credits, tax-exempt financing); or political coalitions (we residents against those owners, we developers against those public officials). Those who choose to fight to defend the status quo will almost certainly face defeat over the long haul. Some risks will be necessary to move to new forms of housing assistance. Those who keep in focus the important long-term goal—decent, supportive housing for those who cannot afford to pay for it on their own—will help to create the new entities, financing ideas, programmatic initiatives, and housing forms that will earn and deserve public support. Finally, these will form the programmatic base that will better serve the families whom the public housing initiative has always supported.

Strategies for a Positive Future

Given these ten principles, what strategies might public housing practitioners pursue to generate the most positive outcomes for the residents? A wide variety of options exists from which to choose, depending on the community, the state of the PHA, the state of the housing stock, the needs of the low-income residents of the community, and other variables. But there are a few constants to any strategy.

- *Preserve the assets (housing units, land, streams of cash, etc.).* Physical assets that are lost in these hard times will be extremely difficult, if not impossible, to regain. In the best of worlds, units will continue to be rented to low-income residents, either because subsidies continue or because other resources can be found. In other cases, the units may have to be rented to households with somewhat higher incomes in order to pay the bills. This may be a difficult accommodation for those who have long served the poorest of families, but it is preferable to giving up the buildings. At least these homes will be available to serve low-income residents in the future when subsidies are again available. At a few particularly troubled developments, many of which are very prominent, the only asset worth retaining is the land. The buildings are unfit for human habitation and should be torn down. They are a blight on the program, their neighborhoods, and the lives of the residents they house. But it would be a mistake to sell the land. Long-term leases to developers prepared to develop the site as mixed-income housing are a far better alternative. Whatever strategy is appropriate for a particular site, an almost universal principle is "Don't give up the land."

- *Defend the goal—decent housing for households of modest means—not the system.* One of the primary problems public housing advocates have faced over the years is the bad image of their program. They have been forced to defend a system that is seen by many as a failure. In this defensive posture, they have needed to be apologists for some bad housing, some dysfunctional agencies, and some intolerable conditions. This must stop. Universities and hospitals and a few other institutions have developed accreditation systems that have largely eliminated the bad apples. As a result, these industries generally have far greater respect in their communities and in Congress than public housing. The current discussions about an accrediting system for public housing may or may not bear fruit. Accreditation makes a difference only if there are consequences to *not* being accredited, something which HUD (or its successor) must address. But public housing professionals can learn from the principle of self-policing. If advocates focus on the purposes of the program, serious evaluation will dictate that certain PHAs, certain properties, and certain regulations must be reformed or eliminated immediately. At the same time, it will become crystal clear in the vast majority of locations that the local PHA is the best, or among the best, or perhaps the only, organization available to meet the goal of decent affordable housing.

- *Move all the elements of the program into the mainstream.* The Tetreault et al. (1994) chapter in the *Proceedings* volume from the Cincinnati conference on "Future Visions of Urban Public Housing" refers to a quote from a most remarkable document, a 1967 memo written to help define the shape of "A Housing Program for Montgomery County." In this memo, Alexander Greene, a local leader who was working on the establishment of a PHA-like body for that county, laid out a housing policy direction with four major thrusts:

First, subsidized housing development should be consistent and compatible with the County's development plan;

Next, housing programs should be oriented toward assisting families to become self-sufficient and not be reservoirs of failure and hopelessness;

Thirdly, subsidized housing should be dispersed, not concentrated, to avoid segregation by race and income; and,

Finally, in cooperation with other agencies, a full range of social, educational, and recreational services should be provided to assisted-housing residents. (Tetreault et al. 1994).

This thirty-year-old memo is remarkably prescient. It provides four important indicators for how public housing ought to fit into any community, and it is as relevant today as it was when it was written.

Similarly, Peter Marcuse argues persuasively in his outstanding chapter in this book that the goals of the public housing program are likely to be met only if the program elements are integrated into the mainstream of housing and social policy in the nation. Only then will public housing serve its residents, its communities, and the taxpayers who provide the funding in the best manner possible. Such a program will be more comprehensive in the services it provides, more integrated into the community, more efficient in the use of tax dollars, and more politically acceptable. There are several dimensions to the mainstreaming of public housing. In general, most of these elements might go under the appropriate rubric of "deregulation." The cry for this action applies primarily to the mountain of micro-management regulations that specify how small details of the program must be run. But it applies as well to broader aspects of the program. Some of the dimensions are identified below.

❐ *Move the agencies into the mainstream: Allow PHAs to undertake a wider range of activities.* If these public agencies were to become truly a third type of actor in the real estate sector of the local economy (along with private for-profit and private nonprofit organizations), they could be measured by the same standards and have an opportunity to thrive in the same manner. For example, PHAs in Virginia are, by statute, joint redevelopment agencies and housing authorities. As a general rule (and there are always exceptions), these authorities are very well regarded in their communities, have a wide range of resources available to them, and operate excellent public housing programs. Many officials of these agencies attribute this level of success to their broader range of roles and more general involvement in the community.

There is no innate reason why PHAs shouldn't be able to own and manage properties that serve the full range of renters (with a clear emphasis on serving poorer families); administer homeownership programs; borrow wherever it makes sense to borrow; have full access to the equity markets; issue bonds and lend money; undertake studies of housing needs in the community; act as a broker; or use subsidy streams to induce redevelopment efforts.

Some PHAs might decide to own their properties but contract out the management of the properties to other agencies. Resident management options could be included here, though William Peterman's chapter reminds us to set realistic goals for such efforts. Whatever strategies are adopted by a particular PHA in a particular context, the agency should be judged by the standards set by other actors and subjected to the discipline of the "marketplace." When PHAs perform well in their various roles, it will make sense to have properties poorly run by others transferred to them. When the PHAs fail at their work, their resources should be "foreclosed" and given to others who seem more able to serve the needs of poor households at that time. Some PHAs have shown the advantages of this diversity of roles. Richard Best, in his chapter in this volume, describes with sharp insight the mixed experience of British housing authorities as they have become subject to a more competitive environment.

❏ *Move the properties into the mainstream: Move toward more mixed-income properties.* In the same way, it makes sense to try to integrate the lower-income residents that are currently isolated in public housing developments into the overall neighborhood and community in which they are located. Gayle Epp's excellent chapter, as well as the fine work by Lawrence Vale, documents the ways in which PHAs are undertaking this work today—and what the keys to success seem to be. This strategy means broadening the income range of residents in current public housing developments, as well as using certificates and vouchers (or similar elements) to provide opportunities for poorer residents to live in a wider range of neighborhoods. It may also mean purchasing market-rate buildings and converting them, over time, into mixed-income properties.

This is not to argue that some properties that serve 100 percent low-income families don't work perfectly well. Nor is it meant to suggest that mixing the incomes of residents will automatically result in an "uplifting" of the lower-income residents, as Alexander von Hoffman reminds us in his chapter. Good property and asset management is still the key to this goal. The suggestion, however, is that more diverse residential settings are likely to be more successful and more supportive of individual growth over the long run. Particularly if a property is not meeting the needs of its residents as well as it might, a wise course would be to alter the various regulations, financing mechanisms, and ownership entities that would make it possible for the property to serve a wider range of residents.

☐ *Move the money into the mainstream: Allow the money currently flowing into public housing to be used in more flexible ways.* Currently, public housing's financial resources (operating subsidy, modernization money, Section 8 payments, development funds, and special program resources) flow in narrow channels determined by HUD in Washington. A good deal of current legislative discussion is focused on making these separate streams of money into a block grant. Some analysts are concerned about such a change because they feel it may mask a policy decision to reduce the overall level of funding. Although block grants make a great deal of sense, less money does not. There is no rational reason to believe that erasing the boundaries between the types of funding and then reducing the overall amount by 20 percent will get the job of public housing done more efficiently or effectively. At the same time, it is undeniable that greater flexibility in the use of funds might go a long way toward developing, preserving, and improving affordable housing resources in many communities. As one example, using public housing funding to purchase an "expiring use" property may be a far more efficient way to preserve affordable housing than trying to develop an equivalent number of new units or modernize unmarketable and poorly located units. In other cases, using public housing operating subsidies to acquire (and/or lower rents in) a few units in privately owned properties throughout the community may be a very good strategy. This same effort might also be used to encourage the physical improvement of those properties, thus yielding a second benefit. In general, allowing the current funding resources to be applied in the fullest possible range of strategies to increase and preserve the amount of decent affordable housing in a given community clearly makes the most sense.

☐ *Move the residents into the mainstream: Provide a full range of options to poor households so that they can choose the housing solution that works best for them.* The Housing Authority of Burlington, Vermont has joined with five nonprofits and the city's Office of Community Development to create what they refer to as a "ladder of tenure" for households of modest means in their community. These seven agencies develop and operate homeless shelters; transitional housing units;

rental apartments for families, elderly residents, and people with disabilities; cooperatives; and programs for first-time home buyers. The agencies work together to make the housing they develop affordable in perpetuity to the maximum degree feasible. This usually means reducing financing costs to the lowest possible level so that tenants' rents need cover only operating costs. These agencies are attempting to assure there is an affordable resource to meet the needs of any kind of household that cannot afford housing on the open market in Burlington. While there is not *enough* housing in each of these categories, the groups have built a continuum into which new developments can fit. The hope is clearly that many families will move along this continuum as their income grows and that one day they will be on their own. These agencies do not want families to remain in any one type of housing because there are no practical options available for them until they earn a *lot* more money. If each step seems reasonable, it is more likely people will take those steps. At the same time, the Burlington agencies want to make each type of housing reasonable so that when families choose to make a permanent home in any particular place along the continuum it will be a comfortable and affordable choice.

- *Broaden the constituency.* The wider the range of activities in which PHAs are involved, the greater the interest communities, institutions, and residents will have in their continued survival. If public housing money becomes part of more housing properties around the community, more lenders and owners will support the program. If a wider range of residents are the beneficiaries of what is now identified as public housing assistance, public officials will find it more difficult to isolate these residents and ignore their needs for the full range of public services.

Conscious efforts to improve the image of public (and other forms of assisted) housing should reduce opposition to the program and bring additional support. A strategy for eliminating the worst elements of the program will not only mean better communities for those served by public housing, but added respect from others. The full integration of social services into public housing so that residents are further aided in their efforts to move ahead with their lives will win many friends for the program. In general, any effort that shows the community that public housing can be a positive will be beneficial to the future of the program.

- *Recruit and train good professionals.* Any program works only as well as the professionals that operate it. The most carefully designed regulations and funding package in the world will be destroyed by incompetent or ill-motivated staff. Conversely, good personnel will find a way to make even the most underfunded and poorly structured program work better than might be expected. Therefore, although deregulating public housing is critically important, it is also vital to find ways to increase the number of skillful, committed, and well-trained staff who are available to administer housing programs for households of modest means. This requires developing excellent training programs, paying salaries that will attract the caliber of people necessary to undertake the complex and demanding work, and developing clear career ladders. Most important is providing these staff with the freedom and the resources that are necessary to do their work well. No self-respecting professional enjoys working in a context where it is impossible to do the work in the way it needs to be done. Today, the public housing field is fortunate to have a number of professionals whose commitment to their work runs so deep that they are willing to struggle to deliver on public housing promises even in the face of great odds. With some changes in the program, many more of these professionals could be enlisted.

A Vision for the Public Housing of the Future

At its core, public housing is a set of homes—some owned outright and some leased—that are controlled by a public agency and subsidized by the federal government so that they can be made available at affordable costs to families and individuals who earn less than 80 percent of the median income in their area. Which part of this program do we most want to change? If, as a society, we don't like the idea of public agencies owning housing units, we should turn over the millions of units owned by the military to private organizations. If it's the subsidies we're concerned about, we should eliminate the 80 percent of all federal housing subsidies that go to homeowners earning more than 80 percent of median income in the form of income tax deductions. If we simply want people to have only the shelter they can afford with their income, then we should eliminate not only military housing and the homeowner's income tax deduction program, but also FHA insurance and all public assistance for housing for the mentally ill, mentally retarded, elderly in nursing homes, students in dormitories, and so on. In fact, I do not believe we want any of these things. Rather, we are concerned about a few disastrous examples of the ways in which our taxpayer dollars have been misspent in several housing programs. And we have failed to look beyond these isolated mistakes to see what parts of the program are worth saving and which parts must be changed.

One difficulty with the public housing program is that its parts have always been bundled together in one particular fashion. One type of owner (PHA) has received all the funding (development grants, operating subsidies, capital improvement grants,

leased housing subsidies, and special purpose funding) to use for one type of housing (multifamily rental), serving one kind of resident (lower and very-low-income
elderly and family households). What we are learning is that this concept is too narrow. The "public" housing of tomorrow will need to bundle these elements in a variety of combinations. Most of the authors of chapters in this volume believe that
there is a very important place in the future for a renewed and strengthened public
housing program. Their vision of the future includes a variety of ways of blending
the aspects of public housing.

They imagine strong, independent, local public agencies acting as a third force
in local real estate, alongside a vigorous for-profit and an equally potent nonprofit
sector. Each of these actors would nominally have the capacity and authority to study
the housing needs of an area; develop, rehabilitate and own real estate; manage property; provide ancillary services; act as brokers; make available various financing options; and, in other ways, serve the shelter needs of the area. Each would center its
work on a different part of the population, though these foci ideally would overlap.
Public housing authorities would pay particular attention to those parts of the population who could not afford private-sector housing or who have some special needs
related to their shelter. The PHAs would determine the best ways of providing housing
for this segment of the population, and it is likely they would conclude that no one
is best served in isolated, exclusively low-income complexes. Therefore, housing authorities would tend to acquire, own, and possibly manage a wide variety of types of
housing (multifamily rental, cooperative, condominium, single-family, sheltered,
homeownership) that serve residents with a range of incomes. They would mix and
match ownership with leasing programs in whatever ways best serve the community. As to the properties they now own, the PHAs would evaluate each of them
and determine which could continue to thrive as exclusively low-income communities and which would work better as mixed-income developments. They would take
steps toward converting the latter. At the same time they would search for other properties to purchase that would lend themselves to the same type of population mix.
Finally, if there are some properties currently owned that simply will not work as
decent housing for anybody, the housing authorities would demolish the buildings
and follow one of several courses: rebuild an improved and viable housing development; keep the land and cause it to be redeveloped for some other more appropriate
purpose; or, in very rare cases, sell the land and use the proceeds to produce more
affordable housing.

In addition to taking on new initiatives themselves, PHAs that strongly pursue
the vision described above will form partnerships with nonprofit organizations as
well as some for-profit developers and other organizations. Social service agencies
will become integral members of some partnerships. Community development corporations (CDCs) will work much more closely with PHAs. Many authorities will
contract with private organizations to perform functions they have previously undertaken themselves. Partnerships with major employers will result in job opportu-

nities for residents as well as stronger capacities for the PHAs. The possibilities are manifold.

This vision of the future for public housing requires an infusion into the housing industry of some new types of public entrepreneurs. The program will not be formula driven but rather one that seeks the right, sometimes unique, solution for each group of residents and each neighborhood that it serves. Many of the stalwarts that have worked so hard to deliver the promise of public housing in spite of all the obstacles will have to let go of some of the most constant elements of the program over the years in order to make the transition. This flexibility will provide a challenge for the new cohort of public housing officials.

Just as PHAs would take on a much wider set of activities and serve a wider range of residents, the financial streams will be used differently than they have in the past. Operating subsidies would be tied to individual properties rather than entire agencies and their portfolios. Agencies would then be forced to function efficiently (using only a competitive overhead measure for their central office costs, for example) or face the possibility of losing some of their assets. In this ideal future vision, the subsidies would be based on a serious evaluation of the needs of each individual property and its unique situation. This operating subsidy would also take into consideration the real capital improvement needs of the development and allow for the rational buildup of a replacement reserve. Again, like all other real estate owners, the PHAs would be encouraged to plan wisely for such capital improvements or face the possibility of losing some of their properties. Leased housing subsidies would go to the agencies (PHAs, other public bodies, nonprofits, or for-profits) that could operate them most efficiently and effectively. Similarly, special funding (Drug Elimination Grants, Youth Sports, HOPE VI) would go to those organizations that could deliver the best outcomes for residents and the community as a whole in those areas of concern.

One critical element in the realization of this picture of the future is how the PHAs act during the current period of transition. If the leadership of the public housing industry sticks its head in the sand and resists change, then not much of this will happen and many elements of the public housing program will die. If this leadership takes the initiative to reshape the program, the PHAs will be able to play a major role in the future of housing in the nation.

Two other forces that will also significantly affect the realization of this vision are Congress and HUD. If Congress continues to reduce funding for those parts of the housing stock that receive federal assistance, then even the strongest properties will begin to fail. Alert owners will be able to save them only by evicting most low-income residents and renting apartments and homes to higher-income occupants, thereby producing the first examples of public housing residents evicted because they cannot pay the rent. No precedent exists for these types of evictions in public housing, and they are likely to cause a significant stir. But by the time the evictions happen, it will be too late to save those units for those residents. If Congress continues to cut funding, we will lose several hundred thousand of the 1.4 million public hous-ing units over the next decade *and they will be almost impossible to recover in the fu-ture, no matter what level of funding is made available.* Once sites are lost and buildings are destroyed it is unlikely that either the higher funding or the political consensus will be available to reestablish these units. Many of the units that do remain will be rented to individuals in the 50 percent to 80 percent of median income range (or even higher). While there is no question these households need housing assistance, many families will be left to fight the unwinnable battle for decent housing in the private marketplace. This scenario will produce a great deal of pain for many people who are today decently housed by the public housing program. According to the well-known Hubert H. Humphrey dictum—"Societies are judged by how they deal with their frailest citizens, the elderly, the children, and the poor"—we are likely to be found severely wanting as a nation.

Further, if HUD (and Congress) continues to overregulate and micro-manage those parts of the housing stock that are overseen or subsidized by public agencies, it is unlikely that any significant change will be able to happen. If these mean-spir-ited alternatives prevail, Congress and HUD will have killed public housing; it will not be the fault of the local actors who, in the vast majority of communities, have labored valiantly to produce decent housing for poor households. If, on the other hand, an adequate level of funding is continued, and regulations are reduced (as seems to be the trend at the moment), then competent local agencies will be able to un-bundle and reassemble the elements of the public housing program in ways that will be responsive to the needs of low- and moderate-income households and the com-munities in which they live. In this case, HUD and Congress can claim an impor-tant role in realizing the needs of a new era in affordable housing and responding in ways that make creative new solutions possible.

Some current legislators believe that the best strategy for affordable housing pro-grams is to have them "devolved" to the states and cities so that these other levels of government will pick up the slack left by reduced federal assistance. This is not likely to be a successful approach. What makes us believe that the "tax-cutting, welfare-reducing, government-shrinking, everybody-fend-for-themselves" politics that is cur-rently in vogue at the federal level of politics will not also dominate the state and local levels of discourse? Why would the voter of tomorrow ask the federal govern-ment to reduce the public housing program at the national level and then vote to have his or her state or local government increase taxes to cover those same costs? Although devolution may have some attractive elements, replacement of lost federal funding with state and local resources is not one of them.

There is one other way in which Congress and HUD can help. They can make certain that there are consequences for both failure and success at the work of hous-ing poor households decently. When PHA-owned properties fail, the properties should be taken from the PHA and given to other actors—nonprofits or for-profits—in the local community. When subsidy streams are flowing to private actors who are doing a poor job—as in Section 8 project subsidies—those streams can be redirected toward public agencies who show promise of being able to perform better. When whole organizations are malfunctioning, subsidies that prop them up can be withdrawn. When entities show long-term success and creativity, they can be rewarded with additional funding and even less oversight. If this formula is followed, the incentives in the affordable housing arena will finally all point in one direction. Serve lower-income people well, and you will be encouraged to do more of this work, given the money you need to do it the right way, and left alone to use your skills. Fail this population, or the taxpayers who have provided you with the resources to do this work, and your money, flexibility, and opportunities will be reduced or even removed.

The chapters in this volume paint a picture of a program that has delivered long and distinguished service to the American public but that is now troubled by a poor image and caught in a valley of political support. There is a great deal of discussion about what should happen next. Some are prepared to abandon the essential elements of the program. Others would fight to defend each and every element as it now exists. The chapter by Irving Welfeld shows clearly that the United States should not discard public housing on the basis of flimsy evidence from one or two voucher demonstrations. Richard Best's chapter shows how Britain's adoption of some of the strategies advocated by public housing's greatest American critics (e.g. the widespread sale of public housing units to their occupants) has produced some results nobody would advocate.

Two primary options are available to those who believe public housing has served our nation well, and can do so in even better ways in the future. One option is to defend the program as it now exists and attempt to survive the current bad times. Those who adopt this strategy will lose. The alternative is to seize this moment to make some of the changes that are long overdue in the program as well as to adopt some of the new strategies that are growing out of current debates about affordable housing policy. With these adjustments, advocates will be in a position to fight aggressively to move public housing into the mainstream of national housing policy and thereby save the essence of the public housing program, rather than its trappings. This path can lead to sixty more years of quality housing for people of modest means, a goal that this nation can ill afford to abandon.

Notes

1. Comprehensive modernization efforts at developments such as Washington Elms in Cambridge, Massachusetts; Diggstown in Norfolk, Virginia; and Lake Parc Place in Chicago have helped to begin turnarounds in these neighborhoods. Buildings serving the elderly have long been seen as stabilizing influences wherever they are built—in small towns, urban neighborhoods, or even the central city.

2. Some of the more public and serious examples include the "Passaic" scandal, where several staff and board members were receiving double and triple paychecks from the authority; the Department of Public and Assisted Housing in Washington, D.C., where numerous

staff were indicted and convicted of selling Section 8 Certificates to applicants; and the large
northeastern authority where a large number of key staff in a poorly performing agency were
also major political operatives for the mayor.

3. This story has been told to the author frequently by PHA staff from across the country and experienced directly in the court systems of Massachusetts, Pennsylvania, and Washington, D.C.

4. For example, in the Boston area, PHAs collect about $200 in rent each month from
a typical resident. Authorities receive approximately $290 in operating subsidy for that same
apartment each month. Add another $150 per month for an average modernization (capital
improvement) grant, and the total operating costs for a public housing apartment come to
$640 per month. Typical Fair Market Rents for the Section 8 program, which are supposed
to reflect about the median rent (actually the 45th percentile) in the area, are $850 for a two-
bedroom apartment.

References

Abt Associates. 1987. *A Study of the Modernization Needs of the Public and Indian Housing
    Stock; National, Regional, and Field Office Estimates: Backlog of Modernization Needs.*
    Cambridge, MA.
HUD System for Management Information Retrieval—Public Housing. 1995. Washington,
    D.C.: U.S. Department of Housing and Urban Development. September.
Joint Center for Housing Studies. 1996. *The State of the Nation's Housing.* Cambridge, MA:
    Harvard University, Joint Center for Housing Studies.
National Commission on Severely Distressed Public Housing. 1992. *Final Report of the Na-
    tional Commission on Severely Distressed Public Housing: A Report to the Congress and the
    Secretary of Housing and Urban Development.* Washington, DC: U.S. Government Print-
    ing Office.
New Community Services, Inc., Reese Fayde and Associates, and Stockard & Engler &
    Brigham. Forthcoming. *Public Housing Children's Impact Study.* Study commissioned
    by the Annie E. Casey Foundation. Baltimore, MD.
Public Housing Management Assessment Program (PHMAP) System for Management Infor-
    mation Retrieval—Public Housing. 1995. Washington, DC: U.S. Department of Hous-
    ing and Urban Development. September.
Tetreault, Bernard L.; Patrick O'B. Maier; and Joyce B. Siegel. 1994. Lessons for the Future:
    What We've Learned in Montgomery County, Maryland. In Wolfgang F. E. Preiser,
    David P. Varady, and Francis P. Russell, eds., *Future Visions of Urban Public Housing.*
    Proceedings of "Future Visions of Urban Public Housing: An International Forum,"
    held at the University of Cincinnati, Cincinnati, Ohio, November 17–20.
U.S. Department of Housing and Urban Development. 1995. Characteristics of Households
    in Public and Assisted Housing. *PD&R Recent Research Results.* Washington, D.C. De-
    cember.
U.S. Department of Housing and Urban Development, Office of Policy Development and
    Research. Forthcoming. *Public Housing Data Book.* Washington, DC: U.S. Department
    of Housing and Urban Development.

Contributors

Richard Best is director of the Joseph Rowntree Foundation in York, England. The Joseph Rowntree Foundation supports a program of research and development in the fields of housing, social care, and social policy.

Gayle Epp is a principal associate at Abt Associates, Inc., in Cambridge, Massachusetts. An expert in the revitalization of public housing, Ms. Epp was the design consultant to the National Commission on Severely Distressed Public Housing. She has been a consultant to architects, housing authorities, and public agencies on planning and design issues for low-income, elderly, and special needs populations.

Karen A. Franck is Professor in the School of Architecture and the Department of Humanities and Social Sciences at the New Jersey Institute of Technology in Newark, New Jersey. She is the author of *Nancy Wolf: Hidden Cities, Hidden Longings* (1996) and coauthor of *Ordering Space: Types in Architecture and Design* (1997). Dr. Frank worked with Oscar Newman at the Institute for Community Design Analysis in New York until the 1970s.

Leonard F. Heumann is Professor of Urban and Regional Planning and Psychology at the University of Illinois at Urbana-Champaign. His current research involves a new home- and community-based care system in Australia. With Duncan Boldy, he coedited *Aging in Place with Dignity: International Solutions Relating to the Low-Income and Frail Elderly,* published in 1993.

Peter Marcuse, a lawyer and urban planner, is Professor of Urban Planning in the Graduate School of Architecture, Planning, and Preservation at Columbia University. His current projects include a history of the New York City Housing Authority and a comparative study of the impact of globalization on the internal spatial structure of cities around the world.

Mary K. Nenno is an expert in the fields of housing and urban development with a research concentration on low-income housing and metropolitan development. In a career than spanned more than forty years of housing policy study, she served on the staffs of the National Association of Housing and Redevelopment Officials and the Urban Institute.

William Peterman is Professor of Geography and Coordinator of the Frederick Blum Neighborhood Assistance Center at Chicago State University. Dr. Peterman, whose research focuses on housing and neighborhood development, is currently completing a book on the relationship between neighborhood planning and community revitalization.

David M. Schnee is an associate with Group 4 / Architecture Research + Planning in San Francisco, California, where he specializes in public architecture and urban design. Mr. Schnee received the 1993 Environmental Design Research Association student award for the paper on which his chapter in this volume is based.

James G. Stockard, Jr., partner in the consulting firm of Stockard & Engler & Brigham, is Curator of the Loeb Fellowship at the Graduate School of Design, Harvard University. Mr. Stockard was a District of Columbia Superior Court-appointed Special Master to the Department of Public and Assisted Housing. In that capacity, he was charged with evaluating one of the nation's most troubled housing authorities and recommending remedies for its revitalization.

Lawrence J. Vale is Associate Professor of Urban Studies and Planning at the Massachusetts Institute of Technology. He is completing work on two books about public housing, one focusing on the history and prehistory of the Boston Housing Authority, and the other a comparative study of public housing in three neighborhoods.

Alexander von Hoffman is a Senior Research Fellow and historian at the Joint Center for Housing Studies of Harvard University, where he is writing a book on community development and the revival of the inner city. His latest book is *Local Attachments: The Making of an American Neighborhood, 1850 to 1920*, published by Johns Hopkins University Press in 1994.

Irving Welfeld is Senior Analyst at the U.S. Department of Housing and Urban Development, Office of Policy Development and Research. He is the author of *Where We Live: A Social History of American Housing* and *HUD Scandals: Howling Headlines and Silent Fiascoes*. He was formerly an attorney for the Department's Office of General Counsel.

Index

Note: Italicized page numbers indicate figures and tables.

Greenwich, Connecticut, 10
Gropius, Walter, 10
Guam, 219

H

handicapped, housing for, 206, 208, 218, *222*, 258
Harbor Point (Boston), 130
Harlem River Houses, 6
Hartford, Connecticut, 15, 227
Hartford Design Corporation, 15
Harvard University, 206, 207
Hellmuth, Leinweber, and Yamasaki, Architects, 11, *12*
Henderson, Peter, 206
high-rise designs, 217, 242
    appropriateness of, 104
    component in urban development plans, 10–11
    condemnation of, 15
    institution-like quality of, 14
    issues in, 107, 125
Hilliard Center, Raymond (Chicago), 13
Hills v. Gautreaux, 226
Hoffman, Morton, 214
Holly Park (Seattle), 131, 133–135
Holmans, Alan, 197
homeless, 25, 26, 249
    assistance, *222*
    in the United Kingdom, 186, 196, *197*
    shelters, 257
HOME program, 205–206, 208, 210, 213–214
Hong Kong, 11
HOPE VI, 50, 126, 143, 245, 261
    See also Urban Revitalization Demonstration (URD) Program
Horn, Stanley, 57
Hosiery Workers Union, 6
housing
    authorities, 38. *See also* public housing authorities (PHAs)
    industry, 4
    new directions in federally assisted—, 222–223
    ownership, 53–54, 56, 90–91, 133, 134, 136, 142, 181, 192, 195, 200, 205
    reform, 4
    shortage, 28
    sound and livable developments, 212
        assisted housing, 215–216
        mixed-income, 212–214
        opportunities for household independence, 218–221
        quality and diversity in housing design, 216–218
    stock, 122, 123

subsidies, 38, 182, 262–263
  "bricks-and-mortar," 191–194, 201 n. 2
  "personal subsidies," 191–194
  phasing out general—, *193*
  resident based, 252
suburbs, 17, 18, 226–233
superblocks, 6, 7, 92, *94*
Supplemental Security Income (SSI), 221

T

tax policies, 34
Taylor Homes, Robert (Chicago), 12, *13*, 228, 240
Technical Aid Network, 190
Techwood Homes (Atlanta), 6, 131
tenant associations, 36, 37
tenant management. *See* resident management
Tenant Management Organizations (TMOs), 190, 191
"Tenants' Choice," 187–188
Tennessee, 6, 227
Tennessee Valley Authority (TVA), 5, 32
Tent City (Boston), 17
Tetreault, Bernard, 238
Texas, 10, 227
Thatcher, Margaret, 25, 181, 184, 192, 201
Tigerman, Stanley, 15
"To Whom Should Limited Housing Resources Be Directed?" (Nelson and
    Khadduri), 206
Truman, Harry S., 9

U

United Kingdom. *See* Great Britain
United Way, 56
Unwin, Raymond, 6
upper class, *24*, 28, *33*, 37
  housing, 99
Urban Development Corporations, 198
Urban Institute, 208, 211
Urban Redevelopment Program, 215
urban renewal programs, 35
  emerging strategies, 121, 137–138
    development of mixed-income communities, 128–132
    family economic self-sufficiency, 132–133
    Holly Park, 133–135
    Indianapolis, 135–137
    National Commission on Severely Distressed Public Housing, 123–124
      families living in distress, 124–125
      physical deterioration of buildings, 125–126